Professor Peter Coaldrake is Vice-Chancellor and President of Queensland University of Technology (QUT), a position he has held since 2003. A dual Fulbright Scholar, he served as Chair of Universities Australia, the peak body of Australia's universities, for a two-year term to May 2011. He served as Chair of the governing board of the OECD's higher education program (IMHE) between 2011 and 2015, and earlier in his career he was Chair of Queensland's Public Sector Management Commission.

Dr Lawrence Stedman has been the Principal Policy Advisor within QUT's chancellery since 1995. He holds a PhD in mathematics from the Australian National University and, prior to joining QUT, he worked within both the Commonwealth Department of Finance (monitoring higher education) and the Commonwealth Department of Health, where he was Secretary to the Medical Research Committee of the NHMRC.

In addition to the first edition of this book, Coaldrake and Stedman previously co-authored *On the Brink: Australia's Universities confronting their future* (UQP 1998) and *Academic Work in the Twenty-First Century* (DETYA 1999). Coaldrake is also the author of *Working the System: Government in Queensland* (UQP 1989)

RAISING THE STAKES

SECOND EDITION

PETER COALDRAKE
& LAWRENCE STEDMAN

UQP

First published 2013 by University of Queensland Press
PO Box 6042, St Lucia, Queensland 4067 Australia
This edition published 2016

www.uqp.com.au
uqp@uqp.uq.edu.au

Cover design by Luke Causby, Blue Cork
Cartoons by Sean Leahy and Brett Lethbridge
Typeset in 11.5/16pt Janson Text by Post Pre-press Group, Brisbane
Printed in Australia by McPherson's Printing Group

Cataloguing-in-Publication entry is available from the
National Library of Australia
http://catalogue.nla.gov.au/

978 0 7022 5427 7 (pbk)
978 0 7022 5844 2 (pdf)
978 0 7022 5845 9 (epub)
978 0 7022 5846 6 (kindle)

University of Queensland Press uses papers that are natural, renewable and recyclable products made from wood grown in sustainable forests. The logging and manufacturing processes conform to the environmental regulations of the country of origin.

All royalties from the sale of this book are being donated to the QUT Learning Potential Fund. That fund is QUT's major strategic investment to provide scholarships, bursaries and other financial support to students in need.

This book is for
Lee, Emma, Jess, Calum, Mark, Fletcher and Milla

And for
Robyn, Dougal and Lucy

Contents

Chapter One

Tackling myths

In the early decades of the twenty-first century Australia is still a lucky country, blessed with abundant resources, high standards of living for most and a society that has so far managed to avoid the polarising extremes in wealth, economic dislocation and cultural conflict seen in many other places. Yet we cannot assume things will stay this way indefinitely. We are connected more than ever to the rest of the world and are consequently affected by powerful global forces driven by demographic change, economic development in the Asian region, prolonged fallout from the global financial crisis, structural changes in developed economies, ongoing technological transformations and environmental challenges and disruptions. We have only just begun to feel the impact of all these factors.

In this connected, competitive and environmentally stressed world we depend on better understanding and knowledge, but uncertainty seems ever more present. The scope and range of scientific expertise and technology are greater than before, but so too is our awareness of the limitations of what we know. We have faced adversity in the past and a major part of our national response to that was to increase our collective ability to make use

1

of our brainpower. Like many countries Australia emerged from the Second World War determined to improve national circumstances through public investment in education and research, and transforming a fledgling university system was part of that task; however, the situation today is different. While individually, and as a nation, our need for better knowledge to adapt to the challenges we face is much greater than it was, the costs and risks are being borne mostly by individuals and we are struggling to manage and sustain funding for a university system that has grown enormously in size and scope.

There are numerous expectations of universities and many people are sceptical about their capacity to deliver. While universities are considered fundamental for economic, social and individual development, and university places are highly sought after and more widely available than in times past, the institutions themselves are portrayed widely as unsustainable, unfit for purpose, lost in their way and on the brink of obsolescence.

From the viewpoint of government, universities are costly and difficult to align with official priorities, and they are often judged as complacent, self-serving and insufficiently exposed to competition and market forces. Consequently, students now shoulder a substantial share of the cost of their education and, in turn, students expect flexibility, responsiveness and service from their universities as well as excellent academic standards and facilities.

Some worry that the special character of elite universities, those that seek to produce world-class research, compete internationally for top researchers and cater for the most academically adept students, will be lost in a homogeneous system. In other universities there is a widespread view that their supposedly defining characteristics – for example, regional engagement, industry links, modes of teaching, or student demographics – are insufficiently recognised and ought to receive special support. More generally within universities there is chronic discontent with constraints on time and resources, and dissatisfaction with management. Strains are evident in traditional academic cultures with increasing work pressures, more intrusive regulation by government and closer involvement with the world of commerce, as well as diversification of roles and disparities in rewards.

Looming over much of the university policy debate here and overseas is a spectral threat of technology-driven obsolescence. New, nimble and cheap online providers are, we are assured, about to break the traditional university mould. The best lecturers and learning resources from the best universities in the world can be accessed anywhere at any time with minimal cost, avoiding the unnecessary overheads of the place-based, research-involved and labour-intensive university.

While Australian academics are, according to international surveys, among the least content with their lot in the world, the dismal picture just painted is not confined to Australia. Nor is it particularly new. Academics, government representatives and pundits have been fretting over much the same issues for decades. The United States and, to a lesser extent, the United Kingdom dominate the university league tables, but official reports in those two countries, as in most other places, warn of 'falling behind' and 'lagging behind our competitors', and both countries also excel in the production of doom literature, with new works analysing the decline of the university appearing with depressing regularity.

There can be no doubt that these are challenging times, and even institutions as venerable and apparently ancient in form as universities are exposed to forces that will ensure that they have to change. This change will be hardest for public universities, the backbone of the higher education system in many countries, and particularly in Australia and the United Kingdom. The model of the public university with which we are broadly familiar today is no more than half a century old, and it emerged largely from the extension of an older form to fit new circumstances. That extension is now under unprecedented strain and challenge.

The rationale for the expansion of universities was that future prosperity would depend on unlocking the creative and productive potential of a nation's citizens and drawing on the impressive development of human scientific knowledge and technological possibility that had been amply demonstrated since the nineteenth century. In the twenty-first century it has been recast as building knowledge-based economies and societies, and this acquired added urgency as the golden age of post-war economic growth faltered in the 1970s and gave way to significant economic and social disruptions caused by globalisation and technology. The nature of knowledge, though, and its role in economic and social development is not fixed, nor is it self-evident.

Knowledge, or at least information, is constantly growing and reshaping itself and is available in massive quantities anywhere at any time, and authority over knowledge has been muddied and vigorously contested. Universities cannot hope to maintain monopolies over the production and certification of knowledge but, despite the best efforts of governments around the world to design or encourage cheaper and more efficient alternatives, universities remain the preferred choice of students and the locus for undertaking long-term and basic research that add to our understanding of the world and can be used by others.

Australia is now entering an effectively universal phase of higher education: government restrictions on how many may enter public universities have been removed and public subsidies have been extended to a wide range of non-university providers. The percentage of young adults with a degree in this country is already high by world standards, and increasing. And, at least up to this point, the advantages of having a degree continue to make it a worthwhile investment for the great majority. The challenge for the future is to sustain the strengths of the university as an institution available to all in the face of inevitable resource pressures, demands for more accountability and policy reforms that can work against dynamism in the sector.

There are many policy conundrums facing Australian universities and in this book we do not attempt to grapple with all of them. We do not, for example, examine in depth issues about internationalisation, interfaces with business or with the vocational education and training sector, skills shortages, curriculum, changes in the academic workforce, or access and equity. These are all undeniably important, and of course are all mentioned. Our primary focus is on universities as institutions, and on the broad developments that are shaping their future.

The Australian university is based squarely on models drawn from the United States and the United Kingdom, and has evolved over time to take a more or less single institutional form in that it combines in various ways both teaching and research, is a physical home for scholars and is large in size and scope. By the latter we mean that it is broadly comprehensive in areas of study and in awarding credentials from bachelor degree through to postgraduate qualifications (in Australia this includes the doctorate). Within this form there is substantial academic freedom and institutional autonomy, including the power to self-accredit awards and to be self-governing. No doubt many people within Australian universities would dispute that academic freedom is sufficiently uncompromised and, in practice, issues can arise that cause complications – for example when one person's claim to academic freedom may compromise another's or when terminally disruptive and dysfunctional behaviour occurs. Yet academics in Australian universities have substantial control over what is taught and researched and enjoy significant leeway to make public comment without fear of dismissal or censure from management. Issues of governance are also more complicated than the term 'self-governing' might imply, and there are constraints and controls that apply to any institution that relies on public funding, but in essence the principle applies.

While variations on this theme may be found around the world, there has been a general convergence toward the Anglo–US university model, with a number of European countries giving greater autonomy to formerly state-managed institutions, and the vigorous pursuit of 'world-class universities' by many nations. Even at the less than elite level, universities in several formally differentiated systems have grown closer to the norm, in some cases differing only in their capacity to award doctoral degrees.

Despite sustained unease in government circles and in elite parts of the university world, the combined forces of student preference, economic change, public policy and financing, academic norms and institutional strategy have driven universities in a more or less similar direction.

The problem that arises is that if universities are to deliver what they purport to deliver, then this does not come cheaply. Moreover, their basic 'business model' remains dependent on both highly specialised human work and leading-edge technology, both of which contribute to escalating costs. The response by governments, particularly here in Australia and in the United Kingdom which regularly exchange policy ideas about higher education, has been to control the major part of university income, allow limited deregulation in some areas, encourage (or force) the rationalisation of activities and the amalgamation of smaller players, keep the price of a student place at artificially low levels, separate funding for teaching and research, ramp up measurement and inspection of university quality, and make universities bid for new money for capital works or other developments. The effect has been to put

greater pressures on universities, and further increase administrative and compliance costs, but not to change the fundamental
nature of the sector.

There is no shortage of pundits on the future of higher education
who opine sagely that all this is unsustainable, and more reform is
needed. What we need, we are frequently told, is more 'diversity'.
This is a term that has been sufficiently flexible to enable disparate
and sometimes conflicting concerns to be addressed under one
heading, although it should not be surprising that the resulting
policies and implementation have often failed to live up to expectations or have generated unintended consequences.

In the future, we are told, universities will be obsolete, or only
the elite research-intensive institutions will survive, leaving the rest
of the population to make do with cheaper alternatives better suited
to their more limited abilities. Others claim that the market will sort
it out, with private sector competition creating a better match of
needs and means as students operate as savvy consumers, possibly
guided by helpful information on government websites. Or perhaps
the messiness of the current situation can be addressed only by better
planning, or by more reform aimed at teasing apart the different
parts of the university 'value chain' and opening up the university
black box to external scrutiny and more effective external control.

Emerging from these kinds of policy debates about universities
are propositions that are often repeated, and may be sincerely held
to be self-evident by policy entrepreneurs, but are at best half-
truths. Part of our purpose is, if not to debunk them, then at least
to expose them to some critical scrutiny and to flesh them out a
little more realistically. These propositions include that:

- Australia needs to pursue explicit policies to move up the world
  university rankings and concentrate its research resources on
  building world-class excellence;

- new providers, such as massive online courses offered from prestigious universities, are about to transform the higher education scene, hollowing out the university model;
- research and teaching are inextricably linked, or conversely research is an expensive optional add-on that should be separated from teaching for most universities;
- teaching needs performance-based incentives to raise it to be on a par with research;
- the higher education sector's problems can be resolved only by deregulation. Universities can then play to their strengths, better informed markets will enable greater competition on price, and better choices will be made by students and better services provided to students;
- the sector needs more focussed coordination and design by government, through mission and performance-based agreements or by adopting the Californian system, or by encouraging smaller universities focussed on excellence in a specialised field;
- the university sector needs a buffer body to protect it and manage its relationships with the government of the day;
- university vice-chancellors are spineless and complicit in the destruction of public universities and need to be more effective lobbyists for more funding; and
- universities can regain their golden age by resisting the forces of neo-liberalism and managerialism.

Higher education, on the scale operating in Australia where more than a third of young adults hold a bachelor degree or higher qualification, is a remarkable achievement, one which has consistently exceeded past assessments about the intellectual capacity of populations, the relevance of study, or the economic demand for graduates. There is no sign that our national need for highly skilled graduates or new knowledge will decline in the future; in fact the opposite is likely to be the case. It is also abundantly clear that if we are to tackle the myriad social, environmental and other challenges facing us as a nation, and indeed as a species, then we need to know a lot more about the nature of the world we live in, and our relationships with it and with one another. Strong demand for education and research would seem to suggest a rosy future for universities.

Yet there are many signs that universities in Australia, as in most other countries, are under pressure. The stakes are being raised, and not just for students and for governments, which must balance competing demands for public funding. Universities face mounting risks as large, complex and often unwieldy organisations facing global and local competition and higher expectations for accountability and performance. We are moving inexorably away from a public system of university education toward a hybrid that is increasingly privately funded but subject to significant levels of public control and surveillance.

If we are to navigate this transition successfully and derive the best value from our universities we need to move on from myth-based policy-making and acknowledge the complexity of the sector, recognising that it has long moved past the point of yielding to simple systemic solutions. The real work of reform must move to the institutional level.

RAISING THE STAKES

Chapter Two

The role of universities in the twenty-first century

Genius is one percent inspiration, ninety-nine percent
perspiration.

Thomas Edison

If Edison had a needle to find in a haystack, he would
proceed at once with the diligence of the bee to examine
straw after straw until he found the object of his search.
I was a sorry witness of such doings, knowing that a little
theory and calculation would have saved him ninety
percent of his labor.

Nikola Tesla

In the tumultuous rise of human civilisation, universities remain
one of our oldest institutions. This pedigree is emphasised with
ceremonial caps and gowns of medieval origin, and echoes remain
in academic titles such as dean and chancellor.

The roots of today's academic institutions are indeed ancient. The
term 'academic' comes from a hero of the Trojan War, Academus,
after whom an olive grove was named. At that grove Plato founded

his Academy in 387 BC. As the economic historian Donald Stabile has pointed out, higher education in ancient Greece generated conflicts between the sophists, who sought practical knowledge and charged tuition fees, and those committed to 'virtue' in the form of the pursuit of 'pure' knowledge, such as Plato. Plato's star pupil, Aristotle, remained at the Academy for two decades as a leading intellectual figure, but left when he was overlooked in the appointment of an Academy leader after Plato's death, the job going to a much older man. Thus human resource conflicts, like debates about fees and usefulness, go back to academe's origins.

Although greatly interesting in its own right, we will not be tracing the development of the university from its medieval roots as a fixed home for scholars through to the development of the research university in the nineteenth century; that task has been done very well elsewhere.[1] Suffice it to say here that the dominant driver of university expansion since the 1960s has been about that institution's role in knowledge, based on the idea that developing educated people and generating new ideas drives national economic growth and prosperity. These propositions have been used to inflate to unprecedented proportions a model that had evolved over barely a century, one which had grown out of traditions of elite education, a fostering of national culture, and the specialised pursuit of professorial research interests. In the process the university model has been moulded to fit a new set of priorities, providing education for the masses and generating useful research, and has been subject to increasing pressures on funding and external scrutiny. But the university concept has also demonstrated its own adaptability and influence, retaining substantial independence, resisting many attempts to engineer it into policy-makers' preferred forms, at times leading politicians and others to back it in international races for prestige and basic research, and absorbing influences that many have thought would lead to its downfall.

Of course it is easy to find signs of pressure, and many are willing to claim crisis. Forests have been levelled to produce books and articles about the corruption of the ideals of liberal education and the pursuit of knowledge for its own sake, the incursion of managerialist methods and terminology, the fracturing of academic work and the use of non-permanent staff. Some of these are serious scholarly criticisms, others are more curmudgeonly polemics produced by disgruntled academics.[2] From other quarters policy entrepreneurs regularly herald the coming dissolution of the academic monasteries, for nimble online private alternatives will surely rise to swamp them. More recently, as befits these times of global economic uncertainty, there has been talk of a 'higher education bubble' as levels of degree attainment and student debt reach unprecedented heights.

Without doubt we are beyond the stage where grand narratives of the university will do the job that they have done in the past, whether they invoke the purity of knowledge or its usefulness. Knowledge is vastly more diverse, complex and contested than ever before, and public funding for universities is under even greater pressure. This does not mean that universities will become obsolete, after all they have shown considerable adaptability before, but it does mean that it will be increasingly easy for what has been built up over the past half-century to be steadily eroded by a zero-sum competition for resources, changing philosophies of public financing, and competition for credibility and relevance.

After the Second World War, the attention of policy-makers turned to national reconstruction. In Australia and the rest of the Western world they did so in an environment with radically changed perceptions about the power of science and technology, alongside ongoing political concern about the influence and growth of communism and growing egalitarian and democratic social norms. An expanding middle class was emerging as Australia moved from a heavy reliance on primary industries and as corporate and government bureaucracies grew.

An observer had only to look to the United States to see practical demonstration of the industrial, military and wider economic power of science and technology, riding on the back of the world's strongest universities, which had benefitted enormously from the Nazis' gutting of Germany's intellectual capital in the 1930s. The arms and space races between the United States and the Soviet Union yielded astonishing advances in technology and engineering, and prospects for further advances in prosperity through knowledge seemed limitless.

By the late 1950s new theories of 'human capital' were being developed by economists to link the spread of education and research with economic growth. International bodies such as the United Nations Education, Scientific and Cultural Organization (UNESCO) and the Organisation for Economic Co-operation and Development (OECD) spread the new gospel with conviction and the arguments provided were an additional spur to help justify rapid expansion in public funding during the 1960s.

The post-war boom that fuelled the growth of universities in Australia and around the world was driven by demographics, changes in social attitudes and expectations, and economic growth. For the next 25 years until the early 1970s the Australian economy experienced a 'golden age' of prosperity.[3] However, since that time there have been several economic swings in fortune, with a sustained shift away from traditional primary and manufacturing industries as a source of employment, along with rising participation by women in the workforce, expansion of service industries and, in particular, strong growth in professional employment and a shift in financial rewards to favour people with higher levels of skill and knowledge.

One evident factor driving these changes was globalisation and the exposure of national economies to increased competition. In particular, much attention has been directed toward the rise of East Asian economies, beginning with Japan in the 1960s, which were able to draw on abundant low-cost labour to supply global markets with manufactured products that could out-compete those supplied by developed nations. The capacity of firms to outsource elements of their supply chains to countries with cheaper labour has not been restricted to manufacturing, and 'offshoring' has seen significant numbers of lower-skilled jobs in areas such as telecommunications and banking support shifted to call centres in Asian countries. More recently, signs have appeared that professional skills such as IT and legal services might be heading the same way. A related development is the increasing standardisation of aspects of work, for example in accounting standards, technology platforms, management procedures and national and international regulation. These all reduce the value of local, firm-specific and non-specialised skills.

However, it is the development of new technologies which has led to the most profound changes in the ways we work. The nature of these technological developments, and the consequent shifts in the demand for skills as people adapted their needs and abilities around the capabilities of new technology, are far from straightforward. There is not one simple story to be told, not least because the adoption of technology around the world has at different times been influenced by social and political factors – such as opposition by guilds, mercantilist protectionism, or imperial and colonial dominance. Technology's impact on the demand and reward for skills has also played out in complex ways. That said, we will attempt a very broad sketch of what appears to be the pattern.

The most familiar large-scale technological disruption is of course the Industrial Revolution. In the nineteenth century steam-powered advances in machinery and transport reduced demand for highly skilled artisanal labour and replaced it with largely unskilled factory work, a phenomenon that continued into the twentieth century with the rise of the factory assembly line. However, over time advances in electrification, transport and logistics in turn reduced the demand for unskilled routine manual work and led to higher levels of 'white collar' work as well as driving greater rewards for those workers who had higher levels of skills and education. Toward the end of the twentieth century this direction of change was further emphasised by the deployment of computers and new communications technologies, and we saw the demise of many routine white collar jobs such as typists, book-keepers, telephone operators and bank clerks.[4]

This trend over the second half of the last century has been described as 'skills-biased technological change', and has come to be a widely accepted explanation for the counter-intuitive fact that in most developed nations higher education graduates have done and continue to do much better in the labour market than others, despite a massive increase in the production of graduates from universities over recent decades. It has seen a hollowing-out of the more routine medium level of skilled jobs, including 'blue collar' jobs in manufacturing as well as those in the white collar areas which constituted the staple form of employment for much of the middle class that emerged in developed countries, such as Australia, in the post-war period. What we see now is a gradually polarising labour market, with employment growth and increasing pay in jobs which demand high levels of cognitive ability, as well as growth in low-income low-skill jobs which are relatively hard to automate, including personal services such as hairdressing, hospi-tality and cleaning.

Technology continues to develop, due in no small part to the work of engineers, computer scientists, mathematicians and other researchers in universities around the globe who are working busily with various partners to explore ways of further enhancing the scope of computers to undertake more complex tasks. In 2011 two MIT professors, Eric Brynjolfsson and Andrew McAfee, set out the case for the next phase of employment disruption, or as they phrased it 'the race against the machine', a case they expanded upon in their 2014 book *The Second Machine Age*. With ever increasing capacity to collect and analyse data, and greater power for computer programs to simulate human abilities to perceive and manipulate the external world, they saw inevitable inroads about to be made into what might previously have been seen as comfortably safe havens of human employment. They pointed to early developments in automated tutoring, self-driving cars, language translation and speech recognition, health diagnosis, software engineering, financial advice, data analysis, legal services, monitoring of other machines, transport logistics, and even surveillance and monitoring that might reduce the need for law enforcement.

Even more disturbingly they suggest that the traditional economists' view – that people find other jobs when technological changes raise productivity – might not continue to hold true, or at least such new employment might not be keeping pace with the rate of job destruction. This issue is far from being settled, but the general picture of increasing encroachment of computerisation into employment certainly is. In 2013 two Oxford academics, Carl Frey and Michael Osborne, modelled such changes and estimated that around 47 per cent of total US employment is at high risk of being transformed by computers over the next couple of decades, a calculation that has been reproduced for the Australian labour market to arrive at a figure of around 40 per cent.[5] Importantly, Frey and Osborne's model predicted an end to the workforce polarisation that had characterised the latter part of the twentieth century: despite the concerns about the impact on more cognitively demanding professional jobs, their assessment was that computerisation would be mostly confined to low-skill and low-wage occupations. Their take-home message was that the only refuge from automation was for workers to develop stronger creative, social and cognitive skills.

Again, we must emphasise that these changes are not uniform and they do not constitute anything like the full story. If technology had indeed been steadily driving up demand for high cognitive skills and enabling skilled employees to enhance their work then we would expect to see clearer signs of productivity growth across the world than we see in practice. Some scholars argue that the wave of computer use that drove up rewards for skills ended at the turn of the century, at least in the United States, and that since 2000 the demand for cognitive skills has declined, leading more highly qualified applicants to seek less skilled employment and pushing people with lower skills further down the employment chain. Thus the *supply* of educated workers has been a major driver of change rather than *demand* arising from technological change.[6]

Certainly the supply of graduates has been a major factor in the different levels of the so-called 'degree premium' – the wage gap between workers with or without degrees – across different countries. In Australia, for example, rising demand for skilled workers since the early 1980s was met with a strong increase in the supply of graduates, particularly after the Dawkins reforms of the late 1980s, while in the US the increase in supply was much less. As a result the wage premium for workers with degrees did not widen in Australia to the extent that it did in the US.[7] Estimates of the rate of 'return on investment' for obtaining a degree inevitably rely on particular methods and assumptions, and they vary significantly for different courses of study, 'but there is general agreement that investment in an undergraduate degree is highly profitable from an individual viewpoint'.[8]

Policies to expand the number of university graduates were actively pursued in many countries, including Australia. Added impetus to this expansion came from new theories of economic growth that were developed in the late 1980s and 1990s, originating in work by economists Robert Lucas and Paul Romer. Known as endogenous growth theories (where endogenous means an 'internal driver of a system' rather than an 'external add-on'), these models suggested that the development of human capital and technological innovation could interact in productive ways, with the accumulation of knowledge generating increasing returns from their deployment. This contrasted with classical theories, which assumed that stocks of capital had declining returns beyond a certain point.[9] In other words, the total value of a qualified population was more than the sum of the individual parts, and one person's degree could add value to that of another, leading to higher levels of creativity, innovation and productivity. Such ideas were adopted enthusiastically by New Labour in Britain. In 1999 Tony Blair announced the goal of 50 per cent of 17 to 30 year olds in the United Kingdom participating in higher education, and two years later a date of 2010 was set as the target for achieving that goal.[10]

However, the extent of the return on investment to individuals and to the wider public may prove to be tested more seriously following continued rapid rises in university enrolment and graduation. In Australia there was a rapid increase in the university student population after 2008, as a result of the removal of government controls on student numbers in public universities under what has been termed the 'demand-driven' system. Between 2008 and 2014 the total number of domestic Australian university students rose by nearly one third, to over one million. The number of graduates rose by 27 per cent overall, and up to 47 per cent in areas such as health. The demand-driven system had been conceived in more optimistic times before the Global Financial

Crisis (GFC), when a review of higher education predicted strong growth in demand for graduates over the subsequent decade. The Australian job market remained sluggish for some years in the wake of the GFC and in 2014 the annual national survey of initial employment for university graduates, the Graduate Destination Survey, recorded the lowest levels since the early 1980s, with only marginal improvement recorded in 2015. In the past, surveys taken a few years after graduation have shown much stronger employment outcomes than the initial snapshot, which is taken only four months after graduates leave university, and so it is hoped that these subdued results will turn around in due course. Nevertheless, the situation starkly illustrates the heightened risks and raised stakes involved in higher education: university education is becoming more and more necessary, but in at least some fields there is increasing uncertainty about where, or in some cases even if, the expected rewards might be found.

In addition to allowing universities to enrol more students, in Australia there have been fundamental changes in economic and industry policies that have sought to help, or at times force, local industries to adapt to the new globalised and technology-influenced realities. And there have been related efforts to reorient education systems to equip people with what were seen as the necessary knowledge and skills to enable the Australian economy to remain competitive. Over the course of the 1980s and 1990s increasing attention was paid to ways in which developments in knowledge and technology could also play a part in this program of reform.

Undoubtedly and inevitably, government efforts to respond rationally to the ways in which complex global forces impacted on the local scene have involved a level of oversimplification. A focus on identifiable skills and competencies, particularly those of a generic rather than a disciplinary nature, and on meeting the immediate or planned future needs of industry, came to dominate the vocational education and training sector. That focus also influenced universities, though in less prescriptive ways. In addition to attempts to turn on or turn off the tap to supply overall graduate numbers to the workforce, there have been efforts to develop meaningful workforce planning in professional fields and to anticipate and respond to skills shortages in areas such as teacher education, science and engineering, and medical and health fields. These exercises proved to be more difficult than anticipated, although more sophisticated and comprehensive approaches continue to be explored for the health workforce in the present day. And in terms of encouraging innovation, the principal focus of policy that affected universities was on increasing the supply of research and emphasising its commercial possibilities.

Many state and national governments around the world have sought to anticipate which areas might provide competitive advantage and directed investment toward them. These efforts have been valuable in stimulating additional activity, and were intended to identify strategic niches. Most investment, though, has been directed toward a similar set of fields: nanotechnology, biotechnology and information/communications technologies. At least this has been the case over the last decade or so in Canada, several US states, and Queensland and Victoria as the two standout Australian jurisdictions. The prevailing and understandable mindset in all these places was driven by the desire to generate new industries and commercial returns from spin-offs over a relatively short period.[11]

A complex picture of the role of knowledge in promoting innovation and economic growth has emerged over the past decade, involving more than simple stories of old industries being replaced with new technology-based ones, of manufacturing giving way to services, or of an extension of Silicon Valley-style spin-offs from the commercialisation of university research. The *use* and *exchange* of new ideas and technology, not just their invention, are now recognised as important in driving innovation and productivity in all industries. Examining which factors make an organisation good at effectively developing and deploying new ideas or technology is an ongoing topic of scholarly research, as is the exploration of how (or in fact whether) knowledge-intensive industries differ from others. Increasingly, attention has been directed to the dynamics of complex interconnected systems of institutions and people, operating under conditions of uncertainty, in some cases adopting a framework that is closer to biology, and in particular to evolution and ecology, than to traditional industrial research and policy development.

In 2008 the Rudd government in Australia commissioned a study of national innovation, developed by an expert panel chaired by Dr Terry Cutler. Although influenced by wider systems perspectives, both the report of the review and, more particularly, the government's response did not develop clear and consistent positions in emphasising ways of developing greater experimentation and connectivity between the parts of the national innovation system.[12] Instead, the fall-back position was to adopt more orthodox approaches that boosted research spending and rationalised government action only on the grounds of possible market failure as a general principle, or for particular industry sectors such as car manufacturing. For university research, despite aspirations for greater connections with business, the sole emphasis was on 'excellence' as judged by academic peers, and any potential conflict between the goals of excellence and impact was ignored. Since that time changes of government have seen some new priorities identified, and in one of its first statements of policy intent the Turnbull government signalled that renewed attention would be given to stimulating innovation and links between universities and industry. Industry-funded research will be allocated more weighting in calculations of research infrastructure, and there are ongoing efforts to measure and reward research impact, including proposals to include this aspect in the next round of the national university research assessment in 2018.

More generally, the unclear nature of what knowledge is, how it is developing, and how it adds value in complex, unstable, global and local interconnected networks poses dilemmas for policy, and raises hard questions about the role and future of universities. 'We are in a crisis of knowledge,' writes Harvard University's David Weinberger in his 2012 book *Too Big To Know*, which explores the implications of the explosion in networked information and communication in environments of constant uncertainty, change and contested claims to authority. Weinberger points to five basic features of the internet that affect our use and understanding of knowledge:

- Abundance: the sheer volume of data, information, scientific viewpoint and general opinion that is available continuously from around the world;
- Links: connections can be made from one idea to another, embedding any one point in a much larger context, and 'the last word is now never the last word';
- Permission-free: publication is open-ended and largely uncontrolled, and drawing out credible and reliable information from the noise needs new ways of deciding and rating expertise;
- Public: the process of science has been opened up, instead of being communicated through authorised final channels in the form of journals or books, and knowledge is being shown to be a web of human-mediated connections rather than independent absolute truth;
- Unresolved: knowledge is not about the removal of doubt or conflict; 'what we have in common is not knowledge about which we agree but a shared world about which we will always disagree.'

These are not new discoveries about knowledge. To some extent they reflect, though in a much more accessible way, arguments about science and society set out a decade ago by Michael Gibbons, Helga Nowotny and Peter Scott.[13] The authors built on their earlier ideas about the emergence of what they dubbed 'Mode 2' forms of university work, and research in particular. Under Mode 2, the emphasis was expected to shift from departmental, discipline-based formulations to more socially accountable ways of addressing problems in their practical context. Somewhat cryptically they wrote of society 'speaking back' to science under new conditions, where expertise is widely distributed and contextual problems involve opening up science and dealing with uncertainties that are qualitatively different from those traditionally dealt with by scientists.

Many would recognise elements of evident transformations in university research that correspond to parts of the Mode 2 paradigm. For example, there is an increasing tendency to focus work in fields such as the health and medical sciences on particular problems by drawing together the perspectives of different disciplines. There is little doubt that universities have become more densely embedded in society, with multiple forms of engagement, and links formed with business and government. The Mode 2 term, though, has never really taken hold. In part this was because it underplayed the continuing role and reality of traditional discipline-based work, and also because the wider claims of Gibbons and his co-authors about the 'hollowness of the core of science' were either too cryptic or a step too far for either scientists or policy-makers to take.

Challenges to disciplinary knowledge on the grounds of insufficient appreciation of 'context' have not come just from external engagement. The structure of disciplines and the authoritative nature of academic knowledge have been undermined from within via the rise of postmodernist thinking, and related ideas in education such as constructivism. These movements emphasise that knowledge is not separable from human beings and their social context, and it does not come simply from the observation of reality without the intervention of human-constructed frameworks for interpretation, so truth cannot be determined in an absolute manner. In more extreme forms some proponents have argued that reality is a meaningless concept, that all knowledge is politics and no form of knowledge should be 'privileged' over another, so that people should simply be assisted to construct their own 'meanings' rather than be drawn into academic disciplines. Not only have looser versions of this thinking invited ridicule, particularly when expressed in unnecessarily dense jargon and when drawing on poorly understood scientific concepts, but they also have been prone to sterile analysis and have proven to be ineffectual in the face of more practical and powerful interests that have their own reasons for wanting disciplinary knowledge downplayed in the curriculum.[14]

Postmodernism has evolved within the academy, and these days it is less flamboyantly radical. While the fundamental insights about the frailty and social origins and forms of knowledge remain, reason has not been entirely dethroned and natural scientists still go about their business as if there is a real world they are studying with real atoms and galaxies in it. Scholars of people and society can also ply their trade as if their work might actually involve generalised ideas and drive useful change. If anything, the rise and dominance of the Western form of the university based on knowledge, and scientific knowledge in particular, shows that the tide has been, and continues to be, against the kind of local contextualised 'knowledges' talked of by Mode 2 proponents. The university as we know it offers a universal framework for understanding and responding to the world and makes authoritative knowledge accessible, and presents it in a form that certifies that graduates have at least some grasp of what it entails. Sociologists

David Frank from the University of California and John Meyer from Stanford University argue that it is precisely this search for participation in an individualised and globalised framework that has driven the rise of universities around the world and not, as commonly believed, the meeting of increasingly complex social and economic demands for skills. They see this as explaining the survival of the university 'over all the technically superior competition that is supposed to undercut it in the current period', as well as the considerable degree of similarity displayed by universities around the world. For them, worries about the corruption of the academy by the intrusion of outside interests overlook far more the thorough 'destruction of what was once thought of as local 'society' by a universalizing academy'.[15]

This global reach of universities, in a form recognisably based on Western institutional models, has been clearly illustrated by the dramatic growth of higher education and research in Asia.

Building critical mass in Asia

This is expected to be the Asian century. The links between universities and economic growth have long been acknowledged by the most dynamic economies in the region, with explosive growth in a number of East and South Asian countries' university systems over the past two decades. While some countries, such as OECD members Japan and South Korea as well as non-OECD Singapore, Taiwan and Hong Kong, have well-established higher education systems that combine, to varying degrees, mass access with quality, other vigorous emergent economies are moving rapidly in that direction. Most important among them is China. In addition, since the late 1990s several Asian countries, including China and South Korea, have massively expanded university research in an effort to drive greater economic innovation and to achieve parity with (and ultimately surpass) Western nations' capabilities in future knowledge economies.

The template for Asian universities varies to some extent but is based on Western models, reflecting either colonial legacies or, in the case of Japan, the evolution of German ideals of the research university. Western universities, and those in the United States in particular, exert powerful influences both through their provision of education to international students and through their current dominance of research. In most Asian countries strong emphasis is placed on applied research and practical knowledge, in line with firm government driving of the 'universalising' knowledge of science. However, it would be a mistake to assume that Asian higher education and research are necessarily converging in all respects to a Western model. These are, after all, times of transition and development.

A number of scholars have pointed to particular characteristics that distinguish higher education in those jurisdictions that share a Confucian cultural heritage: China, Taiwan, Hong Kong, Japan, Korea, Singapore and Vietnam. These include:[16]

- strong national government influence;
- a high value placed on education by people from all walks of life, with education seen as a crucial part of social mobility but accessed via competition rather than by right. 'Meritocratic elitism' based on success in high-stakes tests has its roots in civil service examinations used to select government officials, and it has extended into the modern era through university entrance exams. This develops strict institutional hierarchies, but elitism and stratification are widely seen as legitimate and necessary to maintain prosperity and harmony;
- families in Confucian traditions play a central role in financing and driving students, unlike countries such as Australia, which

emphasise student choice in a system sustained by public funding. Surveys in China have repeatedly shown children's education to be an important reason for family saving, and private tutoring is widespread to gain an edge in highly competitive schooling systems. Private provision of higher education is a major part of the sector, particularly at the lower end, with most public subsidies flowing to those attaining prestigious spots at top universities; and

- partly as a corollary to the high level of private contribution to the costs of tuition, some of these nations have been able to direct large amounts of public funding toward scientific research and the development of 'world-class universities'.

Such features have enabled massive growth in university systems in a relatively short period of time. For example, China in 2014 had at least 27.3 million students across its 12,529 higher education institutions, representing a participation rate of some 37.5 per cent, on track to meet a target of 40 per cent by 2020. The OECD projects that on the basis of current trends, China and India will account for 40 per cent of all young people with a tertiary education in G20 and OECD countries by the year 2020, while the United States and European Union countries will account for just over a quarter. By 2030 China and India are expected to supply more than 60 per cent of the G20 workforce with a qualification in science, technology, engineering and mathematics. Nor are those two the only Asian countries pursuing rapid growth: Singapore also has a 40 per cent participation target by 2020, and has set ambitious investment targets for R&D investment as a share of GDP.

Progress in the development of university systems in Asia has led to an upward movement in league tables based on examination results (such as the OECD PISA[17] measures of secondary school students) or on research output. Growth in immigration by people from Chinese and other Asian cultures in Australia has also seen their children come to dominate elite levels of school performance and university entry. This has led to alarm in some quarters, and concern that other Australians could be left behind. Asian examples also have provided a source of leverage for arguments about the need for the Australian government to lift its investment in research and, for some, to imitate strategies of increasing investment in selected universities. More positively, the fact that much of the knowledge produced by universities is open and a public good should mean that the growth of Asian universities is not a zero sum competition but, rather, provides an opportunity for greatly increased collaboration and growth.

On the other hand, there are signs of some vulnerabilities in Asia's race to achieve parity with the West. There are good reasons for not necessarily wanting to emulate Asian national strategies simply because we fear falling behind. In the first place, the ideals of the Western university do not necessarily mesh easily with Confucian-style strong government, a desire for social stability or respect for authority. Much has been written about different styles of communication and of teaching and learning in Asian countries and, while some have taken issue with stereotypes about rote learning and lack of creativity, there are genuine differences in expectations and learning styles. Many Asian students studying in Australia have experienced difficulties with individual learning, plagiarism policies, constructivist pedagogies, and group and class participation. In China there has also been persistent criticism of traditional didactic teaching methods.

Philip Altbach, a leading scholar of international higher education, has pointed to the constraints inherent in the lack of flexibility and innovation in many higher education institutions in China, the subordinate role played by students in strict academic hierarchies, and the restriction of research and graduate studies to an elite few. The Chinese system has seen significant and robust debate in recent years over university outcomes, entry procedures and a questioning over whether the higher education system is delivering the results needed for China's future. As is the case in Australia, but on a much larger scale, rapid expansion in graduate numbers has coincided with a lack of immediate job opportunities for new graduates. In 2013 nearly one in four of China's seven million new graduates was unemployed, and millions more form what has been dubbed the 'Ant tribe' of graduates working in unskilled and poorly paid positions.[18] In addition, the relatively single-minded focus of research on applied scientific and technological fields may not pay dividends to the extent envisaged unless it is broadened into more fundamental and discipline-based inquiry and into wider areas such as bioscience, social sciences and other creative fields.

Perhaps most importantly, the elite and hierarchical nature of higher education in a number of Asian countries may derive cultural support from Confucian values, but as the middle class grows and, in all likelihood, as elite privilege becomes more entrenched and concentrated, reliance on this support may prove increasingly misplaced. A focus on educational equality is already becoming apparent in Chinese education, but efforts to make practical inroads may be difficult while wider cultural and economic causes of inequality remain in place. This is a phenomenon that has long been observed in the West.

All large countries that seek to develop mass higher education systems will be confronted with the dilemmas inherent in balancing elite and research-intensive activities against the need to provide good quality education for those who participate. While some of the Confucian-heritage Asian nations have the resources and organisation to make headway in dealing with these issues, others are struggling. Altbach has highlighted the parlous state of higher education in India that, despite massive growth in enrolment over the past decade, faces many challenges.[19]

Indian economic growth has been underpinned by domestic consumption and a large services sector rather than low-cost manufacturing-driven exports. The services sector is becoming more knowledge intensive, making quality expansion of the higher education sector a necessity for continued growth. While India is blessed with a young population and most projections of the growth of the Indian economy are based on this factor, the nation's leaders have realised that this demographic dividend could easily become a social nightmare if India fails to properly educate its youth.

In terms of sheer numbers, India has a very large higher education sector. However, it is of highly variable quality. While the elite institutions are world class, mainly because they are among the most selective institutions in the world, the quality quickly deteriorates as one proceeds down the reputation pecking order. There are other peculiarities of the Indian higher education sector. Apart from a few notable exceptions, India does not have high-quality, comprehensive, research-intensive universities. There has been a tendency to create discipline-specific elite institutions beginning with Indian Institutes of Technology (IITs), Indian Institutes of Management (IIMs) and, more recently, National Law Schools and Indian Institutes of Information Technology (IIITs). Again, apart from a few elite institutions the research output of Indian universities is low. Some of this can be attributed to the historical focus on national laboratories for much of the country's research needs. These are also some of the reasons that Indian universities do not perform well in global rankings.

The Indian government has made expansion of the higher education sector a priority and has been looking at a number of avenues in this regard. One of the earliest steps taken by the government was to relax the requirements for setting up universities by private providers and giving these institutions the status of 'deemed' universities. This measure has been the most significant contributor to the quantitative expansion of the Indian higher education system. To address the question of quality, the Indian government has developed a program to establish a number of national world-class universities and the creation of several more IITs and IIMs. The biggest challenge facing these new institutions has been their ability to attract quality academic staff. This is because India has not made the requisite investment in doctorate-level education. To address some of these issues, the Indian government introduced *The Universities for Research and Innovation Bill 2012*, however, this Bill lapsed in the transition to a new government.

Another proposal to enhance the quality of the Indian higher education system has been to open the sector to overseas institutions. There has been serious opposition to this move and the *Foreign Educational Institutions Bill* – originally tabled in the Indian parliament in May 2010 after being cleared by the cabinet – has not progressed. Also, the government's aim of establishing new institutions has also encountered challenges resulting from delays in land acquisition and disputes between central and state governments over the location of these institutions.

Achieving reforms to Indian higher education and research will not be easy. The Indian political process is both complicated and chaotic, and not assisted by the confusing though powerful role of the Indian judiciary in regulating the landscape of Indian higher education. But India's culture is also extraordinarily entrepreneurial, and new and politically confounding experiments are occurring regularly.

Against the backdrop of the Indian government's inadequate attempts to address the mismatches between supply and demand, the private sector appears to be filling some of the gaps. There has been an explosion in private sector activity in higher education in the past decade. Again, much of it is of variable quality, but there are some notable experiments that could point a way forward for India. Companies such as InfoSys now provide world-class training facilities for their employees that act as finishing schools for poorly prepared university graduates. Private institutions such as Manipal have developed commercially sustainable models for providing quality professional education and are expanding overseas. There is a great deal of experimentation with new business models in the private education and training sector, and it is very likely that trends such as online learning and new ways of assessing quality of learning as demanded by employers could lead to some disruptive business models that may have consequences far beyond India.

A good example is the emergence of a private company, Aspiring Minds, established by Himanshu Aggarwal and Varun Aggarwal and now a Harvard Business School case study. This company, which has financial backing from eBay founder Pierre Omidyar, is essentially a graduate brokerage service for industry and employers, and its formation reflects a high level of frustration on the part of employers regarding the skills of graduates and the reliability of qualifications. In this context, Aspiring Minds – the tagline of which is 'employability quantified' – works with employers to identify the skills they need in graduates. The company then designs skills tests that university graduates may sit. An initiative like this is highly relevant in an era where certification of massive open online courses (MOOCs)-based ventures is an active issue. Aspiring Minds entered into a partnership with edX in 2013 and has since expanded into China, the US, Southeast Asia, Sub-Saharan Africa and the Middle East. It has recently acquired Letintern.com, India's largest online and mobile internship platform, and plans to expand its scope globally.

There can be no doubt that higher education and research across Asia will continue to develop rapidly and new approaches will emerge too as countries grapple with issues such as quality and the balance between mass and elite activity. Certainly selected Asian universities will grow their share of global research output and, in doing so, they will exert powerful influences on universities around the globe. Asian higher education systems have absorbed many of the forms and norms from the West but are both reworking and rethinking them and reflecting back to the rest of the world the importance of universities as engines of economic and social development.

We have deliberately focussed in this chapter on the role universities play in economic development. Of course there are wider rationales to do with private and public development from which benefits can and have emerged in the past, from university research, critique and education. Simon Marginson covers a number of these aspects in his reflections on the nature of public good in higher education.[20] One of the key points he makes is that universities have great potential as creators of global public goods, and a focus on that aspect could offer some escape from both capture by private interests and narrow steering by the state. Certainly there is no shortage of global challenges; a rather alarming summary has been provided by the World Economic Forum cataloguing a series of global economic, societal, technological, geopolitical and, perhaps above all, environmental risks.[21] Coming to grips with these will require breakthroughs in knowledge and understanding and will require us to break out of the straitjacket of individual or national self-interest. The wider benefits of university education and research may ultimately be more important than immediate employability or industry innovation, and many students are driven by curiosity and a desire to make a positive difference to the world, not just simply to secure a well-paying job. However, it is probably the case that the contemporary university will stand or fall on perceptions of its economic benefits. Preparing students for more challenging and uncertain working lives and generating useful knowledge remain the cornerstones of public and private support for universities.

Yet there are serious questions about purpose and structure. Are universities really necessary and are there better alternatives? There is no firm resolution of the nature of the intertwined relationships between higher education and the economy, and this includes lack of clarity as to how universities should balance their obligations to the here and now with their obligation to prepare people for the economies of the future. The endogenous growth models of Romer and Lucas suggest that knowledge drives growth, while the functional idea that an increasingly complex economy drives demand for higher education remains widespread. Yet it is exceedingly difficult to measure how much value higher education actually adds to people's prospects and to the wider economy. There is little doubt that people who are more educated do better, on average, in all sorts of ways, including in lifetime income. What is more contested is how much of this is due to the quality of their education, as opposed to education acting as a sorting and signalling mechanism of basic ability. Proponents of the signalling hypothesis suggest that employers look to university graduates because they have shown the ability to complete a degree and the more selective the university the better. From this perspective higher education is more of a zero-sum competition than a snowballing benefit to individuals and society.

Alison Wolf took a sceptical look at the links between education and growth in her book *Does Education Matter?* Writing in 2002, she noted the drive for more university education and vocational training around the world, particularly in the United Kingdom at that time. While acknowledging some benefits she argued that such expansion had led education to become over-bureaucratised, stretched too thinly to the point where quality was in jeopardy, and too narrowly focussed on economic return. For her, the main impetus for university growth was student demand fuelled by signalling effects: the higher the percentage of a person's peers with degrees, the more the need to have one to make it to the job interview, because employers will interpret degrees as signs of ability.

It is likely that some such element of signalling is part of the picture. But while it is always possible to find contrarians who take strong positions on the signalling function of education, it is both highly plausible and in line with a considerable body of research evidence to conclude that university education can and does make people more productive in particular ways associated with what is taught. In other words, engineers and other graduates have actually learned things at university that equip them with skills and abilities that allow them to be more productive than if they had not gone to university. In turn, their productivity helps to raise that of others. As the Edison and Tesla quotations that open this chapter suggest, theory is useful precisely because it helps us to understand the nature of a task better and to be vastly more productive by building on the formally developed insights of many others.

One would hope that graduates develop a deeper and broader understanding of the world beyond technical or generic skills related to their prospective employment, not least because they will have been involved in an environment that has challenged their preconceptions and led them to realise how little they know. Of course this is an ideal that is more recognisable by its absence than its pervasiveness, and it is likely to be impossible to secure broad agreement on which areas of study should constitute a curriculum that truly prepares graduates to take their place in the globalised transformed future. Nonetheless, while some degrees will be of more value than others, the general value of higher education is becoming more and more apparent, certainly over the alternative of not holding a degree. As the proportion of people holding degrees increases, though, we are hearing louder questions about cost and value, and alternatives to the university-as-we-know-it are being more vigorously sought.

At the heart of the university as it has developed in Australia is a series of propositions, which we cast in a consciously pragmatic way – that is, they are not about personal growth or culture but about how universities can be useful to individuals and society, as that usefulness has been the rationale for their growth and without it they can only drift:

- in a world of uncertainty, instability, political spin and influence, a world that is facing complex social, economic and environmental challenges, there needs to be a home for scholars to pursue new knowledge and to question the status quo in open environments; that is, not directed by short-term or proprietary interests or subject to intervention and control by those who might not like what is being examined;
- higher education is about the interface between what is known, which is almost always subject to revision, and what is not known, and so it should involve some element of exposure to research through the kinds of scholarly communities referred to above;
- breadth rather than specialisation is desirable because the deep pursuit of an area relies on disciplinary methods and knowledge that need to be integrated to develop an appropriate perspective. Narrow or shallow training in a limited number of areas does not equip people with what is needed to flourish in a complex changing world; and

- universities link particular places with global knowledge. Universities provide a physical (and increasingly virtual) focus not only as a home for scholarship but as an education and research bridge to the world for local and regional communities and economies, including Australia's various key regional sites of economic and social production. Universities must be internationally oriented. While they can have multiple local foci, they are also vehicles for universal knowledge without which nations and individuals would be left behind.

These propositions are being challenged and scrutinised more closely than ever before. Is it affordable to have institutions that reflect these principles catering for a universal system? Is academic knowledge provided by local universities really so relevant in a wired and globalised world? Do people really need to turn to universities for meaning and broad understanding of the world rather than acquiring generic and professional skills in order to secure a good job? How much education is enough and what sort of education is useful? Do institutions providing degrees really need to 'do research', or at least research across all the areas in which they are involved? Can the process of higher education be re-engineered to be more cost-effective and who should pay the bill?

Chapter Three

Models of the Australian university

In many respects Australian universities are baby boomers. Up to the 1950s Australia had seven universities but these were small, and while they produced some eminent figures in the advancement of science they played relatively little part in national life or economic development. In university education, the prevalent ideal – one held dear by Prime Minister Robert Menzies – was the English concept of elite preparation for gentlemen coupled with select professional training (particularly in law and medicine).

In Australia this ideal was supplemented by a more practical orientation and commitment to industry and community service along the lines championed by the US land-grant universities. All this was set to change in scale, scope and fundamental type as Australia, along with almost all other developed nations, embarked on a period of massive expansion in publicly funded higher education and research.

The big bang and binary systems

The rapid expansion of higher education in the 1960s was framed in terms of a principle set out in Lord Robbins' review of UK higher education and later reflected in a parallel Australian review headed by Professor LH Martin, the head of the Australian Universities Commission (and, like Menzies, a great admirer of the English university system): 'courses of higher education should be available for all those who are qualified by ability and attainment to pursue them and wish to do so.' This lofty principle immediately raised questions about how many and what sorts of people might have such ability, and whether the elite and relatively expensive university was a feasible way of delivering such courses.

In 1947 a major US federal study commissioned by President Truman claimed that 'at least 32 per cent of our population has the mental ability to complete an advanced liberal arts or specialised professional education'.[1] However, experts in the United Kingdom and Australia evidently had a lower opinion of their populations' distribution of brainpower, with the first director-general of the Australian Council for Educational Research (ACER) allowing in 1939 that perhaps 10 per cent were capable of university study, an estimate that was raised to 15 to 20 per cent by the economist John Vaizey in 1962.[2] Both the Martin and Robbins reviews ultimately settled for something around this level, but neither in Australia nor in other places was it delivered by simply expanding the scope of universities.

Present-day concerns about rapid further expansion of university education are certainly not new. In the United States, around the time of the report to Truman, the chancellor of the University of Chicago expressed alarm at 'the proposed pile-up of reluctant learners'. Then, as now, conservative commentators viewed with some alarm the thought that pearls were being cast before swine, and Kingsley Amis, author of the satire on 1950s UK second-tier university life *Lucky Jim*, put it succinctly and spoke for many when he stated 'more will mean worse'. But such concerns could not turn back the tide of overwhelming demand and continuing economic development.

The expansion of higher education in Australia was shaped by both cost considerations and a desire to protect the perceived special nature of universities. These special characteristics drew on two broad university traditions. The first was articulated by Cardinal Newman, who championed the cultivation of the able and deserving individual through classical education, a feature Menzies saw as the shining virtue of the English university. The second tradition was the independent pursuit of research and scientific knowledge by professors and students in departments based on academic disciplines. This latter model grew out of the German universities of the nineteenth century, pioneered by Wilhelm von Humboldt in 1810 with the establishment of the University of Berlin.

While Menzies reluctantly conceded that the pre-war university model would have to change, he was adamant that it would not change too much. Martin had originally proposed, like Robbins, expanding higher education through universities, but he was given clear direction by Menzies that this would not do[3] and the final 1965 Martin Review justified the creation of non-research higher education institutions on the grounds that new knowledge might be valuable to those working in industry or commerce, but it was incidental and it was 'important that students receive the kind of education best suited to their innate abilities and purposes in life'. Thus was born the binary system and, in 1973, the new vocational and technically oriented advanced education sector was further supplemented by the addition of state teachers colleges.

University enrolments in Australia rose steadily until the mid 1970s, and new universities were established to accommodate the demand. However, growth slowed after the financial troubles of that time, with the emphasis shifting to the advanced education sector. By the mid 1980s the numbers in both sectors were about equal, with the advanced education sector funded at around 15 to 25 per cent less per student than universities, the difference being (loosely) attributed to research and postgraduate training.[4] It might also be noted that in those days academic pay was based on recommendations of the Academic Salaries Tribunal, which had looser prescriptions for university lecturers and recommended that the chief executives of universities be paid more than the heads of advanced education institutions (notwithstanding the view that the latter institutions were supposed to require more management). In Australia, as was the case in other binary systems, the official line was that there were 'separate but equal' sectors, but over time it became clear that neither part of this formulation was true in practice.

By the mid 1980s, some two decades after the establishment of the binary system, the national education policy environment had changed dramatically. Lofty ideals of equality of opportunity in education had been whittled away at the secondary school level, with selective independent schools entrenching their position as desired places for the schooling of the children of the aspirational middle class as well as the wealthy. While university fees had been abolished in the mid 1970s and the Labor Government of the mid 1980s maintained an emphasis on access and equity in universities, participation in higher education remained dominated by those who were better off.

The economic outlook was also very different. Severe recessions in the 1970s and early 1980s had accentuated problems with longer-term shifts in the Australian economy and employment. These shifts were not confined to Australia and public policy responses drew on new approaches to public financing and management that were emerging in the United States and elsewhere and which, along with a general recognition of the need for higher order skills in a changing economy, emphasised close scrutiny of efficiency and more structured quasi-scientific management of government outlays.

At this time of high unemployment, constraints on public funding and major structural change, controlling the growing cost of higher education assumed an even higher priority. The Commonwealth Tertiary Education Commission (CTEC), a national body with powerful advisory and administrative responsibilities across higher education, was charged in 1985 with the task of reviewing efficiency and effectiveness in the sector. The 1986 report of its review committee, which included the doyen of university education and former Martin committee member Professor Peter Karmel, considered the future of the binary system, noting considerable overlap in a number of areas, and problems with inflexible credit-granting by universities. However, it continued to maintain that universities were inherently different, arguing that if it were not for the advanced education sector there would have been less recruitment of middle and lower-income students and less vocational commitment, because presumably these were not the province of universities. The report went on to say:

> Finally, it is disturbing to note the extent to which some academics and institutions in both sectors are concerned with matters of status. Reference has already been made to the trend in universities to give inadequate recognition for work carried out by students in the advanced education sector, and to the excessive concern of some advanced education academics to upgrade continually the level of their courses. In many cases this tendency is stimulated by professional bodies and learned societies which tend to upgrade progressively the levels of award they will accept for membership purposes. Public funding is not provided to enhance status ... (p. 199)

While the CTEC Review Committee allowed for the possibility of some expansion of applied research in the colleges, the report recommended that doctoral programs be permitted in a particular college only if a university was not already offering PhDs in that field within the relevant state, and preferably any such program should be under the accreditation of a university.

The assumption that the stresses on the binary system arose mainly from upstart colleges chasing prestige was widespread at the time and, of course, was not entirely without foundation. However, many of those in universities who condescendingly referred to 'aping' or 'mimicry' conveniently overlooked the fact that, far from ceding the lucrative growth in vocational and professional education to the colleges, universities had developed their own programs, which by the late 1980s had well and truly crossed the binary divide.

This was a long way removed from the original plan. Indeed, the first chair of the Advanced Education Commission had commented in 1969 that 'by the end of the century I picture them (the universities) rather as ivory tower institutions, with the colleges being much more practical and training students for chosen vocations and professions ... Thus I envisage a gradual movement away from vocational training in the universities.'[5] This convergence of higher education activity was also due to more than simple mimicry (or, as more polite and theoretically minded scholars would put it, 'institutional isomorphism'). It arose in part from a series of amalgamations between universities and colleges in the early 1980s, and the creation of institutions like Deakin University in the 1970s from non-university component institutions. More fundamentally, the notion that new knowledge and research were appropriate for only a few elite professions, while more or less fixed knowledge and skills were sufficient for others, was increasingly hard to sustain in the face of developments in the real world. Nor could the traditional universities be expected to be the sole source of new knowledge for the wider range of professions; after all, their distance from these fields was the premise on which the binary system was built.

The 1988 Dawkins White Paper, which brought the binary system to an end, was issued at a time of ongoing economic turmoil, with strong pressure for university expansion. Growth would be accommodated, but in a way that was efficient, simplified and managed by the Commonwealth government. Advanced education institutions were not simply redesignated as universities, unlike a similar process that took place in the United Kingdom a few years later. Rather, the entire Australian higher education sector was reshaped along lines perceived by the then minister, John Dawkins, as more manageable. Size benchmarks were set, which effectively drove all institutions to seek amalgamations, and the terms of amalgamation and new university formation were driven strongly by settings dictated by the Commonwealth government.

By 1990 much of the present-day university landscape was in place. It marks out Australia as having a single institutional form to cater for the great bulk of higher education. This form is that of the large, comprehensive public university with the ability to offer degrees through to doctorate level. Defenders of the old binary system claimed, as some still do today, that the new model would be too costly, but several mechanisms were put in place to manage this possibility. Key among these were continued control over the overall price of undergraduate education, the introduction of student contributions to be repaid through the tax system depending on graduate income, deliberate indexation of grants below the level of actual cost growth, and steady separation of funding for teaching and research. Nevertheless, pressures continued to mount as student numbers grew and stronger cases began to be made for increasing research funding.

The Policy Discussion Paper that preceded the 1988 White Paper on Higher Education suggested for indicative purposes that the annual output of graduates might increase from around 88,000 at that time to about 125,000 by the end of the century.

As it turned out, that figure was attained by 1994 and the actual number of domestic students completing in 2000 was more than 10 per cent higher, rising to over 150,000 by 2002. Much of this growth was driven by more students staying on until the end of secondary schooling, which added to a demographic spike in the number of school leavers. It was also contributed to by the transfer of nursing to the higher education sector and strong demand fuelled by continuing economic problems and the evident financial returns enjoyed by university graduates compared to those with lower-level qualifications.

This growth levelled off after 1996, when the Howard government took office, and over the subsequent decade domestic student numbers grew slowly, even declining in 2000 and 2004. In part this reflected demographic factors, as well as wider opportunities for young people in an economy riding another mining boom and an inflating global financial bubble. Political factors were also undoubtedly in play, as the Howard government repeatedly emphasised the benefits of non-university education, and relations between the university sector and the government were at times very strained. Some commentators found it deeply significant that the prime minister during 11 years of government never once visited the Australian National University, just across Lake Burley Griffin from Parliament House. But this viewpoint might be slightly precious. Both John Howard and Dr Brendan Nelson, as the minister for education, ushered in significant reforms of the sector and have since received honorary doctorates from leading public universities.

After the election of a national Labor government in late 2007 growth in domestic higher education provision was actively encouraged and student numbers grew quickly, rising by more than a quarter from 2008 to 2013. The key factor was the government's decision to remove limits on undergraduate student places by 2012, in line with a national target of having 40 per cent of 25 to 34 year olds holding a degree by 2025. While it was known that government spending would inevitably rise with increasing enrolments, the actual level of spending driven by vigorous growth in new enrolments significantly outstripped budget estimates. The financial sustainability of this growth was a key factor in the rationale for the deregulatory reforms proposed in the Abbott government's first budget in 2014. But while deregulation of fees and withdrawal of public funding were controversial, uncapped expansion was not.

As for research, it should be noted that it was never the intention of government that research funding would keep pace with student growth when new institutions were designated as universities, and certainly there was no plan for research funding to be equalised in the new system. The outcome has certainly not been equalisation. Over the period from 1992 to 2013 the share of total external research income (excluding the Australian National University, which receives special block funding arrangements) for the seven oldest research giants has barely shifted, staying at over two-thirds and has even increased for competitive research grants. There have been some movements within that group, however, with the University of Queensland, Monash University and the University of Melbourne growing their relative share. The share of some of the second-tier older universities, such as Flinders University, La Trobe University and Macquarie University, has fallen as some of the newer universities have staked strong research claims. But this has been through competition not favouritism.

It is worth noting that this picture of relative shares obscures an important rise in research activity across almost all universities. During the same 1992–2013 period, external funding for university research increased more than four-fold in real terms, and all but eight Australian universities attracted annual external research income above the $10 million mark. More significantly, a considerable amount of research work is undertaken as a fundamental part of academic work, and so research has generally expanded with growth in the academic workforce. However, it is far too simplistic to assume that the traditional academic workload breakdown of 40 per cent teaching, 40 per cent research and 20 per cent service applies across all academics and all universities; if that were the case then most of our research would indeed be driven by student demand for particular fields of study. In reality there is enormous variation within and among universities in the balance and intensity of various aspects of academic work.

Since the 1990s overall government-controlled funding more than kept pace with inflation, but in universities, as in healthcare, the actual costs associated with highly skilled labour and the use of advanced technology grew much faster. This has translated to pressure on staff numbers and staff time. The growth of external research funding in relation to base funding has meant that it has driven wider research activity in directions unrelated to student demand for education. Nonetheless, the ongoing expansion in undergraduate numbers does drive a demand for more academics and, in turn, an increase in research expectations and demand.

With these mounting pressures it is not surprising that heightened levels of intra-sectoral competition have emerged, and the attractions of a return to the 'good old days' of formal differentiation remain strong for many, particularly the likely beneficiaries of such a return. To this day we hear periodic calls for government to reinstate a formal pigeonholing of institutions, most often by reference to differentiated systems that remain in place in some other countries. Overseas models of differentiated higher education systems can provide useful examples of alternative possibilities, and there are two that recur time and again, though usually the comparisons are not pursued in any depth. Instead they are held up as unproblematic paragons that we should emulate. It is therefore worth considering each of them a little more closely.

The University of California system

In the 1950s California's planners were well aware of the demographic, economic and social factors that would drive the coming great expansion in higher education. As was the case in Australia, the existing system was wholly unprepared to take on the expected growth but, unlike in Australia, the field of play was within one state that contained an existing mix of established and aspiring players, all jockeying for position. Moreover, the future was not bound to British models or ideals. California had on hand a number of gifted educational leaders, prominent among them the University of California President Clark Kerr, and together they developed the 1960 California Master Plan for Higher Education. Under this Plan there was clear demarcation of roles among three sectors:

- The University of California (UC): this is essentially one entity with multiple campuses (currently ten) governed by a single Board of Regents. Under the Plan, the university would take the top 12.5 per cent of high school graduates and one-third of its intake would be students transferring from community colleges who would be guaranteed transfer if they had completed 30 units with a grade point average of 2.4. UC alone has the roles of a traditional research university including the right to award PhDs, to pursue research development and to offer degrees in the prestigious professions of law, medicine and veterinary science;
- The California State University (CSU): as with UC, this is a single entity with multiple campuses (currently 23) governed by a Board of Trustees. Its mission is similar to Australia's

former advanced education sector, dominated by undergraduate programs in teacher education, technical education and a range of other applied higher education areas. It provides certification up to Masters level, although in recent years controversial moves have been made to include PhD awards in education. CSU is meant to draw from the top one-third of high school graduates. Under the Master Plan one-third of its intake would be students transferring from community colleges who would be guaranteed transfer if they had completed 24 units with a B average;

- The California Community Colleges: these take all other high school graduates and provide vocational programs similar to those offered by Australia's VET sector, typically two-year associate degrees. The Master Plan provided for most of the future expansion in Californian higher education to be in its community colleges.

The resultant structure is not only immensely appealing as an exercise in rational central planning, it has generally worked in practice, though is now under serious strain. UC Berkeley is the only public university ranked in the top ten of the prestigious research-based Academic Ranking of World Universities developed by Shanghai Jiao Tong University, while seven other UC campuses are in the top 100. Over more than 50 years mission differentiation has been preserved, at least until relatively recently when cracks have begun to appear, and California has always ranked among the top US states in the number of high school graduates, the number of younger people going on to college, and the number gaining a tertiary degree.[6]

The system was designed, in Clark Kerr's words, to develop 'a universal access segment, a designated research segment (a 'flagship' campus), and a polytechnic segment' to serve 'an egalitarian democracy, a technocratic economy and a meritocratic society'.

However, it relied on a combination of political will, visionary and coherent leadership, economic and labour market conditions that fitted the mould, a within-state perspective on student access to higher education and, above all, money.

By the end of the century Clark Kerr was able to look back with satisfaction but forward with some trepidation. 'The plan's big test now lies in the next twelve to fifteen years,' he wrote with some prescience, noting that the percentage of Californian public spending that went on the Master Plan had fallen from 11.3 per cent in 1960 to 7.8 per cent in 1995, while over the same period spending on prisons had risen from 2.4 per cent to 7.1 per cent and medical expenses for the aged had risen from virtually zero to 14 per cent.[7] The premise that the public would be more likely to fund a planned system rather than a set of institutions of which only one or two would be attended by any one taxpayer's own children seemed to hold while times were good, but the good times seem an increasingly distant memory.

In the wake of the global financial crisis, Californian state funding to UC was sharply reduced, with a cut of 20 per cent in 2009 (partially offset by federal stimulus money), followed by restoration of about half that cut in 2010–11 and then a further reduction of US$650 million in the UC base in 2011–12. In 1990 UC enjoyed per student income of more than US$21,000 in 2011 dollars, 12 per cent of which came from students. By 2011 this had fallen to just over US$17,000 (still well above that for Australian universities), of which students contributed 49 per cent. Average full-time undergraduate tuition fees had already begun to climb sharply in the early years of the new century, but skyrocketed from 2009 before being frozen in 2012–13 for three years. In late 2014, despite the objections of Governor Jerry Brown, the UC Board of Regents sought some relief by conditionally approving five years of relatively modest tuition fee increases, leading to conflict with the State and a push for efforts to pressure the university to operate at lower cost. The tidy apportioning of roles also is fraying. For some time community colleges have chosen to de-emphasise their role as feeders to the university campuses. In addition to the introduction of teacher education PhD programs in 2005, one CSU institution has chosen to develop a collaborative PhD program in engineering with Mississippi State University. A landmark change came in late 2014 when legislation was passed allowing 15 community college districts to offer four-year bachelor degrees. While this is initially a limited pilot in vocational fields not offered by CSU or UC, a precedent has now been established.

Pressures to devolve governance to individual campuses are also growing as the state becomes a minority funder and strategies to develop new funding streams become essential. Others argue against such proposals, claiming that the Board of Regents has not sufficiently exercised its role in keeping UC campuses in their boxes: 'not every place can be Berkeley and UCLA'.[8]

While deeply troubled, the Californian system remains strong and its travails are to some extent more about adjusting to a reality already faced by other higher education systems than a terminal threat to its structure. Whether a tight lid can, or should, be kept on mission differentiation remains an open question, but one downside to its rigidity is that there is little room within public institutions to cater for further expansion in the way needed for the future, which will require greater variety in types of advanced education and depth across many fields rather than a shift to shorter vocational degrees. Further breakouts along the engineering PhD line may eventuate, or possibly new reformulations of managed diversity. One such reformulation has been proposed by a leading US higher education scholar, the Berkeley-based John Aubrey Douglass, whose plan for a refreshed system includes four-year degree-granting community colleges.

The strongest advocates for replicating a Californian-style differentiated system in Australia are those in government who see it as a way of containing costs and those in elite research-intensive universities who see it as a way of limiting competition and funnelling more resources to their own institutions. However, the California Master Plan was a product of economic and political conditions of more than half a century ago and barely made it to fruition in the face of the institutional hurdles in place at that more expansionary time. It was never intended to deliver cheap university education for the state, and it remains under considerable pressure. Keeping such a system together would be a great challenge for any potential replicator, and perhaps this is one reason why, despite widespread admiration, the Californian system remains the exception in the world of higher education and not the rule.

The German model

> I am strongly of the opinion that we need to re-create
> a new class of institution similar to the German
> *Fachhochschulen*, where emphasis is placed on technological
> and practical training closely associated with the short-
> term needs of industry and commerce.
> *John Lovering, vice-chancellor of Flinders University, 1991*

German higher education, like that of the United States, is largely state (*Länder*) based. Like many countries it established a binary system in the 1960s with the *Fachhochschulen* (FH) created mainly from reworking existing engineering colleges or business academies with the intention of catering for greater student numbers and providing applied degree programs.

Unlike the Californian system, or even the Australian system (which, though state based, is strongly driven by the national government), the German binary system did not have strong coordination, and things did not go entirely to plan. Rather than most students going to the FH sector, the university sector continually and haphazardly expanded, becoming large in size, stretched in funding and with high dropout rates, while constraints on the FH meant they were unable to respond effectively.[9] The FH, nonetheless, have managed to establish strong professionally oriented higher education programs; substantial numbers of their staff hold doctorates and the FH have built applied research programs of increasing scope and quality. Known now in English as 'universities of applied sciences', they are converging in many respects to a university model that is recognisable in Australia, particularly for dual sector universities that combine TAFE with higher education offerings. One fundamental difference, as with the Californian system, is a prohibition on offering doctoral programs. Another is the industry environment within which they operate and the depth of the links between businesses and institutions of higher education and research. In Germany, unlike Australia, there is a strong manufacturing sector with many medium-sized businesses that are heavily involved in innovation. This helps to explain the high number of doctorate holders in the German workforce, which is more than twice that of Australia.

As the birthplace of the research university, German universities remain strongly wedded to the Humboldt ideal of close integration of teaching and research through strongly autonomous departmental units with research expectations for all academics. The Humboldtian principle of 'solitude and freedom' prizes the 'disinterested pursuit of knowledge, uncontaminated by any obligation to train for a profession, or to apply knowledge to useful ends'. Not surprisingly this has rendered German universities strongly resistant to contemporary management reforms, and has led to concerns about stagnation, which may only be partly addressed (or even possibly exacerbated) by recent new injections of research funding. By contrast, FH professors do not seem to regard management and market-oriented reforms as a threat to their professionalism.[10]

It also should be noted that the binary higher education system in Germany reflects a hierarchical school system, with very early streaming of students. As early as age ten, students are directed into differentiated school streams: one for the academically weakest students (only up to grade nine), one for those with average grades (up to grade ten, normally followed by vocational training or education, which can lead to higher education) and at the top the selective Gymnasium (up to grade 12), which leads to direct access to universities. Seventy per cent of German school leavers enter Germany's so-called dual apprenticeship system, which leads to respected and rewarding employment in trades and similarly regarded occupations. The system entrenches social inequalities, with migrant children over-represented in the lower division schools and the children of parents in white-collar, high-skilled occupations having a four-fold greater chance than those with parents from blue-collar or low-skilled occupations of making it to university, even if they display the same level of educational performance at an early age.[11]

Germany has been a latecomer to universal higher education. While in many developed countries (including Australia) more than 30 per cent of 25 to 34 year olds have degrees, in Germany the figure is 19 per cent. There is also little variation in attainment across age groups, whereas many other countries, including Australia, have higher rates among younger people, indicating growth in the numbers who hold the qualifications needed to underpin knowledge economies for the future. Germany's low degree-holding profile is shared by Greece, Italy and Portugal (although the latter two have more growth in the younger age group) and, coupled with ageing populations and declining youth cohorts, the prospects for economic vitality look less than optimal.

Of course Germany is nowadays a major economic power on the back of a strong manufacturing sector, with innovative mid-sized firms of the kind rarely found in Australia, and it has taken steps to revitalise both university research and higher education in recent years. However, the sclerotic nature of German university decision-making and the costly and inefficient mode of university operations, mean that progress in driving further economic growth from the work of its universities may be slower than anticipated. There may also be risks for Germany as one of the few countries which have swum against the global tide by returning to an entirely publicly funded system after experimenting with tuition fees over the past decade. Low participation rates enable such exclusive government funding to some extent, as of course does a strong economy, but German higher education is drifting into a system comprised of research elites mixed with poorly funded mainstream institutions, raising the stakes for investment in those elites to deliver tangible returns for the nation.

The Californian and German models illustrate the strengths and limitations of binary systems but neither is a template that would transfer easily to Australia, even if a return to centrally planned system engineering was deemed to be worth pursuing. Universities and university systems do not exist in isolation: they are part of wider ecologies of schools, cultures and industries, and it is naïve to imagine that simply transplanting one part of that ecology to a different setting could reproduce particular features that some might see as desirable. The task of balancing mass higher education, affordable higher education and elite higher education and research is a global one, and formal institutional separation was a logical step 50 years ago at the start of the educational big bang. However, the original rationale for dividing sectors along vocational and theoretical lines has weakened and both the Californian state universities and the *Fachhochschulen* have converged toward a model current in Australia with the exception of PhD awarding power. It would not be surprising to see institutional ambition, student demand, industry expectations, and university inflexibility combine to further weaken that last barrier in coming years.

One can still find binary systems in a number of other European countries, but they too have struggled to hold the line on role definitions in the face of mergers and moves to harmonise degree structures across Europe. Denmark is one country where the line has been held, but the price has been very limited movement or cooperation across institutional divides[12]. Similarly, Norwegian higher education mergers in 1994 were intended to cement a binary system, and in particular to keep two large colleges from becoming universities, but as colleges became larger and developed their programs a number merged with, or became, universities. By 2014 the binary system in that country was much more integrated than structurally separated.[13]

Other forms of US higher education have from time to time been put forward as possible models for Australia. During the period of higher education reform that began a decade ago a senior government official asked in the course of consultations why Australia could not have liberal arts colleges, institutions that concentrated on high-quality undergraduate education (Australia has one self-described Roman Catholic liberal arts college, Campion College in Toongabbie, western Sydney, which enrolled around 400 students in 2015). The reasons why we do not have more are complex and involve quite different trajectories of education reform and philosophy across the two countries, as well as issues of student demand, employer demand, government policy and academic status. However, it is worth mentioning a few features of US liberal arts colleges that may be underappreciated: they are not 'teaching only' institutions and many staff maintain active research profiles, albeit without PhD students; and while quality varies greatly the liberal arts colleges that admirers hold up as worthy of emulation are far more expensive than public alternatives. Perhaps most importantly, the tradition of 'liberal arts' education, that is, broad undergraduate education with no link to any particular vocational outcome, has never taken root in Australia. It has evolved in the United States over more than two centuries, aided by endowment funding of higher education and strong academic norms, but even there it is under some pressure.[14] Adopting something like it would require a mix of market power, pragmatic compromise and financial incentive and, in 2005, one Australian university announced that it would go down something like this path.

The Melbourne model

Almost one year after taking up his post as vice-chancellor of the University of Melbourne, Glyn Davis issued a discussion paper that set the scene for a radical restructuring of the curriculum, shifting the university's vocational and professional education to the postgraduate level while instituting broad general education at the undergraduate level. What became known as 'the Melbourne model' had both principled and pragmatic drivers. It espoused the merits of breadth in undergraduate education and of breaking the immediate link between school achievement (in turn closely linked to socioeconomic privilege) and elite careers.

A move to lengthening the duration of professional education had been underway for some time in a number of areas, and the move from four- to six-year undergraduate degrees in areas such as medicine to graduate entry undergraduate programs (such as the Bachelor of Medicine, Bachelor of Surgery [MBBS]) began nearly two decades ago. The shift to postgraduate education as the standard for professional entry has been more recent, and has taken root in professional programs such as medicine, dentistry and architecture in a number of universities. In 1964 Macquarie University was established with just arts and science undergraduate degrees, with vocational and professional programs offered either as a graduate entry undergraduate program or as a postgraduate program. However, over time Macquarie moved closer to the then norm for Australian universities, and the University of Melbourne was the first institution to systematically overturn this norm in the contemporary Australian higher education environment.

Advocates have argued that extending the education of professionals such as doctors to postgraduate specialisation on top of a more general undergraduate degree would produce more rounded and effective practitioners. Whether it is true or not that US doctors have been generally better practitioners than Australian doctors by virtue of graduate training is not clear, and it might be conversely argued that for a given age, undergraduate trained doctors would have additional relevant experience and knowledge.

Originally it was envisaged that there would be two undergraduate degrees: arts and science. Practical considerations intervened and ultimately a suite of six emerged, with the addition of commerce, biomedicine, environments and music. Students were required to undertake 'breadth' subjects from outside their main degree field, but there too some adjustments had to be made to original aspirations. Originally one-quarter of the degree was to be in breadth subjects, but that was scaled back in 2011 to a requirement of between one-sixth and one-quarter, with problems arising from perceptions of lack of coherence and depth.[15]

In 2005 Australian non-research postgraduate education was mostly full fee-paying, though subsidised places had been made available principally where a postgraduate course was required for initial professional registration. It was expected that the University of Melbourne would move from being nearly three-quarters undergraduate in student load to around half by 2013, a goal that was achieved. The scale of this move prompted a tectonic shift in the policy landscape, with the Commonwealth government allowing the transfer of large numbers of subsidised places from undergraduate to postgraduate level, particularly for the University of Melbourne. This gave strong support to the model but in the process established a problematic precedent and an anomaly that became a substantial policy headache when undergraduate places were deregulated from 2012. The full financial implications of the removal of limits on funded places at undergraduate level were seriously underestimated by the government, and it never intended for a similar open-slather approach to occur at postgraduate level. However, by allowing a piecemeal bleeding across the two levels of public subsidies, one being capped and the other uncapped, Commonwealth authorities found it hard to establish a consistent basis for limiting and allocating subsidised postgraduate places among universities. In addition, the government found itself providing lengthier public subsidies to University of Melbourne students than to those studying in similar areas at other institutions.

To give one example of the resultant anomalies, registration to practice as a general dentist requires around five years of study. There are three possibilities: a five-year undergraduate program such as is offered by the University of Adelaide; a three-year undergraduate program plus a two-year postgraduate program as is offered by Griffith University; and a four-year postgraduate masters-level program with doctoral title to which the University of Melbourne (Doctor of Dental Surgery) has moved. The cost implications for students and the government are significant, with total study time lifted from five to seven years or longer and the fees for postgraduate programs in 2016 to around the $50,000 mark, which for two-year programs would require near to the maximum possible loan coverage from the Commonwealth government. But the cost exposure of students is not consistent. A prospective Adelaide dentist (assuming they did not pay upfront) would leave their undergraduate program with a debt of around $52,000; meanwhile a graduate from Griffith University's postgraduate program could accrue a debt of over $100,000 on top of an undergraduate HECS-HELP debt of around $25,000 to $30,000. The pathway under the Melbourne model would lead to over $260,000 in costs for fee-paying students (twice the limit for government loans) on top of the undergraduate debt. Those fortunate enough to secure a postgraduate Commonwealth-subsidised place would, on the other hand, generate a postgraduate debt of some $42,000 on top of their undergraduate debt.

The University of Melbourne had some additional issues to resolve with the transition of students to the new professional postgraduate programs. In principle, one of the virtues of the process was to break the immediate link between school results and entry to professional programs but, in practice, a number of high-achieving prospective students were unclear about the hurdles they might need to clear in order to gain a postgraduate place. Guaranteed entry to Commonwealth-subsidised postgraduate places in all but the elite programs of law, medicine, dentistry and optometry is now provided to high-achieving students who graduate with at least a 65 per cent GPA, with the very highest echelons (Chancellor's Scholars) also guaranteed entry to a subsidised place in the elite programs. The university is also finding it hard to offer postgraduate programs within the funding rates for places subsidised by the Commonwealth in programs with few if any full fee-paying students, such as teacher education. This is, of course, a difficulty for all Australian universities, but the extent of Melbourne's exposure makes the problem more acute. In 2005 the University of Melbourne had 9.6 per cent of the national pool of Commonwealth-subsidised postgraduate places, behind Monash at 10.7 per cent, while the next highest was the University of New South Wales (UNSW) at 6.3 per cent. By 2013 Melbourne had 15.5 per cent, Monash 5.5 per cent and UNSW 3.9 per cent.

Late in 2008 the University of Western Australia announced that it too would move to something like the Melbourne model, and from 2012 it has offered four broad undergraduate degrees (arts, science, commerce and design) and a Bachelor of Philosophy (Honours) as a research-oriented degree available to the top 2 per cent of prospective students. At least four units (one-sixth of the total) must be taken in one or more areas of knowledge outside the degree-specific major, including some that focus on 'some aspect of the globalised and culturally diverse environment', which includes languages other than English.

Such moves are courageous in a climate where most Australian students have particular preferences and views about relevance when undertaking undergraduate study. Academic critics have argued that breadth subjects would force unwilling or uninterested students to take subjects that would be populist rather than exposing them to depth in another discipline, and standards would inevitably decline as a result. Others anticipated that students would look elsewhere for more specific and immediately relevant programs offered by competitor universities. Certainly undergraduate applications to Melbourne initially fell significantly with the advent of the Melbourne model, to the advantage of places such as Monash University. However, the University of Melbourne's first preferences recovered strongly with its guarantee of entry to professional programs for top-scoring students. No significant fall in demand was seen when the University of Western Australia adopted its postgraduate professional model, possibly because no Group of Eight[16] counterpart was nearby to attract students seeking the usual undergraduate route.

The Melbourne model was always intended to appeal to a particular group of students, and some shift in demand was both anticipated and unproblematic for that institution; in fact, Melbourne intended to hold growth in the student population fixed at around 2010 levels, although by 2014 its total domestic student enrolment was some 13 per cent higher. As for concerns about standards or impacts on staff arising from the teaching of students taking subjects outside their main area of interest or ability, and the additional costs to students (or to the government in the case of students accessing subsidised postgraduate places), it is too early to make conclusive judgements and no doubt various adjustments and improvements will continue to be made. Bold moves are to be encouraged, and governments of all persuasions understandably will be tempted to support what they see as actions to sharpen market differentiation and increase competition. As we shall see in a later chapter, however, sector-wide funding implications and broader policy considerations also need to be carefully weighed.

The regionals

The structural fault lines of Australian higher education do not run solely along research–teaching or pure-applied lines: at least one other significant feature of the Australian scene is the impact of geography, as well as history and politics, and that relates to what have been dubbed the 'regional universities'. Australia's population is highly clustered around its metropolitan centres, but the economic and social significance of the rest of the country is undeniable and the provision of university education and research in the regions has been a prominent and long-standing feature of policy. It is also the case that regional universities tend to be, together with the defence forces, the largest employers in their local areas, and thus critical to the local regional economy.

While distance education and online provision provide some redress for the tyranny of distance across the country, the desire of local politicians and business people to have their own university or university campus remains very strong. Of some 220 Australian domestic university campuses, around half are within 20 kilometres of a capital city, and two-thirds are within 100 kilometres, meaning that there are many campuses located in the outer metropolitan and rural areas of the nation. While most universities have one or more outer metropolitan or regional campuses, around ten have their main campus in what could be considered a rural or regional area.[17] In many instances there are problems with sustaining these facilities in fields of weaker demand for relatively small student populations, and claims have been made about higher travel and other costs, and difficulties in attracting academic talent and international students.

Universities with regional campuses receive an additional funding loading for teaching students, although not on a per capita basis. In 2010 the proportion of Commonwealth funding represented by the loading was under 5 per cent for most recipients with the exception of Charles Darwin University, where it amounted to some 14 per cent. In 2012 the loading was almost doubled, but allocated according to a new formula, which emphasised more remote areas and concentrated the funding on fewer institutions and campuses. Following the 2010 federal election the Labor Party led by Julia Gillard struck agreements to establish a minority government with the support of several independents from rural electorates. One element of those agreements related to special university funding for rural and regional areas. Specifically, substantial capital works and other funding was to be set aside for regional and outer metropolitan campuses and additional assistance provided to students from regional areas. Regional universities were also the target of special 'hubs and spokes' research funding designed to link them with more research-intensive institutions. In the 2013–14 attempts to deregulate the sector, concerns about rural and regional students and universities dominated discussions with newly elected independent senators whose votes were vital if the reforms were to be passed. The vice-chancellors of rural universities and some senators who were sympathetic to rural issues supported deregulation subject to special assistance being offered to the regional universities in the form of transitional and continuing support. A proposal put forward by one senator was the option of regional universities being able to 'opt out' of deregulation if they chose to.

The significance of regional universities and campuses for the structure of Australia's university system is that they provide a counterbalance to the play of market forces – campuses are kept open despite weaker student demand and marginal viability – and to the concentration of research funding. They have powerful political resonance and it would be unacceptable at several levels for them to be relegated formally to second-class standing in the higher education system.

Why Australian universities look the way they do

The Australian higher education system has been shaped by both global and local forces and, as a result, Australian universities are both reflective of an international type and distinctive in their orientation, scope and broad similarity of purpose. They have – more readily than many of their counterparts in other countries – adapted to cater for part-time and older students, for working adults seeking additional qualifications, and for students who are far away from metropolitan centres. All combine the purely academic with the professional and vocational, and have drawn international students from around the globe in numbers that are very high by overseas standards. The environment in which they have evolved, particularly over the past three decades, has been marked by:

- a strong Commonwealth rather than state influence;
- amalgamations to secure economies of scale and scope;
- steady tightening of public funding with growth in grants held below growth in costs and consequently increasingly limited scope for cross-subsidising programs;
- increasing exposure to market forces, with fee-based programs for international and postgraduate students;
- increasing influence of student demand at all levels, in a market that is relatively small and localised by some international standards and where students are seeking employment in an economy dominated by service industries;
- increased separation of funding for teaching and research;
- price control on undergraduate places and equalisation of funding rates for subsidised places across all institutions; and
- a historically strongly unionised workforce, though significantly less so today, and high levels of staff mobility among universities.[18]

These influences have led us to have the kinds of large and comprehensive universities that distinguish Australia today. In large part this is because they have been created that way by government policy, funding arrangements and by student demand. Institutional and academic aspiration have undoubtedly also played a role: all universities want to pursue the full university mission as best they can, and few academics would choose to restrict themselves to teaching large undergraduate programs with students of mixed motivation and ability. There are high levels of stratification by research activity, but most universities offer similar types of courses because it is those courses that students demand. Conversely, those courses that have weak demand have struggled to maintain their existence, creating difficulties in fields that are deemed to be of local or national significance.

A return to formally structured roles for institutions with limitations imposed on some by government mandate appears unlikely. However, to some the current scene is insufficiently exposed to bracing competition, while to others it needs to be made more orderly and efficient by planning and design. The uniformity that has to a large degree been created by government policy has, since the mid 1990s, come to be cast as a problem that now needs to be solved by more government policy reform. The operative term is *diversity* – it is argued that to better serve the needs of students and the economy we need more diverse university missions. As we shall see in the next chapter, however, this concept is surprisingly slippery and several, sometimes conflicting, agendas are at play within it.

Chapter Four

Driving mass diversity

The underlying motive of many Socialists, I believe,
is simply a hypertrophied sense of order. The present
state of affairs offends them not because it causes
misery, still less because it makes freedom impossible,
but because it is untidy; what they desire, basically,
is to reduce the world to something resembling
a chess-board.

George Orwell, The Road to Wigan Pier

While the United States is widely described as having the most diverse types of higher education institutions in the world, the term 'diversity' is used there in higher education circles almost exclusively to refer to the access and participation of different racial and ethnic groups in universities and colleges. In Australia, as is so often the case, the focus on diversity is on *institutions* rather than students, and the term has come to be invoked regularly by those who appear to worry that in our post-binary system 'all our universities are essentially the same'. For example, Stephen King, an economist and a former dean at Monash University, wrote in 2012 that, 'unlike universities in many countries, Australian higher education has become a homogenised product where diversity appears to be actively discouraged by government policies'.[1]

Concerns with the supposed homogeneity of universities should be clarified. There are many ways one may view diversity in higher education, looking at variations in characteristics of the student population, modes of teaching, geographical spread, courses of study on offer, patterns of research activity, and relationships with local communities. However, in most of the discussion at the national policy level about higher education diversity, these sorts of differences are briefly acknowledged but then deemed either immaterial or insufficient, usually on the basis of sweeping assertion rather than specific evidence of shortcoming or market need. This was illustrated more than 15 years ago, some eight years after the Dawkins reforms had led to a single university system in Australia, when diversity was made an explicit policy concern in the 1997 National Review of Higher Education Financing and Policy, led by Roderick West. The discussion paper issued as part of that review looked at diversity through the lens of market-oriented reform:

Australian public universities are all comprehensive institutions of higher education. While there is considerable diversity in mission, clientele, mode of delivery, educational philosophy and style within the system, far greater differentiation is possible and desirable. One of the fundamental issues that must be confronted in this context is that of price differentiation. (p. 19)

Restricting public funding to a certain set of 'public' institutions represents one of the greatest impediments to the development of a private higher education sector in Australia. The highly subsidised nature of education at public universities makes it difficult for private institutions to compete for students in terms of price. Australia stands to benefit from the diversity which would be offered by a wider range of providers. (p. 21)

The first questions posed by the West Review under the heading of pressures for structural change were somewhat broader in scope:

- How many providers does Australia need to optimise its delivery of higher education services?
- What kinds of services should each provide?
- Is a system composed mostly of large, comprehensive providers (as the current system is) best, or would it be better if there were more room for small providers focussing on excellence in particular areas?

Nevertheless, it ultimately proposed that deregulation and market forces should do the job:

> In our view, the prospects of an optimal higher education structure delivered by government fiat, in the complex and dynamic environment of the next century, are not high. Attempts at prescription are fraught with high uncertainty. Centralised decision-making becomes more difficult the larger and more diverse the system. Our policy framework must allow greater freedom for the structure of the sector to evolve naturally in response to the changing needs of its clients and the continually increasing range of possibilities which the new technologies open up for the production and distribution of higher education. (p. 64)

The advent of a new minister in the person of Dr Brendan Nelson, less driven by a preference for deregulation, led to another round of reviews of the sector in 2002, with diversity again a prominent feature. A series of discussion papers was issued, including *Varieties of Excellence*, which emphasised the desirability and possibility of specialisation, supporting the notion with extracts from submissions from across the sector. Noting that there were many different types of students with many different needs, it made the fairly obvious point that 'it is a significant challenge for any one institution to be able to cater for the varied demands of all students. Within the network of higher education institutions, Australia needs a variety of institutions capable of catering to an increasingly diverse range of student needs.' (p. 3) However, as with the West Review the remainder of the document failed to specify just where students were being short-changed and where greater specialisation was needed. It noted that considerable diversity already existed, but went on to assert:

> there is also evidence that Australian universities demonstrate diversity which is 'phenotypic' rather than 'genotypic': variations within a species rather than differences between species of institution ... What is the species? It may be argued that the species in Australia is the large, research-intensive, campus-based institution offering a comprehensive suite of undergraduate and postgraduate courses.

Such an assertion had to rely on a blind spot regarding the distance education, open learning and nascent online activities of a number of universities, as well as an extremely liberal definition of the term 'research intensive'. The paper then drew on other assertions from various submissions, including several from members of older universities that were definitely of the comprehensive research-intensive species (but who argued that others should not be), as well as newspaper reports that noted other countries had different types of higher education institutions. It ultimately concluded that diversity was a good thing, that it was already present but not in institutional type, that there were no specific mechanisms to drive diversity, and that this was a problem that needed solving.

A few years later, the new minister, Julie Bishop, indicated that diversity was high on her list of priorities for the sector, noting in a 2006 interview that 'we've got neither the population nor sufficient high-quality academic staff to maintain 37 comprehensive universities which are all undertaking teaching, scholarship and research across a similar and very broad range of disciplines'. She went on to explain that she was not advocating for teaching-only universities, but for entities such as the French and Swiss specialist institutions for engineering and science, as well as the development of particular areas of strength for existing universities.

Without doubt changes to the financing of higher education brought about by the Nelson reforms have greatly facilitated diversity in the Australian higher education landscape beyond the system of public university provision. Public subsidy of fees through various loan mechanisms drove a rapid expansion in new and established private-sector and non-university providers over the first decade of this century, although growth slowed (and in some cases reversed) with the uncapping of places at public universities that began in 2009. It is difficult to be precise about numbers as there is no comprehensive reporting: the government has only required reporting for those receiving Commonwealth subsidies from 2007, and since 2011 most of the publicly available data for private providers are aggregated. However, it can be noted that in 2010 there were 89 private providers listed in the national data collection and in early 2016 some 128 non-university providers of higher education were registered with the national regulator TEQSA.[2] So far as new categories of students being catered for, much of the activity was in business studies, preparation of international students for university study, and various creative arts courses, none of which had been particularly ill-served by the public university sector. However, significant increases in enrolments were also recorded in religious studies (one in six of the new providers is a religious college) and in alternative health (the Australian College of Natural Medicine doubled its student load between 2007 and 2010 and by 2010 had a domestic student load level that was 89 per cent that of Bond University).

None are the kind of nimble online provider envisaged at the time of the West Review or the kind of specialist science and engineering institution suggested at other times. They do, though, provide opportunities for students seeking higher education qualifications without the research and scholarship 'overhead' costs of a university, and in some cases they operate (as does Bond University) a trimester system enabling three-year, six-semester degree study to be compressed into two years for full-time students.[3]

A change of government at the end of 2007 brought to office a prime minister, Kevin Rudd, who was publicly committed to an 'education revolution' and the deputy prime minister, Julia Gillard, was given responsibility for the education portfolio. One of their early actions was to establish a major national review of higher education, led by Professor Denise Bradley, former vice-chancellor of the University of South Australia. This review focussed on three key themes. The first was a return to explicit concern with access and participation issues by students from disadvantaged backgrounds, the second was expanding the production of graduates in response to expected economic needs in the future, and the third was about bringing the national regulatory framework up to speed to cope with the rapid diversification that had been introduced over the past decade in the higher education sector and across the wider postsecondary education field.

The report of the Bradley Review marked a break from the diversity rhetoric of previous years:

> The panel is not drawn to recommend a formal process to restructure higher education in line with any prescribed model. Such a process

would be a prescription for increasing levels of government intervention in the affairs of institutions. Instead the panel's preference is to establish a national framework which allows progressive change in the structure of the sector to occur over time as institutions and governments respond to emerging trends in the environment. Such a framework should permit a diversity of approaches by institutions while also encouraging excellence, innovation and accountability. It should also encourage institutions to both work together and compete with each other, while meeting the nation's needs for high-quality, tertiary-educated citizens. (p. 2)

The government accepted almost all of the Bradley Review recommendations for its 2009 Budget, with the notable exception of one, which recommended an immediate boost to per-student funding. However, the subtle distinction between 'permit' and 'facilitate' diversity became manifest in a series of proposals that amounted to having the government and the relevant Commonwealth department continue an active interest in trying to mould the sector. Annual discussions between universities and departmental officials, which had taken place in one form or another since the Dawkins reforms two decades earlier, were recast as 'compacts', which would 'facilitate greater specialisation within the sector and greater diversity of missions'. In part this would be achieved through the use of performance-based funding. Further, the government expected that the removal of restrictions on publicly funded places for public universities 'will encourage universities to respond to student demand and will encourage greater diversity to attract students'. In addition, the introduction of a new scheme for assessing the quality of university research would be used to further concentrate research funding, although special support was provided to build research facilities and activities in regional universities.

The change in political leadership from 2008, along with the deflation of overseas student numbers, expansion of public provision and tightening of regulation, slowed the growth in private provision of higher education. However, Commonwealth government efforts to bring about greater diversity in the public system through compacts or competition were not noticeably successful, although, since the terms of success were never defined clearly, this is neither surprising nor particularly troubling.

The return of a conservative government in 2013 swung the pendulum back to the deregulatory perspective of the West Review, and rather than seeking to engineer a diversified public sector the government proposed to abolish altogether the distinction between public and private institutions by placing all providers on the same footing, provided they were registered by the national regulator TEQSA. We will revisit these reforms later in the book, but with their rejection we will never know to what extent, if any, they would have materially changed the nature of the Australian university landscape. Barring the much-anticipated disruptive apocalypse, for the time being Australian higher education looks like it will stay dominated by large, comprehensive quasi-public research-and-teaching institutions.

While concerns about the make-up of the university system in Australia have been played out largely at national level, most universities are creatures of state governments. Up to 2012, states were responsible for assessing new providers of higher education but for the most part they did not concern themselves too much with the operations or structure of their universities, particularly since the bulk of the funding burden had been transferred to the national purse in 1974. But in at least one state the idea of diversity in higher education provision was actively fostered as a political goal.

The South Australian approach to diversity

Some time in the early part of the last decade, then South Australian Premier Mike Rann, together with two leading South Australian luminaries – Howard government minister Alexander Downer and then chancellor of the University of Adelaide Robert Champion de Crespigny – resolved to transform Adelaide into a 'university city', the 'Boston of the south', by attracting overseas universities. Adelaide might not seem the most likely venue in Australia for this plan. Demographically the traditional university population of younger people was projected to remain flat or even fall over the period to 2020, and the city's economic growth and appeal for international students lagged behind that of the eastern part of the country. Sceptics could also hear echoes of past grand schemes such as the multifunction polis, a proposed futuristic city development conceived by the South Australian government and Japanese investors that was announced in 1987 but failed to eventuate. The idea that allowing prestigious universities to establish even a limited operation might produce flow-on benefits was not implausible, and was in line with the aspirations of places like Singapore to become 'education hubs' in the region.

In late 2005 amendments to Commonwealth legislation were passed and these enabled overseas universities to operate in Australia. Carnegie Mellon was the first cab off the rank, opening two schools in Adelaide, one a branch of the prestigious H John Heinz III School of Public Policy and Management and the other a branch of the Entertainment Technology Center (ETC). It was expected that around 200 domestic students would be enrolled by 2009. Further announcements followed. These included a partnership launched in 2007 between the University of Adelaide and UK-based defence specialist Cranfield University, a proposal put forward in 2009 for a university to be established by the Kaplan group, and a school of the University College London (UCL) to be set up in 2010.

Significant public subsidies were allocated to drive several of these developments, with very mixed results. For Carnegie Mellon, some $23 million was initially provided by the state and 20 annual federal AusAID scholarships allocated with a cost to the tune of $8 million over four years. By 2010 the state opposition estimated that the total cost of subsidies was around $43 million but enrolments had fallen well short of expectations, with only 106 students enrolled in 2010, most relying on public scholarships. The ETC closed after two years, the Cranfield campus closed in 2010 and in 2011 Kaplan abandoned its plans for a new university, although it maintains a range of interests in higher education in Adelaide and elsewhere across Australia. The small UCL campus with around 60 students in 2012 was for a time more successful, with its high-fee (over $64,000) postgraduate courses developed for the mining industry. UCL also drew on strong assistance from companies such as Santos and BHP Billiton to support research and student scholarships. However, this close relationship with the mining industry exposed the new campus to higher risks when the mining boom ended, and in 2015 UCL announced that its Adelaide campus would close within two years, although a partnership has been signed between UCL Engineering and the University of South Australia to maintain ongoing collaboration in teaching and research.

While Kaplan had withdrawn its plans for a new university, another US-based international university company, Laureate, had been sounding out possibilities in Australia, including an initial exploratory foray in Brisbane. Kaplan cited bureaucratic obstacles – no doubt its code for government requirements to meet particular standards for being a university. Such standards were being redeveloped nationally during 2011, with a new national accreditation agency due to start operation in 2012. Laureate evidently found South Australia provided the most amenable route to university status and in late 2011, just before the new national arrangements began, the South Australian government approved the establishment of Australia's third private university. This was to be known as Torrens University Australia and was initially proposed to begin operations in 2013, then deferred to 2014. Torrens is not receiving a direct public subsidy, and as a condition of approval it must invest $20 million of its own money, with a further $10 million if its enrolments reach 500. It offers high-cost (around $60,000 and upwards) undergraduate courses in media design, commerce, broader business and in nutrition, as well as a range of postgraduate programs up to the level of masters. It aims to build to 3,000 students within ten years, half of these to come from overseas.[4]

While some states have chosen in the past to invest in higher education and research, South Australia stands out as having opted to do so without building directly on the existing infrastructure of its own public universities. The new entrants had links, of course, with places such as the University of Adelaide, and if the vision of a more vibrant and diverse university city had come to pass there could well be spillovers that would benefit all. To date the value to South Australia of these developments is hard to gauge. Adelaide is not Singapore, and its ambition to be a hub of new universities was an aspirational stretch that has undoubtedly fallen well short of expectations. Substantial public subsidies have been provided with some evidently not returning good value; others may have potential to bear fruit.

Defining diversity

Making sense of the various calls for diversity requires clarity about what we mean by a university. Formal definitions of what constitutes a degree and other qualification levels have been in place for some time, and in Australia, as in most other countries, there are organisations other than universities that can and do offer degrees. However, as pointed out in chapter two, the definition of a university has shifted over the years but has come to rest on ideals that are about providing education that is in touch with the complex and fast-moving frontiers of knowledge. This implies going beyond specialised teaching and imparting what is already known in order to incorporate wider perspectives and exposure of various kinds to what is unknown or unexamined; that is, to research and critical thinking.

Like all ideals, these are not always realised in practice, but with more and more aspirants pushing to gain access to the prestige perceived to be associated with the name 'university' it became more important, even if solely for reasons of consumer protection, to formalise a definition. In 2000 National Protocols were agreed in Australia and these required that a university should award qualifications 'across a range of fields and set standards for those qualifications which are equivalent to Australian and international standards' and that teaching and learning should 'engage with advanced knowledge and inquiry' with 'a culture of sustained scholarship extending from that which informs inquiry and basic teaching and learning, to the creation of new knowledge through research, and original creative endeavour'.

Clearly there was much open to interpretation in this definition, but diversity in terms of smaller specialised operations appeared to be ruled out. Changes made in 2007 allowed for 'specialist universities' to offer courses, including research masters and doctoral, and to undertake research, in one or two fields of study only. Provision was also made for 'university colleges' that are required to undertake research and research training in only one field. With the establishment of a more structured system of accreditation and standards setting, and following the Bradley Review and

its acceptance in the 2009 Budget, culminating in the establish-ment of the Tertiary Education Quality and Standards Agency in 2012, these definitions have been largely carried across with some refinement. In effect they rule out the possibility of 'teaching only' universities and will make it hard for the kinds of for-profit universities that have emerged in the United States to establish themselves here. To date only one specialist university has been sanctioned, with the Melbourne College of Divinity becoming the MCD University of Divinity from the beginning of 2012.

Rethinking agendas

There are many agendas behind the diversity debates. One is about what students might need, another is about what institutions might want (including limiting the missions of other institutions), and a third is about what governments and officials might prefer (a more affordable sector, a more orderly sector shaped by plans or incentives, an 'education hub', or more private providers).

The first of these has been the least well argued, but in prin-ciple ought to be the most important. If the agenda had really been about needing more business and IT courses, or better meeting the needs of students of alternative health therapies and religion, then the developments of the past decade or more have been on track. It is possible that Australia needs more growth in higher education provision, and certainly a case can be made that smaller and more specialised providers could help fill gaps that the large comprehensive public universities could not. But smaller providers have struggled to maintain viability in the past, and experience both here and overseas has shown that where public subsidies are provided, entrepreneurs will rush in. Care needs to be taken to ensure that students and those who subsidise them (including the public) can be confident that they are getting what they pay for.

The second agenda, that of institutional jockeying for position, recognition and funding, has led to the formation of various groupings of universities and a multiplicity of policy ideas (many of them self-serving), media releases and submissions to government reviews. As public funding tightens, and it surely will do so even more, we can expect this trend to continue and we can expect that governments will continue to pursue their own agendas by selectively drawing on the range of institutional lobbying that emerges. We can all agree that not all universities can or should be the same, and that we cannot afford 40 Harvards (we cannot afford even one from the public purse). But we should recognise the limitations in the capacity of governments to intervene and shape diversity directly: the opposite of 'one size fits all' policy is often not diversity, but government intervention, inefficient protection of a favoured few and special dealing.

One alternative to direct intervention that has gained considerable favour over the past decade has been to drive institutional change by altering incentives and allocating funding on the basis of 'excellence'. Such approaches are attractive to all political parties and are seen as having a number of virtues. Key among these is the idea that they will focus the attention of universities on what funders see as important and provide incentives for improving measured performance. Through such means policy-makers hope to steer universities in desirable directions, change cultures, and set the conditions that will allow institutions to adopt different missions. The technique had been conspicuously influential in changing research behaviours within universities and it seemed only logical that it should also work for teaching. Whether it would is the focus of the next chapter.

Chapter Five

Funding for performance: The case of teaching

The combination of some data and an aching desire for
an answer does not ensure that a reasonable answer can be
extracted from a given body of data.

John Tukey, statistician (1915–2000)

The use of performance indicators to allocate resources has for
many years been advanced as a way of introducing more objec-
tivity in decision-making and placing a greater focus on outcomes
rather than inputs. Designers of such indicators hope that recipients of performance-based funding will respond to new incentives
and shift their behaviours as a consequence, moving away from
internal, vested interests. Developing performance indicators for
university work grew in the 1980s, and a series of reports was issued
to explore possibilities. In Australia additional impetus was given
to the task by the 1988 Dawkins White Paper, which proposed
the use of performance indicators for internal university decision-
making. Subsequently, the Commonwealth government supported
a trial of indicators across a range of academic and non-academic
activities, though in that most important area of university work,

teaching, only one indicator of quality was available and it was based on surveys of graduates, which sought views about their entire completed coursework experience. Later work attempted to develop further measures of teaching quality, from the level of the individual teacher to the institution as a whole, but careful study showed the limitations of existing indicators and the difficulties of developing new measures that might capture such a broad and complex activity as university teaching with some validity.

Difficulties in measuring teaching quality would not indefinitely delay efforts to bring the perceived benefits of performance-based funding to something that was seen by the government, and by many within the sector, as essential but underappreciated. The allocation of some research funding in the late 1990s on the basis of performance undoubtedly concentrated the minds of institutional managers on the indicators used, for better or worse[1], and despite the lack of suitable indicators a decision was made in the early years of the new century to do something similar for teaching.

The Learning and Teaching Performance Fund (LTPF) was announced in 2003 following a national review of higher education that commenced in March 2002 under the leadership of Dr Brendan Nelson, the minister responsible for the sector at that time. The stated purpose, as set out in the *Our Universities: Backing Australia's Future* policy paper, was 'to reward those institutions that best demonstrate excellence in learning and teaching. The Fund signals the Commonwealth's commitment to learning and teaching and will support institutions that choose to focus on excellence in learning and teaching for undergraduates.'

A year later an issues paper was produced, which elaborated some of the LTPF aims. It noted that excellence and performance were used to allocate research funding, and that in the past there had been no counterpart for teaching; instead 'the main driver of excellence in teaching and learning is currently universities' and individual academics' desire to offer a high-quality learning experience to their students'. The LTPF would, it was claimed, drive cultural change 'by enabling excellence in learning and teaching to achieve equal status with research excellence in terms of contribution to Australia's knowledge systems'. It further indicated that it expected that 'an increased focus on learning and teaching will foster diversity'.

The paper acknowledged there was no straightforward way of measuring the quality of learning or teaching (much less excellence) but, undeterred, it chose to assemble a bundle of proxy indicators that might conceivably have some relation to the educational process, and ran a series of statistical adjustments to account for variations that might be due to a host of factors that were part of the national higher education data collection. The indicators were in three categories: student satisfaction, student outcomes, and student success. The first two categories were based on the annual Course Experience Questionnaire (CEQ) and Graduate Destination Survey (GDS), administered to graduates some four months after they finish their degrees. Meanwhile, the 'success' category was measured by the commencing student load passed as a proportion of load attempted each year as well as a student retention rate (inverting the student attrition or dropout rate). These indicators were to be on commencing students only 'because it was argued that the first year progress rate is highly indicative of the progress rate for subsequent study years, and the likelihood of a student discontinuing study is highest in the first year'. The CEQ data comprised 55 per cent of the total score, the GDS data 22 per cent and the success data 23 per cent.

For the first round, institutions were ranked against each of the indicators, and the weightings then applied to arrive at a total score. The results were announced in 2005 with funds to be allocated in 2006, with some $54.4 million to be distributed among the successful applicants. Five institutions were designated as 'best demonstrating excellence in teaching and learning' and they shared $30 million, while the remainder was divided among nine universities in the second band. Twenty-four participating institutions received no funds. Each successful institution was awarded a $1 million base grant and the remainder was allocated according to the size of its undergraduate student load.

The results were swiftly presented as a league table by *The Australian* newspaper. Unsurprisingly there were at least 14 universities deeply unimpressed by the outcome and the implied finding that they had no excellent learning and teaching practices. Some critics highlighted the strong weighting given to subjective student opinion surveys and anomalies, such as the inclusion of the small specialist Australian Maritime College in the top tier when it had barely more than 100 survey responses, or the fact that some successful institutions had fewer than a third of their graduates surveyed. Others pointed to the impropriety of ordinal rankings, which blew out minor and statistically insignificant differences into artificial distinctions between universities.

In response the government issued a discussion paper and convened an advisory group to examine the method. For the 2007 round significant changes were made, including equal weighting for the seven indicators used, standardisation instead of ordinal ranking and, most importantly, a measure of institutional performance across four broad discipline groups: science, computing, engineering, architecture and agriculture; business, law and economics; humanities, arts and education; and health.

This enabled a greater range of institutions to feature in the 2007 allocations, even though, despite the intention of reporting under broad discipline groups, it did not stop the publication of league tables by the press. A total of $83 million was shared among 30 universities, with the allocations pool dominated by the research-intensive Go8 universities (with the exception of the University of Adelaide), although the University of Technology Sydney (UTS, which had not featured in the 2006 round) and the University of Wollongong were also handsomely rewarded.

For 2008 further changes were made. In response to concerns about the opaque nature of the regression analyses used to adjust the performance data, the department commissioned ACER to review the model and, as a result, the number of factors used in the adjustment was greatly reduced. For example, the survey data was reduced to the narrow field of education on the grounds that other factors showed only weak or inconsistent influence on the survey results. The use of 'imputed' data for the surveys was also discontinued for the LTPF; this referred to the practice of universities submitting data for students who did not respond to the survey but whose pathways subsequent to graduation were known, for example, when they had enrolled in further study. The expert panel also decided to change the way in which it rewarded universities for scoring above the national average: only large differences would be rewarded.

The resultant 2008 allocations of $83.4 million caused particular angst for two universities. The University of Queensland, which had come second in 2007 with $8.1 million, was pushed well down the list with only $500,000, while Macquarie University received no funding and was reported in the media league tables as falling from 15 to 37 (only 37 institutions were eligible). Macquarie's vice-chancellor blogged furiously on the outcome, describing the process as 'fatally flawed' and took issue with the UTS vice-chancellor who, after the continued success of his university in the LTPF, had published an article in *The Australian* praising the fund and claiming the result as a reward for the investments and approaches adopted by his university.

In October 2008 the department published a rather cursory internal evaluation of the LTPF. It presented whatever positive

evidence it could find along with some of the negative feedback from universities, without really addressing the original aims of the program as set out in the 2004 issues paper. To recap, these were to signal the Commonwealth's commitment to learning and teaching, to support institutions that choose to focus on excellence in learning and teaching for undergraduates, to promote diversity, and to enable teaching and learning excellence to be valued equally with research excellence. Of course after only a few years it would be difficult to claim much progress toward those fundamental aims.

The department's evaluation relied mostly on feedback from institutions indicating that the LTPF had directed attention to learning and teaching matters, particularly at senior management and governing board level. It also included some weakly supported analysis of movements in the performance indicators involved. Over four years the outcome data had barely changed and with four data points the claimed statistical significance for any increase was practically meaningless. Overall, CEQ results for Good Teaching did increase slightly, but this was the continuation of a trend that had been evident since the mid-1990s. The quantitative analysis concluded, with no justification whatsoever, that 'it is reasonable to assume that between 2004 and 2007, changes to the indicators may have been influenced by improvements in university learning and teaching, possibly driven by the LTPF'. Of course there is a considerable lag between any action that an institution might take (particularly for first-year students) and the results of surveys of graduates. But this was at the heart of one of the main objections to the LTPF: it was not responsive to institutional action.

Some heightened attention given to the measures by university management was undoubtedly driven by the LTPF, although nobody was much the wiser at the end of the process about how particular initiatives to improve the quality of learning and teaching might actually make a discernible impact on the indicators. Looking back some years later it is hard to say that a cultural shift took place within universities, either at the academic or management level, to lift the status of teaching compared to research. If anything, government research policy has further heightened competition for research funding and raised its significance as a scarce commodity and the prestige associated with it.

Writing after the 2007 allocations were announced, higher education researcher Leesa Wheelahan noted the dominance of the Go8 (seven of this group featured in the top ten recipients of LTPF money):

> It is hard to see how this contributes to institutional diversity; rather it reinforces the existing hierarchy of universities, in which those universities that are the oldest and richest as a consequence of decades of public investment receive the most resources, just as they do in research ... student outcomes and student success at the Group of Eight universities is higher because they recruit the highest performing students from the highest socioeconomic backgrounds, who are already privileged because they come to university with the highest levels of cultural capital, and the highest levels of social capital. Such students are more likely to continue to further study and to obtain jobs with higher salaries after graduation.

As for the argument that the adjustment process accounted for these factors, the results speak for themselves. Regression analysis at the institutional level is a crude tool for disentangling the complex interacting relationships and variations involved in university teaching. At the aggregate university level a number of the influences that might bias the results could well average out, but students are not randomly assigned to universities and the structures of courses are not the same across all universities.

Factors that are inconsistent in their effect at national level can and do have an influence at the institutional level.

Ultimately it is not surprising that a process that defines excellence or otherwise in terms of comparisons with their national averages of a basket of unrelated indicators (none of which directly measures student learning) will not only fail when it comes to measuring something as nebulous as 'institutional teaching quality'; it will also fail to encourage institutional diversity.

While the Bradley Review panel was working in 2008, another round of LTPF money was distributed, with further changes made to the method that allowed money to be allocated for improvement rather than for achievement alone – something which the previous government had explicitly ruled out on the grounds that it diluted the ideal of excellence. As a result, almost all universities were able to claim some share of the $73.1 million reward – the exception being Charles Darwin University, an institution in the Northern Territory that, it might be noted, has the highest proportion of Indigenous students of any Australian university, again underlining the disparity between success in the LTPF and the social capital of students.

The Bradley panel, like the earlier Nelson reformers, saw performance funding for teaching as counterbalancing research: 'The funds allocated for research are generally performance based and there is a case for some funds being allocated through a similar arrangement on the teaching side.' Noting some of the problematic aspects of the LTPF, it recommended that the fund be discontinued and proposed that instead of trying to identify and reward excellence by comparing institutions, the government should negotiate targets with each institution and reward them accordingly.

And so it would be. The compacts process that the government proposed in its 2009 Budget response to the Bradley Review was set out as a methodical and unproblematic matter of agreeing indicators, negotiating 'challenging' targets in 2010, and then rewarding good performance for those that met their targets and negotiated new ones. A total of $135 million per year was to be allocated this way from 2012.

Several key questions had lurked since the Bradley Review was finalised:

- How would the government be able to negotiate targets against indicators?
- Would they be realistic, reflecting the uncertain and fluctuating nature of the measures involved?
- How would they balance flexibility with fairness, avoiding situations where one university might have 'stretch targets' while another might set the bar lower?

The answer to these questions became apparent: one size would pretty much fit all and issues such as measurement error, random noise, time lags and uncertain relationships between actions and outcomes would be ignored. For the recruitment of students from poorer backgrounds, a five-year 'aspirational goal' of a 2.5 per cent performance improvement for each university would be set, with annual targets of 0.25, 0.65 and 1.25 per cent scores above the baseline over the first three years. Those universities already above their state-adjusted share of the five-year target would be deemed 'excellent' and receive reward funding provided they stayed above that level. Similar arrangements were proposed for the CEQ indicators, despite the fact that annual, more or less random, fluctuations in these measures were often greater than the proposed target increments.

New indicators were decided on: a University Experience Survey (UES), expected to be run in 2011 for use as a baseline for 2012 targets; a Composite Measure of Teaching Quality (a poorly defined mixed index based on unspecified proxies, presumably along the lines used for the LTPF); and an adaptation of the US Collegiate Learning Assessment (CLA), which was expected to measure 'value added' by assessing improvements (or otherwise) in students' generic skills. Development of this Australian CLA was intended to begin in 2011, with baseline data gathered in 2012 for targets to be set in 2013.

The ground shifted again in 2011 when, in response to mounting financial pressure on the Commonwealth budget, a package of savings of $6.8 billion was announced against expected future spending. For the higher education sector this included an announcement that $240.8 million would be saved over four years by not proceeding with funding for the student experience and quality of learning outcomes components of the reward funding. Under normal circumstances, the removal of nearly a quarter of a billion dollars from the higher education budget would cause howls of outrage. In this case, however, there was as much relief as there was concern.

The development of the new indicators was not dropped, though. Work would proceed with a view to implementing them as quickly as possible and posting the results on a new government website, *MyUniversity*. With the removal of inappropriate high-stakes funding and the questionable associated method, no objection was made by universities to this proposal. However, as a report on the development of the UES noted, further work would be needed to make the data useful for prospective students instead of, as originally envisaged, for performance funding purposes. Toward the end of 2012 a further change was made when the minister, Senator Chris Evans, announced that the government would not proceed with developing the CLA.

The proposed deregulatory reforms announced in the Abbott Government's first budget in 2014 ushered in yet another reformulation, known as the Quality Indicators for Learning and Teaching or QILT project. This was to draw on and adapt the existing UES and graduate survey data, as well as continuing with a newly trialled Employer Satisfaction Survey (ESS). QILT was launched in late 2015, though the employer survey was initially not available, since the full survey needed further development. The data have been more carefully presented and made available to the public in a more flexible way. However, the statistics still have limited power to inform: students or parents wanting information about specific courses will have to make do with patchy information about broad fields of study. Nevertheless the information is still moderately useful and is presented as part of 'market information' that could underpin a deregulated higher education sector, rather than as evidence that might drive government intervention.

Lessons learned

It is easy and politically attractive to use bold rhetoric about performance funding for teaching and learning driving institutional action that will result in immediate and measurable quality improvement, greater institutional diversity and better outcomes for students. It is also evidently easier to over-promise and under-deliver. We may also note that assumptions that teaching and research will be placed on an equal footing if they are both 'incentivised' with formulas and money are persistent, not only in the minds of politicians and government officials, but also in many parts of the sector itself.

This latter point rests on a fundamental misunderstanding about why research is seen as more prestigious than teaching within universities. Research is not valued because there is performance-based funding that incentivises institutions. It is valued in large part because high-quality research is a scarce commodity, with funding

for it tightly rationed. Moreover, the pursuit of new knowledge is intellectually stimulating for those involved and requires higher levels of cognitive skills and effort than any other form of activity, placing those who do it at the top of the academic meritocracy. Intellectual stimulation and effort can be found, of course, in other forms of academic work, including teaching, synthesising and reviewing knowledge, and in applying research knowledge and methods to new problems. But there is a basic distinction between an activity at the pinnacle of cognitive work that is scarce and rationed, and one that is almost a universal expectation.

This can manifest itself in unfortunate ways, resulting in an academic pecking order where top researchers explicitly or implicitly hold to George Bernard Shaw's aphorism, 'those who can, do – those who can't, teach'. Such views are still prevalent today, and echoes can be heard in the language of academics and government – students are referred to as 'load', with the implication of a burden. Also, academics seek 'relief' from teaching in order to pursue research as they would take medication to relieve a headache. It is part of the challenge of contemporary university management to foster a climate that does not reinforce or support a subordinate position for teaching. The situation is not helped when resources for teaching are continually squeezed and it can be exacerbated in mass systems that require academics to manage ever increasing numbers of students with changing and diverse needs, backgrounds and attitudes to study. At the same time, ever-higher levels of competition in research make it harder for researchers to devote scarce and valuable time to teaching.

This state of affairs will not be reversed by attaching money to formulas that at best relate vaguely to the quality of teaching and which are applied at the institutional level. Student learning is a complex matter: it is not bestowed on individuals by an institution, but co-produced in a complex and layered social environment.

Students come to different universities from different backgrounds with different expectations and diverse levels of preparedness. They learn not just from contact with teachers, but from their peers and from both designed and undesigned activities that vary greatly across the many different disciplines and professional groupings that make up an institution of higher education. The difficulty of capturing quality or excellence in this kind of environment is easily underestimated, and it will only be made harder as higher education is subject to future change and disruption.

It is instructive to compare the situation of university education with that of secondary schooling. A large and vigorously debated body of practice and research has sprung up over recent years in an attempt to measure the quality of school teaching. In this context the curriculum is simpler and more structured than in universities, and there is a lower expectation that students should be responsible for their own learning. In addition, data are based on standardised tests of what students have learned and are available at the level of individual students and teachers. Yet it is proving extremely difficult to find valid and reliable measures of teaching performance at the secondary school level. Moreover, performance-based funding incentives for schoolteachers have repeatedly proven ineffective. Is it any wonder that meaningful measures of teaching quality and effective applications of what we can measure are proving elusive at university level?

The concept of performance-based funding is an attractive one, and we should laud attempts to develop more meaningful measures of the quality of teaching and the extent of student learning. However, failure to appreciate the complexities all too often leads to a waste of time and money, and impedes rather than assists efforts to deal with the underlying issues. Performance-based funding can be useful, for example as a mechanism for providing managerial feedback or signalling a high priority for particular matters. But the further removed it is from the activity being measured, the less credible are the measures used. And the less immediate control the funding recipients have over the outcomes being measured, the less likely it is to be effective. We need good measures of teaching quality, but efforts to measure this activity at institutional level and to understand what the measurements mean are not helped by attaching high stakes to undeveloped instruments.

Performance-based funding has been adopted in a number of US states for several years with, at best, mixed results.[2] At times problems have been caused by overdesign, as US higher education policy expert Peter Ewell has noted:

> The most notorious recent example was an ill-fated approach in South Carolina in the US, which attempted to allocate all available resources to institutions on the basis of thirty-seven statistical performance indicators. Not only were the resulting funding benchmarks burdensome to calculate, they also failed to send a clear message to institutions about what the state actually wanted them to do. Because of associated burden, complex resource allocation approaches will always encounter resistance and this inherent pushback will generally triumph as soon as the political champions of the original venture, for one reason or another, disappear from the scene.[3]

Ewell went on to observe that recent institutional resource allocation proposals in the United States, such as those paying for course completions as well as enrolments, 'have the contrasting merit of being simple and transparent'. One of the longest-standing higher education performance funding systems has been that of Tennessee, which has refined and reworked its approach over more than three decades, and from 1997 has focussed on retention and graduation rates. A recent evaluation found that between 1995 and 2008 there had been no significant movement in those rates, and even when the money was doubled in 2005 no change took place. The researchers did not conclude that this invalidated the idea of performance-based funding. One possibility was that the money at stake should be even larger, and in 2010 Tennessee increased the stakes again, allocating around one-third of public college funding according to various outcome measures, though not on purported measures of teaching quality. This was later extended to all state funding above a base operational amount.[4]

While there are good grounds for being sceptical about the value of performance-based funding for teaching quality, it is reasonable to keep an open mind on the issue for other measures such as retention or completion rates, particularly with Australia's capacity now to track individual students. However, even here it would be wise to tread carefully. It is all too easy to rush ahead with a new scheme that simply ends up providing windfalls for universities for being what they already are and for attracting the kinds of students they already attract. If we are serious about inducing desirable change then we need to understand much better than we do at present the forces that underlie the currently observed patterns of whatever it is we are measuring and how they might be beneficially altered.

Ideally, whether for 'market information' or for the use of benevolent overseers of higher education sectors, we would like to measure how well students have learned what they are supposed to have learned, across a wide range of areas, and in addition we would want to know how much influence a university might have had on these outcomes. Unfortunately in practice we do not have standardised definitions of what students are supposed to learn (and with constant changes in knowledge this is not a bug, it is a feature) and disentangling the various factors that influence student learning is a formidable task. As a consequence, we have to weigh very carefully the costs and benefits of seeking inevitably imperfect answers.

The most ambitious effort to measure what students have learned comes from the OECD, which in 2006 decided to proceed with the Assessment of Higher Education Learning Outcomes (AHELO) project in order to measure both discipline-specific and 'generic' higher education student learning across nations. A trial was conducted under the joint auspices of the Program for Institutional Management in Higher Education (IMHE) and the Education Directorate Policy Committee (EDPC). By the end of 2012 reports were available on the results of a trial, which tested the concept for the disciplines of engineering and economics as well as the use of an adapted form of the CLA for generic skills.

The IMHE and a group of technical experts reported back to the EDPC noting that while some elements of the trial showed promise, there were fundamental problems with the attempt to measure generic skills and that formidable obstacles were evident more broadly. Some of this was no doubt due to the need to cut back costs of the trial in the aftermath of the global financial crisis, but it was also clear that a full-scale exercise would be very expensive and could well fail to yield the anticipated clarity of globally comparable information. Despite this advice, in 2014 the OECD Secretariat announced plans to prepare for a full scale implementation of AHELO, confident that their experience in conducting international surveys of school and adult literacies and basic competencies would enable them to extend these to more complex levels of higher learning, whatever the feasibility study might have found.

This confidence was not shared by a number of the countries which had initially provided support and funding for AHELO, including Australia, which had been an enthusiastic advocate of the project. In late 2014 it was clear that there was insufficient support for a full-scale exercise to go ahead as initially proposed, but in early 2015 OECD officials continued to lobby for support. Andreas Schleicher, the OECD's director for education and skills, argued that AHELO could serve both institutional needs ('you cannot manage what you cannot measure') and also serve as a ranking, along the lines of the PISA survey of school learning, which could give countries, for example those in East Asia, 'who basically have no chance to compete on traditional rankings ... a fantastic opportunity to make a jump-start and put themselves on the map'.[5]

However, the announcement in mid 2015 that the UK would not take part in an AHELO main study appears to have effectively ended the project. To some observers this was a case of vested interests, particularly in the established research universities, killing off prospects for accountability and competition for reputation. But that view overlooks the fact that decisions were made by country officials, not universities, and their concerns were squarely based on the expected return on very large investments, particularly where they could not control levels of participation. Those hoping for comparative measures of learning to serve as an accountability mechanism, instead of a benchmarking exercise for institutional self improvement, eventually had to accept that a globally standardised approach was simply unworkable.

The quest to measure university learning is not over. After announcing it would not be part of AHELO, the UK government revealed plans to develop a teaching counterpart to England's research assessment exercise: a Teaching Excellence Framework. With echoes of Australia's LTPF, the announcement was made as if this was a task that could be done in a relatively short time, with results robust enough to influence funding and drive institutions to value teaching as highly as research. We can only hope the UK learns lessons from the Australian experience, although the early stages of the process appear to be following a similar path: using unsuitable indicators to make weakly justified distinctions among institutions providing higher education.

The OECD will no doubt continue to advocate for something like AHELO. In 2015 funding was provided by the European Union to examine the feasibility of an alternative approach to developing comparable measures of student learning. Unlike AHELO, the proposed Comparing Achievements of Learning Outcomes in Higher Education in Europe project (CALOHEE) will use assessment frameworks that are tailored to different institutional contexts, rather than following a single mandated structure. Thus it is not intended to produce internationally standardised institutional data, but in time this initiative might lead to more robust and comparable ways of looking at student learning in different settings.

It is not the case that teaching and learning are just too complex for outsiders to concern themselves with, and that everything should simply be left to universities to sort out. We do need, however, to avoid the false comforts that can come from simplistic measures of complex phenomena. Student feedback and comparative institutional and discipline-level data are useful and necessary to collect and analyse, and they should most definitely be part of the scrutiny of institutions as part of national regulation and quality assurance. If we cannot have finely calibrated measures of teaching quality that allow us to build sensible league tables then so be it, but we must be able to tell if and when some operator is exploiting students and offering a worthless service. Beyond this, while government-designed funding incentives are unlikely to bring teaching and research into parity of esteem, there are good grounds for raising the profile of, and respect for, high-quality teaching through parallels with research mechanisms that provide external reference points for peer recognition. This is particularly valuable for informing academic promotion decisions. In addition, there is value in having bodies that advance research into how teaching and learning can be made more effective (this might include developing better measurement instruments) and that provide forums for focussing effort on cross-institutional or sector-wide issues. When it comes to university teaching, even if the activity cannot be measured in a globally standardised fashion it can still be managed and measured in more contextualised ways.

In Australia a series of bodies has been developed over the past two decades to advance these tasks, beginning in the early 1990s with the Committee for the Advancement of University Teaching (CAUT), and most recently in the Office for Learning and Teaching (OLT). Such bodies have made some progress in recognising outstanding teaching and building more professional communities and, importantly, in fostering collaboration to encourage ideas to be shared. But tangible progress has been hard to nail down. This leaves such entities vulnerable to regular restructuring and also means they only have very limited resources compared to those available to bodies measuring research performance. In 2011 the national body charged with improving university teaching, then known as the Australian Learning and Teaching Council, operated as an independent company. In 2012 the Labor Government reduced the size of its functions and transferred it to the Department of Education. For a few years various programs of teaching support and recognition were run by the government under the name of the Office for Learning and Teaching (OLT) but in 2015 the Abbott Government announced that those functions would be transferred, again, with a significant reduction in budget, to a university-based consortium. This latter shift might be consistent with reduced direct involvement by government in university matters, but if the government of the day wishes to expand national efforts to boost the quality of university teaching, then greater support and stability for professional development and recognition through bodies such as the OLT is likely to pay greater dividends than renewed efforts to pin down teaching quality through measurement.

Chapter Six

Being world class

Until now, we've been the undisputed leaders when
it comes to finding new ideas through basic research,
translating those ideas into products through world-class
engineering, and getting to market first through aggressive
entrepreneurship. That's how we rose to prominence.
And that's where we're falling behind now.

Norm Augustine, former CEO of Lockheed Martin,
quoted in Forbes, *2011*

Australia is falling behind the rest of the world
in investment in research and only a Rudd Labor
Government will address this problem.

Senator Kim Carr, 2007

Developed and developing nations are increasingly
prioritising research and higher education as they seek to
create more skilled workforces, stimulate socioeconomic
mobility and strengthen their economic competitiveness.
There are already signs that the UK could be falling behind.

Wendy Piatt, director-general of the UK Russell Group of Universities, 2011

Why do we need to pay scientists when we make the best
shoes in the world?
Silvio Berlusconi, prime minister of Italy, 2010

The concept of lifting some universities to 'world-class' status
has been a preoccupation of a number of countries, particularly
in Asia, for many years. However, the publication of global
university rankings, an exercise barely more than a decade
old, has accelerated this ambition and extended it to almost all
nations. The rationale is straightforward: elite universities are
needed to attract global intellectual talent, in the form of research
superstars and top students. Given that there is wide acceptance
that the successful economies of the twenty-first century must
be 'knowledge-based economies', it is easy to join the dots from
the best research and smartest people to the best innovation to
economic advantage and prosperity. After all, the United States
stands as the shining example; it is economically dominant and it
dominates the university league tables.

Within nations, 'world class' has also become a central consideration in assessing research quality and efforts to target research
funding. The overriding emphasis is on enabling institutions to
position their research within a global context, to compete with
international colleagues and to produce research that has impact
on the global academic community. This is evidently a good thing.
After all, who would not want all their country's research to be at
the highest possible standards? If that means that some universities
are squeezed out of significant research activity, then who cares?
The answer depends on why we expect universities to undertake
research in the first place.

For most universities, and certainly those in Australia, some relation between higher education and research is a defining feature.
In general terms the rationale is that higher education is about

learning more than a settled body of knowledge; ideally graduates should know that much of even our best knowledge is provisional and incomplete. In the original Humboldt concept both learners and educators are engaged in an 'unceasing process of inquiry', while in more instrumental terms the cognitive skills that come from grappling with research (if not actually 'doing research') should help build the kind of flexibility and innovative thinking that goes beyond the simple matching of skills with particular tasks.

Such rationales arguably lose some of their force at lower levels. As part of Australia's regulatory system we have an Australian Qualifications Framework (AQF), where all levels of education are defined structurally and shoehorned into a set of descriptions of 'knowledge', 'skills' and 'application'. In this formulation, the expectation of bachelor degree graduates does not extend much beyond possession of some designated knowledge and ability to apply it, except for some 'initiative' in such application, as well as a level of critical-thinking skills and 'responsibility and accounta-bility for own learning and professional practice'. We do not intend to revisit here the extensive (and mostly inconclusive) body of work that has been published on the relationship between research and teaching. While the notion that good research in itself leads to good teaching (or vice versa) has been debunked, as has the claim that the best teachers are necessarily good researchers, research can and does enhance university education in a variety of ways, many of which depend on individual and organisational commit-ment and focus. In any case it is an industrial relations reality that most Australian university academics are expected to be involved in teaching and research, with around two-thirds of those engaged on a non-sessional basis employed in the 'teaching and research' category.

For most of these staff, the underlying source of support for research comes from an apportionment of their time, and a corresponding portion of their salary, but in nearly all cases external funding is also needed. Such funding can come from a variety of public or private sources, including highly competitive grants from Commonwealth agencies such as the Australian Research Council (ARC) and the National Health and Medical Research Council (NHMRC). In addition, so-called block grants are paid to universities as a lump sum each year to contribute to the costs of supporting competitively awarded grants, as well as for support for research students and general research development.

The rationale for such external research support is for the most part unrelated to educational considerations, other than the component for supporting PhD and other research-degree students. Instead, it rests on other benefits that are expected to be derived from research. In the case of public funding the benefits are wider and generally more long term in nature than those of privately supported applied research. And, increasingly, the focus has been on health research and on some assumed links with economic development, particularly from science and technology, which are widely regarded as essential ingredients for a 'knowledge-based economy'.

Despite widespread fears in the academic world, such a focus does not necessarily imply a shift of government funding toward 'applied research'. While there has been a general move toward research that may be classified as 'strategic', in the sense that it has some ultimate practical purpose, the great majority of university research is still driven by the interests of researchers. For example, medical research receives substantial public funding because we want to improve human health, but the bulk of funding goes to basic research into the workings of the human body and its interactions with the outside world, with the agenda set by what researchers feel will yield results. This is as it should be. There is certainly room for applied research, for example in clinical settings, but there is a huge amount we simply do not understand about how the body works, or about how health is determined by socio-economic factors, and so more fundamental knowledge is needed before we can expect to tackle the things that may go wrong. Governments are also willing to provide large sums of money for university research in areas such as deep-space astronomy or the search for the Higgs boson, where arguments based on economic or social returns would have to rely on the drawing of a rather long bow. Nevertheless, funding is limited, and government views about the merits of research are not always clear and consistent.

Periodically Australian policy-makers rediscover the fact that compared to many other countries Australia has low levels of business investment in research and development, and relatively fewer links between universities and industry. Nor is development of new technology-based industries in Australia of the scale and scope found in some other places. While university researchers boast about 'punching above our weight' they can also be quick to issue dire warnings about falling behind, and governments soon find that increasing funding for research generates demands for even more. Black holes are not just objects studied by physicists; they are metaphors for the demands of scientific research, and so while governments generally accept that research is somehow connected to prosperity, concerns about the value that the public is securing for its growing investment have been steadily increasing.

In Australia, as in the United Kingdom, this has led to long-standing preoccupations with selectivity and concentration in research policy. The first refers to the idea that research funding cannot be shared evenly among potential claimants, and so rationing of some form is needed, for example by competitive bidding, priority setting or linking allocations to performance. The second is about concentrating resources on particular areas or institutions, in effect picking potential winners. In practice selectivity will lead to concentration, as those who do well are rewarded with more money and so can do better than those who are not.

Encouraging selectivity by priority setting has been adopted in many countries, and in Australia for more than two decades. The difficulty has been that priorities are usually described as broad areas that need investigation, and governments are reluctant to designate areas as low priority – at most they are implied by omission. With a little ingenuity many areas of disciplinary research can be subsumed under broad outcome or 'challenge' headings, and there is a risk that if a priority area does not already have high-quality research activity then second-rate opportunistic projects may secure funding in fashionable areas. Nevertheless, a case can be made that nominating important areas for national research should make it possible to identify potential opportunities or lacunae that ought to be filled in the national interest. Professor Ian Chubb, Australia's Chief Scientist from 2011 to 2015, has vigorously championed this cause, and was instrumental in driving articulations of such priorities in 2012, under the Gillard government, and again in 2015 under the Abbott government. The 2012 list specified 15 priorities across five broad national 'challenges', while the 2015 version was more specific and aligned to designated industries such as resources, energy and advanced manufacturing. Such priorities will remain uncontroversial as long as additional funding is provided, or as long as areas outside them do not experience corresponding reductions in support. But with a stated intent to allocate 'a proportion' of existing research funding more directly in line with the new priorities, complaints about 'picking winners' and moving goalposts are sure to ensue.

Governments can also promote selective investment in research by allocating funds in line with measurements of past performance. Unlike teaching, university research is externally visible, usually expressed in the form of tangible products linked to the effort of individuals or small groups, and much of its funding is competitive. This gives rise to reasonably valid quantifiable measures of performance, and enables peer judgements to be made about the quality of research results. This, in turn, can allow national and, more recently, international assessments and rankings of research to be developed, which can drive both institutional ambition and policies of selectivity and concentration.

Ranking research

The idea of a national assessment of university research was first implemented in Margaret Thatcher's Britain in 1986 under the title of the Research Assessment Exercise, or RAE. At that time the UK Treasury was concerned about the rising cost of scientific research and, initially, an exercise of identifying quality was intended to be applied in that domain only. However, arts and social studies academics were worried they might be seen as unimportant and so demanded that these domains be included, a demand that led one of the architects of the RAE to comment 'they are bloody fools and they will live to regret it'.[1] His reasoning, borne out by subsequent experience, was that exercises such as the RAE are enormously time consuming and potentially divisive. Opening up parts of the university to external scrutiny necessarily invites intervention, and with measures of quality it is hard to resist the tendency to insist that 'only the best will do'.

The RAE was run five more times between 1986 and 2008 before being recast as the Research Excellence Framework and run again in 2014 with the addition of a new component assessing the 'impact' of university research. From the outset the government, regardless of political persuasion, has made it clear that it intended to use the results to drive selectivity and concentration, and it has done so with increasing vigour, with the effect that research is being concentrated in an ever-smaller number of institutions. More than one-third of the UK block grant funding for research is now given to just five of more than 125 universities. By 2003 Universities UK, the national university representative body suggested that the level of concentration of research funding in the sector had gone 'about as far as it should go', and that any further significant concentration would damage the health of UK research. Yet despite the 2008 RAE showing pockets of excellence around the sector, government policy drove concentration further, cheered on by the elite institutions that were able to grab an increasing share of the available money. By 2010 Universities UK was again warning of the dangers of over-concentration, while the noted professor of higher education Sir David Watson was more blunt, writing of 'the stark conclusion that in the UK we have concentrated public funding of research to the point where it has become dysfunctional'.[2]

In Australia consideration had been given for some time to the possibility of running something like an RAE, but for many years it was dismissed as being unlikely to prove worth the cost, given the scale of university research in this country. In 2005 the Commonwealth government announced that it would develop a Research Quality Framework (RQF), although this had not moved beyond the planning stage before a change in government took place in late 2007. The new government abandoned the RQF work and announced instead that an assessment, to be called Excellence in Research for Australia (ERA), would be conducted and after a trial in 2009 the full exercise was run in 2010, 2012 and 2015.

ERA combined peer review with measures of research quality, and looked at university research across eight discipline clusters, with research that exceeds a certain volume examined at the level of groupings defined by the Australia and New Zealand Standard Research Classification. Evaluations were made using four broad categories of indicators: measures of peer review, including citations of published work; indicators of research volume and activity; measures of application, such as commercialisation income; and indicators of peer esteem. Among the measures initially used for research quality was a ranking of academic journals, developed after an extensive process of consultation and with thousands of hours of expert input. While there would always be concerns about the credibility of any system of ranking journals, the end result proved a manageable way of making broad assessments of the quality of publications. Not only was it used in ERA, but also found its way into arguments for academic promotion within universities and into the suite of performance indicators used by some universities.

The latter was apparently a step too far for the minister, Senator Kim Carr, who announced in 2011 that the journal ranking would be discontinued. The setting of targets for publication in A and A* journals by institutional research managers was, according to the minister, 'inappropriate', 'harmful', 'ill-informed' and 'undesirable'. While there were good arguments to be made about the adverse effects of journal rankings, there was some confusion in university circles because responsiveness to metrics was being directly encouraged in institutional compacts as a way of improving performance in other areas. Also, it had been made clear that journal metrics were intended as a measure of quality and would, as part of ERA, significantly influence future research funding. And many academics expressed exasperation at the wasted time and effort that had gone into developing the rankings.

These matters aside, ERA went ahead to produce an interesting and useful snapshot of the range and extent of university research occurring Australia-wide. From one perspective the results have not been surprising, with the highest concentrations of top level research being found in the eight universities that had for decades received the highest concentrations of research funding. Yet it can also be noted that within the Go8 there were very significant differences in performance – the ANU, the University of Melbourne and the University of Queensland had significantly stronger results than their counterpart institutions in that group, while the University of Western Australia and the University of Adelaide fared noticeably less well.

Overall the national ERA profile reflects what was broadly known from analyses of citations of Australian academic publications: our university research is very strong in several of the physical, chemical and earth sciences and is also good in a number of areas of the biological and medical sciences. However, we are weak, on average, in most of the social and behavioural sciences, including business studies, some areas of economics and education research. It is difficult to know how much of this is due to the difficulties associated with assessing world-class standing in the more contextualised and locally-oriented social sciences, and the rules for making such judgements are not entirely transparent. But there is clearly a considerable tail of weaker performance in those general areas.

ERA also makes useful distinctions between research income and research activity, two elements that are frequently confused, and also between research activity and the distribution of student load. While research income is highly concentrated in Australia, with eight out of some 40 universities commanding more than two-thirds of the resources, this is in part due to their dominance in higher-cost research fields such as physics and medicine. The ERA distribution of quality in research showed that not only are 'pockets of excellence' found throughout the sector, but also that the dividing line between the top eight and the rest is not so marked as income levels might suggest. For example, the proportion of fields where research is assessed as world class or above shows a much more linear gradation in university performance than is widely appreciated. However, the published ERA data do not include measures of volume of activity, so an institution might, for example, score badly in an area where it is involved on a relatively small scale. Thus it is difficult to develop a clear picture of the effective patterns of research activity within and across institutions. This did not, of course, stop newspapers from publishing rankings of universities based solely on the quality scores.

ERA provides activity data at national level, showing that while in some areas the proportion of research activity (expressed in researcher time for those who made it over the threshold level of activity) corresponded roughly with the distribution of university students, in other areas there were marked differences. In particular, as might be expected, the proportion of research activity in medical and public health and biological sciences was much higher than the proportion of students in those areas, while for business and law the opposite was the case. While nearly a quarter of university students were in business courses, only a little over 10 per cent of the ERA-assessed researcher staff time was in business-related fields.

Meanwhile, the Australian Government's shift of emphasis in late 2015 toward 'innovation' – informed by, for example, Ian Watt's Review of Research Policy and Funding Arrangements and the Academy of Technological Sciences and Engineering's Research Engagement for Australia – has implications for the funding of ERA and Australian university research. The newly-installed Prime Minister, Malcolm Turnbull, signalled his government's intention to elevate the importance of industry engagement relative to publication quality and quantity, heralding replacement of the 'publish or perish' mantra with an invocation to academic researchers to 'collaborate or crumble'.

The meaning of 'world class' in the ERA assessments is significant. The term has been a preoccupation of university policy, particularly in research, for at least the past decade and was widely canvassed in a 2002 issues paper, *Varieties of Excellence*, published as part of the reforms initiated by then minister Dr Brendan Nelson. Noting that a number of business luminaries and vice-chancellors of elite universities had suggested Australia's universities were not sufficiently competitive, Dr Nelson asked 'under the current policy settings, would Australia ever be likely to achieve a world ranking on any league table of comparisons?' His question would soon be answered.

Global rankings

While research exercises such as the RAE and ERA are relatively recent in origin, national rankings have been a feature of the higher education systems of a number of countries for many years. In the United States and England they can be traced back to the start of the twentieth century, originating in the efforts of psychologists to work out whether great men were made great by their education or whether they were simply born that way. Until the 1960s, assessing the pathways of eminent men was the principal means of judging university quality, but in that decade the focus shifted to assessing doctoral programs by surveying academic opinion. The pioneering work was done by Allan Carter, then vice-president of the American Council on Education, in 1964. It is noteworthy that his work, like that of a follow-up study undertaken in 1970, focussed on departments and did not rank institutions, but these data were swiftly turned into institutional rankings by others.

By the beginning of this century annual national comparative assessments of universities and other higher education institutions were available in many countries. In Australia the *Good Universities*

Guide has been published for more than two decades, initially by Dean Ashenden and Sandra Milligan and later by Hobsons, a company that grew out of the UK's Careers Research and Advice Centre and is now part of the Daily Mail and General Trust. The Commonwealth government in Australia also publishes reams of data on universities and these national rankings attracted (and continue to attract) considerable attention from university officials. However, unlike the United States with its sprawling and diverse higher education system, Australia's relatively neat and small sector experienced few movements over time and diminishing returns in attempts to shift position motivated solely by rankings.

A new era was begun in 1998 when, at the one hundredth anniversary of Peking University, the then president of China initiated the so-called 985 Project aimed at building world-class universities in that country. Among the first institutions to be selected for development was Shanghai Jiao Tong University, where chemistry Professor Nian Cai Liu and three colleagues applied themselves to the task of benchmarking the top Chinese universities with US research universities in order to explore what the notion of 'world class' might actually mean. Their work was assisted by the growing availability over the last two decades of the twentieth century of a range of new sources of data on institutional and individual research performance. The development of the field known as 'bibliometrics' is particularly significant. Databases of publications and counts of the number of times they are cited by other researchers in subsequent publications have been developed and made available to the international community. The first Science Citation Index was published in 1961 and over the next few decades the scope and depth of citation data increased dramatically, along with developments in information technology that, through the 1980s and 1990s, led to the widespread availability and use of such data in assessing research.

The Shanghai Jiao Tong University work led to a report in 2001 for the Chinese Ministry of Education, which, in turn, encouraged it to apply its methods more widely. The University took this opportunity and in 2003 published a list, known as the Academic Ranking of World Universities (ARWU), of the top 500 universities drawn from a global sample of 1,200 institutions. The list was updated annually and in 2007 rankings were further broken down into five broad disciplinary groups. The ARWU rankings are strictly objective and squarely aimed at research, avoiding any reputation surveys and relying instead on measures of research performance: publications, citations and winners of Nobel Prizes in the sciences and economics and Fields Medals in mathematics. Ten per cent of the score is derived by use of a per capita adjustment, but otherwise the score is dominated by size, science and staying power. With a 30 per cent weighting for Nobel and related prizes, Professor Liu has cheerfully acknowledged that universities established after 1911 'do not have a fair chance' and he has also acknowledged a number of other biases and limitations, such as the favouring of natural science and medicine. The method also means that a few individuals can affect the whole university's ranking – an additional Nobel Prize winner results in a move in the top ranks and many of the universities making it into the lower ranks of the top 500 have done so in large part because they house one or two highly cited researchers. Nonetheless, the objective and transparent nature of the process renders it highly influential and relatively credible among the various global rankings.

The year after the ARWU rankings appeared *The Times* newspaper in the United Kingdom, in partnership with educational and careers advice company Quacquarelli Symonds (QS), published its own global ranking of universities, based predominantly on global surveys of academics and employers. While this had considerably less credibility and transparency than the ARWU, it had more impact in Australia as its methodology (initially at least) favoured UK and Australian universities. By expanding its scope beyond research it allowed a number of other universities to make it into the top few hundred.

In 2010 *The Times* and QS parted company, and each published their own world university ranks. The QS set essentially continued the earlier methodology, although it supplemented its database of survey respondents considerably, while *The Times* teamed with Thomson Reuters to develop its own new approach, which drew on a wider set of indicators but still relied for more than a third of total weighting on reputation surveys. While QS continued to publish a list down to 500 with individual ranks, *The Times* published only the top 200 in unbanded form. *The Times* method changed again in 2011, providing a few nasty shocks for institutions such as the University of Adelaide (which fell from 73 to below 200), the University of Science and Technology of China (from 49 to 192) and the University of Virginia (from 72 to 135). However, no complaint was heard from the University of Amsterdam (from 165 to 92) or Monash University (from 178 to 109).

In 2010 the Centre for Science and Technology Studies of Leiden University began its own research rankings, the Leiden Rankings, based on citation counts of publications in the sciences and social sciences. Unlike the other global rankings mentioned here, Leiden does not produce a single official rank, but allows users to select criteria and to adjust for factors such as university size. Other international ranks have been developed, including the National Taiwan University Ranking, which began in 2007 driven by the Higher Education Evaluation and Accreditation Council of Taiwan; Webometrics, developed by the Spanish National Research Council in 2003; and SCImago Institutional Rankings, which began in 2009. However, to date the ARWU, QS and *The Times* remain the most prominent.

The impact of league tables

The initial *Times* rankings generated considerable controversy and allowed some interesting positions to be highlighted. These included the scoring of RMIT University at 55, above the University of Adelaide, the University of Western Australia, the University of Auckland and the University of Warwick in the United Kingdom. Sadly for RMIT, and through no fault on its part, subsequent versions of *The Times* ranking changed method and RMIT fell from 55 to 146 in 2006 and 206 in 2008. Macquarie University suffered a similar fate, falling from 68 in 2004 to 189 in 2009. In general, Australian institutions experienced most down-grading in *The Times* ranks as its methodology changed, possibly reflecting the excessive weighting initially given to them for inter-national student recruitment. Of the 27 universities that dropped by more than 50 rank points between 2006 and 2009, seven were Australian (39 per cent of those in the 2006 ranking); four were from The Netherlands (33 per cent), three from the United Kingdom (7 per cent) and five from the United States (5 per cent). *The Times* ranking did not bother with the statistical niceties used by the ARWU, which banded universities into broader group-ings below the 1–100 range because the distinctions were not very reliable. The artificial precision provided by *The Times* enabled movements in the lower tiers to continue to excite both public interest (newspapers love a story about a 'slide in the rankings') and institutional alarm.

Wounded national pride arising from the rankings has undoubt-edly played a part in the response of France and Germany. Both countries are large in population and economic clout (around 4 to 6 per cent of global GDP each) and both had university systems that were officially and in public perception deemed to be undif-ferentiated and not in competition with each other. However, in both countries universities are part of a highly differentiated postsecondary education system, and in the case of Germany a binary system based on early streaming of school students into academic and non-academic pathways. Another common feature was that in the post-war period France and Germany had both developed major research institutions outside the university system.

In Germany's case, the initial ARWU rankings came as a shock. The country that originally developed the ideal of a research university in the nineteenth century had only five universities in the top 100 and its best ranked, the University of Munich, came in at a modest 48. After protracted and complex negotiations between federal and state authorities (the latter having legal and financial responsibility for higher education), a €1.9 billion Excellence Initiative was to be launched, funded by the auction of licences for mobile telephony. Beginning in 2006 the Excellence Initiative involved a competition in three categories: graduate schools; clusters of excellence to carry out strategic research in interdisciplinary teams with various partners, and special funding for select universities. Ultimately nine universities were successful in this last category, out of a field of some 300 applicant institutions, each receiving up to €13.5 million annually for five years.

A second and final round of the German Excellence Initiative was approved in 2009, which extended the program to 2017 and involved some €2.7 billion in additional funding. The impact of the Excellence Initiative has been dramatic, showing that even supposedly lethargic university systems can react entrepreneurially to the prospect of new funding, and demolishing long-standing myths about the equality of universities. Predictably, those regions and institutions that have not shared in the new riches have been less enthusiastic.

France fared even worse than Germany in the first ARWU ranking in 2003: only two institutions secured a spot in the top

100 with the best ranked at 65. This situation was described as 'The Great Misery of French Universities' in the daily newspaper *Le Monde*. *The Times* rankings in 2004 did little to soothe Gallic pride, with only eight French universities in the top 200 compared to 14 Australian universities and 30 from the United Kingdom. The situation prompted a review of the complex and heavily state-controlled French higher education and research system, which is highly stratified and has weak links between research and the bulk of university teaching.

In a 2011 interview, the French higher education minister Valérie Pécresse stated that the rankings showed that 'the problem is that the world model is a university. If you have a ranking, you rank universities. For a long time we thought we had a French model that was different from the others and was working better. But now we know that good research and good teaching means you need a multidisciplinary university.'[3] A year later, President Sarkozy said:

> France is a very special case. Just after the Second World War, we created agencies separate from the universities to do basic research. At the time, such a set-up was found only in Communist countries, in particular the USSR and China. Now, even these countries have abandoned this model. In the United States, the vast majority of research operators are universities. That is not yet the case in France, but it is our goal. The research organisations are expected to become more like real funding agencies, serving the universities and research institutions.

Mr Sarkozy described the granting of greater autonomy to French universities, which previously did not have the power to offer new degrees, open new laboratories, hire their own scientists or set their own salaries, as the main accomplishment of his presidency.[4]

Beyond those reforms, President Sarkozy set out to emulate the German support of elite universities. In 2009 he announced a €7.7 billion university Excellence program, known as Idex, as part of a €35 billion stimulus package. The aim was to encourage collaborations between the various education and research agencies, amalgamate a large number of existing institutions, and develop eight universities as elite research powerhouses. Each of the selected institutions (three were picked in 2011) will receive an endowment of €1 billion, to generate income of €35 million to €40 million each year. As with the German initiative, as part of the deal the winners will also be expected to work more closely with business and to improve commercialisation of research findings.

Denmark's reaction to the arrival of the rankings train is also worth mention. In 2010 the Danish government announced new immigration rules that would favour graduates of universities featured in the QS university rankings. Applicants for a Greencard entitling them to work in Denmark need 100 points, and graduates of universities in the top 400 receive 5 points, those from the top 200 are allotted 10 points and those from the top 100 get 15 points.

Dramatic responses to global rankings are not confined to Europe. In 2015 higher education scholar Jamil Salmi identified a total of 37 national governments implementing excellence initiatives in the rankings area in the period 2005 to 2014, including 14 in Asia and the Pacific.[5] China, for example, has invested heavily in long-term, multi-phase initiatives since its much-heralded Projects 211 and 985 that ignited global interest in the nature and achievement of world-class universities. Such economic responses are often accompanied by aspirational political rhetoric.

In Malaysia, after the top two universities in that country slipped by almost 100 places between 2004 and 2005 in *The Times* listing, the leader of the opposition called for a Royal Commission of Inquiry and the vice-chancellor of the University of Malaya (UM), the country's flagship university, was forced to resign. In 2007 the prime minister was again greatly concerned that no Malaysian university was in *The Times* top 200, and the parliamentary opposition leader noted that UM had 'plummeted 54 places to 246th'. In 2008 the situation was described as a matter of 'national shame', though the vice-chancellor of Universiti Kebangsaan Malaysia was more optimistic, predicting that up to three Malaysian universities could break into the top 100 by 2015. Undaunted by past volatility, in 2011 the vice-chancellor of UM announced that his principal target was to break into the top 100 of the QS ranks by 2015 and the top 50 by 2020, while the Higher Education Ministry backed this latter target and also called for 'at least three local universities to be ranked among the world's top 100 universities'.[6] While critics might have been more pleased with a rise for UM to 180 in the 2009 ranks, UM could only manage 151 in the QS list by 2014 and no Malaysian university has featured in the top 400 of the new (post 2010) *Times* ranks.

The idea of such targets has widespread appeal, and a number of politicians and university leaders have set out their own versions of plans for moving up into the top echelons of world rankings within a time frame of a few years.[7] For institutional leaders this is not simply the chasing of status for its own sake: while it is easy to identify weaknesses with rankings it is increasingly difficult for universities to ignore their implications. Officials in a number of countries have indicated that they prefer to deal with universities that register in the global ranks, and the higher the better, and a significant percentage of international research students indicate in surveys that they take a university's placement into account when choosing where to study. In addition, position in the ranks can become self-perpetuating, particularly for the reputation-based *Times* and QS ranks where Bowman and Bastedo (2011) have demonstrated that reviewers base their assessments on the existing standing of universities, even to the point of giving high ratings to prestigious universities in areas where they do not have programs. This 'halo effect' was demonstrated in the United States in the 1980s when Princeton was ranked among the top ten undergraduate business programs when it did not offer such a program.

Internationally, universities are employing various strategies to move up in global rankings, including ramping up international research collaboration. Indeed, international collaboration has been identified as 'the fourth age of research' (following individual, institutional and national), not least because of the enhanced citation impact that accompanies international co-authorship.[8] Another rankings-oriented strategy employed by some universities is to increase the size of the institution's research profile through amalgamation. This has been done for example in Manchester, where the 2004 amalgamation of the Victoria University of Manchester (usually without the Victoria prefix), and the University of Manchester Institute of Science and Technology resulted in a ranking in the 2011 ARWU for the combined institution of 38 compared to 89 for University of Manchester in 2003.[9] However, the most ambitious series of university amalgamations is taking place in France, where the reinvention of universities has been driven, as we have seen earlier, by concerns that their post-war model has been unfit for purpose. The largest of the planned mega-universities will be at Paris-Saclay, where billions of euros will be spent to bring together 19 higher education institutions at a campus around half an hour's journey south of the capital. The combined research performance of Paris-Saclay will undoubtedly propel it to a prominent position in international rankings (though whether it meets its target of cracking the top 10 by 2025 remains to be seen), but equally importantly the new mega-university is intended to build links with industry that, it is hoped, will generate a French version of Silicon Valley.[10]

Another strategy is to buy in highly cited researchers. Pohang University of Science and Technology in South Korea reportedly has allocated the equivalent of $130 million for this purpose, to make it into the top 50, although the plan has been described as 'lacking in detail'.[11] In 2011 it was reported in the prestigious journal *Science* that King Abdulaziz University in Saudi Arabia had signed up large numbers of highly cited researchers as part-time 'affiliates' with generous funding, and in 2012 it scored a position in the 300–400 band. King Saud University in Riyadh climbed from outside the top 500 in 2008 to be in the 201–300 range in 2011 (and again in 2012), 'largely through initiatives specifically targeted toward attaching KSU's name to research publications, regardless of whether the work involved any meaningful collaboration with KSU researchers'.[12] Both institutions later responded to the published allegations, vowing that their efforts had nothing to do with chasing ranks but were motivated simply by the desire to strengthen their research. By 2015 both universities were in the 151–200 bracket of the ARWU.

Nanyang Technological University (NTU) in Singapore is a striking example of a young university that has risen dramatically in the rankings as a result of implementing a radical multi-pronged strategy encompassing academic and organisational renewal, emphasis on research, prioritisation of international collaboration and industry partnerships, and embedded interdisciplinarity. Under the leadership of Bertil Andersson, NTU rose from 39 in 2014 to 13 in 2015 in the QS rankings and occupies first place in the QS Top 50 Under 50.

Andersson himself acknowledges that his capacity to deliver a radical performance transformation was easier in the Singapore context than it would have been in his native Sweden where, he half-joked, a president's decision might be seen as an 'interesting addition' to the academic debate, rather than the definitive word.

In the event, about one-third of NTU's 750 professors failed to meet NTU's new tenure requirements and were discontinued on the grounds that they were excelling neither as research nor teaching-intensive academics.[13]

Many universities are actively pursuing the recruitment of top research talent. This practice oftentimes occurs in countries backed by government schemes designed to retain their top talent or bring back expatriates, such as Australia's Future Fellowships or the Canada Research Chairs program. However, this can be a very expensive and risky strategy if the intent is to further particular institutional positions rather than to strengthen the national research base as a whole. Global rankings have greatly increased the value of the relatively small number of research superstars who have published papers that are heavily referenced by other researchers. Such people can command high salaries and demand expensive facilities such as laboratories, research students and support staff, all of which require continuing resourcing. Furthermore, if they are able to be lured from one place to another then there is an evident possibility that they may be lured again by an institution with deeper pockets and a wider and deeper research culture. The University of Manchester not only pursued amalgamation as part of its aim of moving up the ranks, it also invested heavily in research superstars. This latter strategy has contributed to ongoing financial, cultural and interpersonal problems that have made its progress more difficult than originally anticipated.[14] Moreover, Manchester's goal to be in the ARWU top 25 by 2015 has had to be pushed out to 2020, a practical acknowledgement of the challenge of climbing further up the ladder (Manchester ranked 38 in 2011, 40 in 2012, 41 in 2013, 38 in 2014, and 41 in 2015).[15]

The challenge facing Manchester in lifting its ranking goes to the broader point that there has been barely any movement in the ARWU top 25 group since the ranking commenced. Only nine institutions have moved in or out of the top 50, and all of those moving out were initially ranked below 30. This reflects the stability of the ARWU method as well as the long time lags in building citation impacts from past research and in amassing a number of Nobel Prize winners or other stellar researchers. There is more movement in *The Times* and QS ranks, with regular changes in method and more subjective criteria, but even there the top 50 positions have changed only slightly over several years. There is more room for movement in the next 50, and the rankings swing more wildly further down the list, but any notion that these changes are due to systematic changes in quality or strategic action is hard to justify, particularly given the opaque nature of the reputation surveys used.

Consequences

Notwithstanding the loathing for rankings in some quarters, and the paranoia in parts of the academy about the distorted messages they might convey to the public and to governments, rankings are now a fixture of the higher education landscape. It is also the case, for the foreseeable future, that they will continue to be dominated by the established players, because of the self-perpetuating nature of rankings based on past research performance, ability to attract top researchers, or reputation.

Not surprisingly, the ability to discriminate and rank research has led to calls for more resources to be directed to the top, for resources to be concentrated either as a 'reward for performance' or to enable those at the top to compete more effectively with their counterparts in other countries. Evidently there is a need for most if not all Australian universities to focus on those areas that are identified as performing poorly under ERA. It is also

reasonable that ERA's assessments of quality be taken into account in allocating general funding for research.

It is worth noting that Australian research and research funding are already highly concentrated. While we have a reasonably diverse portfolio of university research activity for a small country, by world standards we specialise to a considerable degree in only a few fields, notably the medical and earth sciences, and nationally resources are concentrated in just a few universities. Three-quarters of our block funding for research goes to 13 out of 40 universities, while three-quarters of competitive funding goes to just eight. Nineteen institutions, nearly half of all Australia's universities, account for less than 10 per cent of external research funding between them. Those that performed relatively poorly in ERA are not the beneficiaries of money that is spread about evenly, despite persistent and misleading rhetoric from some quarters. Only six universities conducted enough research to be assessed in more than half of the 179 fields assessed in the 2015 ERA. On average, universities were assessed in only 59 fields and eight universities conducted enough research to be assessed in only 30 or fewer fields.

In his book *The Australian Miracle*, science policy analyst Thomas Barlow writes of his time as a national science policy adviser when he was struck by the persistence of a number of myths about science that were used to call for government intervention. Among these was the idea that our research resources were being 'spread too thinly' and that they needed to be prioritised and concentrated to enable us to compete with the giants of the global science system. Noting that Australia has a diverse research base, given the size of our economy, Barlow observes that heterogeneity has its benefits and specialisation its risks – the recipe being called for was precisely the wrong one. What Australia needs, he argues, is 'not strongly directive priority setting and concentration

of resources, but rather a radical new approach based on decen-
tralism, and a lack of concern about replicating resources and the
apparent inefficiencies of competing innovators'.

Barlow points out that Australia has long indulged in the science
and innovation equivalent of the cultural cringe, comparing itself
unfavourably to countries with large-scale high-tech sectors,
particularly in manufacturing. He argues that the knowledge-
based economy is not a simple morality tale about the replacement
of old industries by new high-tech ones, but instead involves a
pervasive transformation of the economy where adoption, adap-
tion and innovation occur in all fields by the creative use of new
ideas and technologies. Australia, he suggests, is well placed to
take advantage of a world where low-tech industries are becoming
high-tech and where innovation is a more open process, in that
scale is less important as ideas and creativity are sourced from a
wider global base rather than from within single large firms.

There are dangers if we try to drive too much of our national
portfolio from the perspective of worries about scale, national selectivity or even concerns about the amount of medium-level activity
by international standards in some institutions. We should expect
institutions to push for improvements within their own walls, and
not be content with mediocre work, but the notion that 'only a
4 or 5 counts' in ERA could have adverse effects on our national
research. This includes possible effects on our research training
efforts, keeping in mind that most PhD graduates do not go on to
take up academic careers. By all means research degree students
need to be trained well in rigorous research methods, but discipline-
specific knowledge or excellence is not the only criterion that
matters, particularly if we want to disseminate research-trained
graduates more widely throughout society and the economy.

Invention of new ideas is not the only, or even the main, way
that universities support national innovation. Basic research is a

global public good that we need to participate in, but we also need the capacity to develop local knowledge, and to adapt and adopt ideas to suit our circumstances through education and engagement with industry and other organisations. In the past we have looked to an educated elite to lead some professions, leaving a wider populace to be inculcated with defined skills and specific knowledge. In an uncertain, mercurial and rapidly changing world national innovation now demands mass higher education not just to give people higher levels of specific skills, but also to develop familiarity with the changing nature of knowledge and how new ideas can shape our understanding of the world. Linking research with teaching is therefore not just a good idea for the elite.

The idea that we need to give preferential treatment to a select few universities to enable them to compete well on league tables rests on even shakier ground. Here research is turned into something more like the Olympics, where ranking becomes an end in itself. Indeed, sporting metaphors are frequently invoked to justify the concentration of research funding. In early 2012 French President Sarkozy said:

> I'm a big fan of cycling, and I love watching the Tour de France. We've never seen the pack accelerate because those at the rear go faster; the pack accelerates when the leaders accelerate. Similarly, I think the Investments for the Future program, because it rewards the best, will lift the entire French system of research and higher education, not just the winners.

Such parallels are fairly dubious. After all, research is not a short-term highly ordered activity where there is little benefit in not coming first (and, unlike in physical sport, the oldest and richest players in research almost always win). More to the point, the trickle-down effect is not observed in practice – research heavyweights are more likely to be poachers than gamekeepers. For example, an OECD review of tertiary education in the Netherlands noted that 'there are some indications that Netherlands research is less than fully competitive as a national system *qua* system. The spirit of excellence tends to be concentrated at the top of the academic profession, the part directly involved in international research at the highest level, rather than permeating the whole of localised research and scholarly activity.'[16]

We have given one university preferential treatment for decades. The Australian National University (ANU) receives, in addition to the ability to compete for research grants and block funding,[17] a special grant for research, which in 2013 came to $188 million. This has given the ANU relative freedom from many of the costly overheads of competition and increasing demands for accountability, and it has helped that institution attract some fine minds and to undertake research that has lifted it into the top 100 of the research-based ARWU rankings, at position 77 in 2015. However, the University of Melbourne is ranked 44 and the University of Queensland also occupies position 77, results due in part to size but also to active competition particularly in medical research. Should we increase the ANU's block grant to enable it to overtake Melbourne? Should we give all three universities hundreds of millions of dollars in the hope that all might edge closer to the top 50 at some time in the next decade? Basic research, which is the subject of this kind of investment, is a global public good but its value needs to be examined in better ways than narrow reputational competition, particularly when public resources are so tightly constrained.

Other countries are selectively funding elite universities to move up the ranks, with vaguely articulated hopes that this will pay off for them as players in the knowledge economy. However, their circumstances are not those of Australia – for example, Germany

and France are undoing an arrangement where they seques-
tered research away from universities, and operated with little
competition. Australia can and should invest more than it does in
university research – it provides our best chance for fundamental
as opposed to incremental progress on a range of economic and
social issues – but status games make a poor rationale.

Australia, without the benefit of past research assessment
exercises or much in the way of picking university winners, has
managed to develop a selective but diverse portfolio of research
that is of high quality by international standards. Despite being
far distant from the northern hemisphere academic mainstream
our national output is well regarded, with higher citation rates
than Germany or France and with higher levels of publication per
capita, in better journals, than the United Kingdom, Canada and
the United States.[18] We have low levels of interaction between
business and university research, due in large part to our industry
profile, but this will not be improved by concentrating university research on the basis of international academic esteem and
simultaneously badgering institutions to develop greater 'impact'.
Selectivity in research is both inevitable and desirable – we do not
want to be directing scarce resources to weaker work. But the idea
of concentration is a choice that has its drawbacks, particularly
if driven by rankings. Ellen Hazelkorn, an Irish scholar who has
been at the forefront of analyses of the phenomenon of global
university rankings and their effects on national research systems,
points out that rankings have great limitations as guides to the
best investments for developing knowledge economies. In her
2011 book she singles out Australia as a country that has got
the balance more or less right.[19] We have a highly performing
university system, where elite excellence exists without limiting
other universities indefinitely to second-class standing, and
where there is scope for competition, diversity and evolution.

The great majority of Australian university students do not study in the elite handful of universities, and yet we need our students to develop in what the European Union calls the 'knowledge triangle' of education, research and innovation.

We are confident that Australia can and will continue on a path that balances the elite with the broader system, and the pursuit of academic esteem with research that makes a difference to the real world (the two are, of course, not separate). While supporting ERA, which has identified areas where universities need to focus their efforts to improve, some caution must be exercised about the tendency we have to incorporate each and every available measure into formulas for resource allocation. The total cost of the ERA exercise in 2015 was over $40 million in direct funding, and likely in the order of $100 million when all costs are taken into account. This is more than the total external research budget of any non-Go8 Australian university in 2015, and it will certainly be much higher if the impact of research is to be assessed in future rounds. That suggests some thought must be given to the cost-effectiveness of regular repeats of this exercise, which has also been accompanied by accounting exercises that involve researchers completing time sheets and thousands of hours of administrative work dedicated to developing estimates of the full cost of undertaking research. Whatever the problems we have with a tail of mediocre research or with some universities biting off more than they can chew in research grants, it is important that the cure not be worse than the disease.

Chapter Seven

Weapons of mass instruction

Thirty years from now the big university campuses will be
relics. Universities won't survive. It's as large a change as
when we first got the printed book.

Peter Drucker, cited in Forbes Magazine, *1997*

Five years from now on the Web for free you'll
be able to find the best lectures in the world.
It will be better than any single university ...
college, except for the parties, needs to be
less place-based.

Bill Gates, speaking at the Techonomy conference, 2010

Harvard and the other elite universities won't be
disrupted by online learning; for them, it will be a
sustaining innovation, something they add
to their curriculum to make it even better ...
by contrast, institutions without prestige will
have to use online learning to reinvent themselves;
they need to reduce their costs significantly

in order to avoid being disrupted. Online learning will
produce fundamental change in higher education.
Clayton Christensen and Henry J. Eyring,
cited in Forbes Magazine, *2011*

My ambition is to forge in the smithy of my soul the
uncreated conscience of my race. And then see if I can get
them mass-produced in plastic.
Woody Allen, Without Feathers, *1975*

In 1998 a team of QUT researchers produced a report entitled *New Media and Borderless Education*, which covered a variety of emergent forms of higher education provision. Some of these were already established and many others were on the drawing board or predicted to emerge in the near future. Those were heady days for prophets of the transformative power of the internet, and for investors in new tech start-ups that promised to capitalise on such power. In Australia, a review of the national higher education sector was underway, and a discussion paper that was issued as part of the process raised alarming prospects of heightened competition from corporate universities, global media networks, online providers and global extension of prestigious or for-profit universities.

The first Borderless Education report found that while many of these prospects were overstated, there had already been expansion and transformation of long-standing forms of alternative provision, exemplified by open universities and delivered by for-profit companies such as the Apollo Group, and a great deal of ambitious experimentation by publishing companies and corporate educators as well as from established players such as universities and governments. Follow-up research in 2000 and 2001 traced the fate of some of these experiments, including Columbia University's Fathom, which went on to close in 2003, Dow Jones University,

Melbourne University Private (closed in 2005), UNext/Cardean and several other spin-off online programs that emanated from established universities.[1]

Along with entrepreneurial venturing, fear of 'falling behind' prompted the UK government to set up what was known as UK e-university (UKeU) in 2001. Unfazed by evidence from sceptics and the bursting of the dotcom bubble, and untroubled by market research, the UK government commissioned the university funding body HEFCE to oversee this endeavour more or less on an if-you-build-it-they-will-come business plan. Building the platform took longer than expected, and the first courses did not appear until late 2003, when it became apparent that 'they' did not come. Only 900 students were enrolled against a target of 5,600 and when HEFCE wound up the UKeU in 2004 it had consumed £50 million of public money.[2]

While there have been many failures, as would be expected in a rapidly moving experimental field, some organisations have persisted and have come to dominate for-profit online course provision, particularly in the United States and a number of developing countries. Companies such as the Apollo Group, Education Management Corporation, DeVry and Kaplan hold a large share of the non-traditional higher education market, and all were founded before the 1990s, while some newer entrants have moved into higher education from related fields and established a toehold in a number of countries. Among the latter group is Laureate Education Inc., which grew out of the tutoring company Sylvan Learning Systems (established in the early 1990s), and which now has a global network of universities through Laureate International Universities, including Torrens University in Australia which began operations in 2014.

Australia has adopted rules that make it difficult for many of these ventures to set up shop as higher education providers, and particularly as universities. Key tests include whether they can develop viable research across at least three broad fields of study, engage with local and regional communities and demonstrate 'a commitment to social responsibility in its activities'. Australian higher education providers are required to have a 'clear and discernible separation between corporate and academic governance, including a properly constituted academic board and course advisory committees'. Several of the largest for-profit universities in the United States would not meet these criteria. The Apollo Group's University of Phoenix specialises in large-scale standardised professional programs for working adults; it separates the various elements of curriculum development, content provision, teaching and assessment, with each treated as a contractable business process rather than something under the control of a core of academic staff. On the other hand, Walden University, a Laureate-owned institution, also targets working adults seeking professional education but is an accredited online provider of undergraduate through to doctorate education, with scholarly academic staff and an avowed commitment to social change.

For many years for-profit providers dominated the online delivery of higher education degrees in the United States. In 2009 it was estimated they had 42 per cent of online-only students compared to 11 per cent of the total higher education student population.[3] Three-quarters of their students are aged over 25 years, compared to around 31 per cent for public four-year universities, which on average correspond closely on student demographics to Australian universities. Further, many of the for-profit universities, including University of Phoenix, marketed their offerings to lower-income people, military veterans and others who perceived themselves as poorly served by traditional institutions. Clearly they found a particular niche for their operations in the United States, but despite extremely rapid growth in the latter part of the first decade of this century, questions about the quality of the education experience and employment outcomes of graduates together with an escalation of costs and student debt sparked a backlash. In 2011 new enrolments declined sharply for many for-profit providers: by 2015 enrolments in the largest of them, the University of Phoenix, had nearly halved and another large player, Corinthian Colleges, collapsed completely.[4] For-profit enrolments were down to 6.5 per cent of all enrolments in the United States by May 2015, from 8.3 per cent in 2011.[5]

Reviews of online education in the United States have shown that fully online courses remain concentrated in the large for-profit companies and less selective public institutions. Along with the recent decline in for-profit enrolments, there has been a decline in both the total number of students studying subjects fully online and the average price of online study. Some growth has taken place in the provision of online courses in most public universities, but overall the direction appears to be more about incorporation of online education into traditional campus-based education in what has become known as 'blended' delivery.[6] Much of this activity is supported by university-wide 'learning management systems' that provide various forms of online content and communication with and among students. In some universities these platforms were initially developed 'in house' in an effort to tailor them to specific institutional preferences, but the task of linking them with other major university systems and the cost of maintenance and development has seen a widespread move to standardised commercial systems and more recently some open-source alternatives have been developed. Much of the practical advantage and gains in productivity have come from the use of technology for more routine tasks, such as student administration, assignment handling, basic communication and transfer of information. There has also been an enormous amount of work

over the years in exploring the possibilities of using technology to improve student learning. But it is evident that systems designed to support scale, evolving technology and administrative demands have not yet proved an ideal fit with expectations about making higher education more flexible and customised to student needs. Instead we have seen incremental moves toward greater flexibility, with lectures increasingly available in audio or video form, student portals making learning materials and assessment examples available at the start of the course, and some academic staff exploring social media as a way of complementing their teaching.

Technology, as used to date by most universities, has not decreased the cost of formal education; in fact it has often contributed to an increase. There are signs that online course provision can be linked with lower costs in some institutions, but that can come at the expense of quality.[7] It is, essentially, an issue of scale: digital technology works best at scale, indeed the original proposition of universities was to teach at scale. At Oxford in the early days this meant teaching four or five students at one time. Nowadays it may mean delivering education to thousands of students to ensure a return from a significant investment in digital infrastructure. Two decades into the 'internet age', online delivery has not done away with the physical university, as some suggested it might. Instead most universities are using websites, animations, podcasts, online videos and other tools to augment face-to-face approaches, but it is clear that much more can be done. In Australia as in the United States we are only beginning to tap into the possibilities of using new media and technology in productive and effective ways.

Over recent years a number of new developments have emerged that have reignited the hopes and passions of reformers and educational entrepreneurs. While the established for-profit corporations have failed to deliver the kind of mass low-cost access that many had predicted, and while many university efforts to commercialise their offerings through spinoffs have failed to be sustainable, these initiatives aim to make college and university content widely available at relatively modest cost.

Since 2010 there has been a bewildering proliferation of such new enterprises. Rather than provide an exhaustive catalogue of the most prominent players here, we will categorise them into two broad camps. In the first group are those that emerge from high-brand name universities such as Stanford, Harvard and Massachusetts Institute of Technology (MIT). Typically these take the interests of particular professors and aim to make their lectures and materials available to a mass audience, more or less for free (under certain conditions). In the second group are organisations (re)exploring the potential for breaking apart the traditional higher education processes to deliver much cheaper online education.

Elite education for everyone? The rise of the MOOCs

In the 1990s it was assumed by many proponents of the coming internet-driven revolution in higher education that the ability of the highest prestige universities to offer access to millions would simply blow most other universities out of the water. Similar predictions had been made earlier about videotapes, offering 'lectures from the best professors in the world'. However, as noted in the Business of Borderless Education report there was at least one problem with this model: prestige was built on selectivity not massive openness. Harvard would not become an open university even if it was technologically possible to do so while maintaining standards. Nevertheless, prospects for 'monetising' the internet for higher education proved alluring enough for several initiatives to surface, including NYU Online, Fathom (led by Columbia and including several other top universities), Melbourne University Private, and the University of Maryland University College Online. All of these failed to be sustainable.

Not all such ventures were aimed at making a profit. Oxford, Yale and Stanford set up the not-for-profit venture AllLearn (Alliance for Lifelong Learning) in 2001 to provide, for a reasonable fee, non-credit general or 'liberal arts' university courses. Initially available to alumni, the scheme was extended to the general public in 2002, but in 2006 the alliance was dissolved as it proved increasingly unsustainable. The courses had been more expensive to produce than anticipated, and students were not interested in sufficient numbers in pursuing qualifications that did not have the elite university brand directly attached.[8]

While extending the university in such a structured way had proved too ambitious, even if not aimed at making a profit, the idea of developing a modular or 'unbundled' approach to the delivery of higher education was being explored elsewhere. In 2001 MIT announced that it would make substantial amounts of its course content freely available on the internet. It was not the first university to propose such a move, but its prestige and capacity to deliver marked it out as the pioneer of what became known as 'open courseware'. The motives were pure – to make available to humanity the materials that underlay courses at great universities – and it was followed by similar initiatives at other leading universities such as Yale and the University of California (UC) Berkeley. Adding to these developments, in 2007 Apple launched iTunesU, which provides convenient access, at least for those with Apple products, to content from universities such as Stanford and Harvard.

Although wider access to some of the teaching materials and lectures from the very best universities has been a boon to the curious and those motivated to teach themselves, including many graduates, it has not revolutionised higher education to date. In large part, this is because unstructured content and lack of certification place the onus on the learner to navigate their way through, with no tangible return to show for the effort. More structured versions of open courseware are available, notably Carnegie Mellon's Open Learning Initiative (OLI), which, like MIT's OpenCourseWare, was sponsored a decade ago by the William and Flora Hewlett Foundation. Students can study either under their own steam for free, or pay a fee for an academic course where an instructor in an educational institution uses OLI materials. Courses are coherently designed, although not part of wider degree program structure. A growing feature of the OLI system is the development of software to provide feedback and assessment, beyond simple marking of multiple-choice tests. However, no certification is available for those undertaking the free open courses.

In 2011 MIT announced that from 2012 it would, for the first time, offer certificates to outside students who complete freely accessible courses using a new online course platform to be known as MITx. Then, in May 2012, MIT announced that it would join forces with Harvard to use the MITx platform to offer online courses from both universities, with the platform to be known now as edX. Both universities committed US$30 million to the new venture, the intention being to use edX in part as a delivery platform and in part as a tool for research on how their students can learn in a blended environment. In July 2012 UC Berkeley joined the consortium. Notably, certificates of completion were to be issued for those who demonstrated 'mastery of subjects' but these certificates would not be issued under the name of Harvard, Berkeley or MIT. Nor were they intended for use as credit for study at other institutions.

The edX and MITx ventures are considerably more sophisticated than earlier MIT open courseware ventures, providing access to textbook materials, quizzes, and some online teaching assistance. The format and material are close to that offered and experienced by on-campus students.

As it has in other Silicon Valley endeavours, Stanford University is proving a fertile source of spin-offs in higher education. In 2011 two Stanford computer science professors, Daphne Koller and Andrew Ng, offered an online course through a new platform they had helped to create, and found hundreds of thousands of students from around the world who were willing to take part. With the aid of US$16 million in venture capital they created a company, Coursera, which has partnered with many prestigious universities around the world to offer free open courses developed by professors at those institutions. However, the terms of service make very clear to prospective students that enrolment with Coursera in no way constitutes a relationship with the universities involved, and any certification issued is not for academic credit or recognised by the partner universities. In 2016 Coursera, in search of a business model, announced that it would charge a fee for some parts of the service around MOOC certification.

Another Stanford professor who experimented with a globally-offered online open course in 2011, Sebastian Thrun, left his home university and set up a company, Udacity. This company offers its own courses and, on completion, students receive a certificate signed by the instructor.

Since 2012 millions of students have enrolled in such (mostly) freely available courses sourced from prestigious universities, and a new acronym has come to feature prominently in university policy discourse: massive open online course (MOOC).

Low cost online degrees:
An idea whose time has come (again)?

While for-profit online degree education has drifted to the expensive end of the spectrum, even where it has broken up the traditional model of academic control, a number of private not-for-profit colleges and universities are seeking to develop low-cost online higher education programs, among them Southern New Hampshire University. These are distinguishable from MOOCs in that they are not totally open ad hoc extensions of an elite brand, but attempt to develop full online programs that can deliver academic credit and credentials for a program of study.

One member of the Board of Trustees for Southern New Hampshire University is Harvard Business School Professor Clayton Christensen, who in 2011 with Henry Eyring of Brigham Young University–Idaho wrote *The Innovative University: Changing the DNA of Higher Education from the Inside Out*. This book excited much attention, not so much for its rather lengthy exposition of Harvard history alongside some case studies such as Brigham Young University–Idaho and Southern New Hampshire, but because Christensen is a respected business theorist who has made his name studying how established businesses became 'disrupted' by technologies, many of which were not necessarily better in quality but were cheaper and easier to use. The model he espouses involves establishing something like a spin-off organisation to develop more standardised low-cost online programs, using the University of Phoenix approach of 'unbundling' the various components of course development and delivery, and incorporating where possible new technological products and processes.[9]

In a similar manner, although not allied to any one established college, a company known as StraighterLine began business in 2010, offering low-cost online first or second year college level. StraighterLine uses commercial content and a learning management system paralleling that used in many traditional and for-profit providers, and in 2015 it charged students US$99 a month plus US$49 a course. Most significantly, it has negotiated credit arrangements with a number of accredited universities and colleges, although to date it has struggled to establish such credit arrangements with many of the better-known traditional universities and colleges.

One of the groups with which it has established credit is the Western Governors University (WGU), a private not-for-profit institution founded in 1997 with initial funding from governors of 19 western US states and based in Salt Lake City, Utah. The Borderless Education studies, referred to earlier, noted WGU as a promising new development, not least because it intended to pursue higher education on a competency basis; that is, with credits recognised or awarded based on whether students can demonstrate mastery of specific skill sets rather than by being graded on academic knowledge.[10] WGU does not develop its own courses, but instead specifies competencies and assessments and then either licenses course content from commercial providers or takes it from open courseware sites.[11] There is no structured academic calendar. Rather, students can take tests when they feel ready and they are charged tuition at a flat rate every six months, with WGU claiming that it can provide degrees at typically half the cost of comparable regionally accredited online universities and with tuition rates held constant at 2008 levels through to 2015.[12]

WGU initially had a slow start, taking time to establish itself in an environment that was not set up to handle competency-based higher education, but it has grown rapidly over recent years with affiliates opening in Indiana, Washington, Nevada and Texas, and a total student population swelling to more than 60,000 in late 2015. At a time when many US states are under financial pressure and expectations of higher education attainment remain high, the political and financial attraction of the WGU model is clearly very powerful. Its novel approach to granting and awarding credit for study could, in principle, eliminate some of the longest-standing complaints outsiders have with higher education, namely the perceived intransigence of institutions to give credit for study undertaken elsewhere and their inability to provide opportunities for students to learn and progress at their own pace. It could also greatly shorten the time required for students to complete degrees.

Implications for the university as we know it

Computer engineer Roy Amara once said that the impact of technology tends to be overestimated at first and underestimated in the long run. Certainly the first part of this formulation can be seen in the excessive hype about online education that developed in the late 1990s, along with the dotcom bubble. In retrospect much of this talk greatly overestimated the capacity of the technology at the time and underestimated the complexity of the education process and student demand.

It is possible that 'this time it is different'. The dominance of relatively narrowly conceived for-profit ventures in online higher education in the United States is giving way to more open and exploratory initiatives. Certainly, the new developments in online learning that have been springing up within and outside the traditional academy around the world are promising, and the ability to reach large numbers of students is genuinely new. Further, the development of new online environments has explicitly been aimed at improving the capacity of educators to collect and analyse large amounts of data on student learning activities to provide targeted support and feedback for individuals and program development.

While many institutions have developed various forms of such 'learning analytics', the development of MOOCs should see considerable advancement in this area.

The availability of a variety of courses free of charge is something to be greatly welcomed, and it has clearly struck a chord with many people. There has never been a better time for enthusiasts who are keen to teach themselves subjects such as computer science, statistics and various branches of science. Over a remarkably short period of time the MOOCs associated with prestigious universities have attracted large numbers of enrolments from around the globe. Many academics and commentators on higher education have themselves enrolled in MOOCs and become enthusiastic advocates, leading inevitably to a great deal of speculation about whether this might be the ultimate disruption for traditional universities, particularly for those universities below the elite level.

There can be little doubt that the advent of the MOOCs has sparked greatly renewed interest in online higher education, and the level of investment and activity associated with elite brands will give online education a much-needed boost in credibility and exposure. It is clear that technology will enable fundamental changes to be made to university teaching that could trigger deeper changes to the way academics and universities operate. However, some years after the initial surge of speculation about the impact of MOOCs it is increasingly clear that MOOCs do not pose any immediate existential threat to established universities.

To begin with, the purpose of MOOCs is not to disrupt traditional higher education; that hype is largely grafted on by others, although Sebastian Thrun has speculated that in the long run physical universities might be greatly reduced in number. The MOOCs offer open access to short courses developed by leading professors, and in doing so open at least some doors for people who might otherwise not have access to university study, or who are looking for particular subjects that interest them without necessarily wanting a full degree program. This is a valuable and, for the most part, exploratory and altruistic activity, testing out new platforms for education delivery and experimenting with ways of automating interactions with large numbers of people and collecting useful data for the analysis of learning. It has also been spurred to some extent by status anxiety, with prestige universities keen not to be seen to be left behind, and by hopes that student demand (and international student demand in particular) might be stimulated by 'taster' offerings.

But any kind of sustainable business model has yet to emerge. Of course companies like Google did not start out with a concrete business plan, but its ultimate model of revenue via advertising may not be a good fit in higher education, and other pathways need to be found to 'monetise the MOOC' if it is to be sustainable. No doubt avenues for using the vast amounts of information collected as part of their operations are being vigorously explored, but it is hard to see any of the MOOCs surviving indefinitely on their initial value proposition as a source of education for the specially motivated or disenfranchised or as a source of free support or complementary work for students studying at other universities. To be useful, education needs to be certified, and charging for MOOC certificates has become a regular practice.

An alternative might be to develop more comprehensive links between MOOC providers and universities. In October 2012 Coursera struck such a deal with Antioch University, a small private multi-campus provider of adult education, and in January 2013 Udacity announced a partnership with San José State University to pilot the development of online courses in algebra and statistics for a group of 300 students, half from the university and half from local community colleges and high schools. Also in 2013 Udacity teamed with AT&T and Georgia Institute of Technology to offer an online masters in IT. In 2015 the University of Melbourne, Coursera and New York-based investment company BNY Mellon combined to offer a suite of four online finance courses, at a cost of $89 each plus a $69 capstone project. Also in that year edX announced a partnership with Arizona State University to offer a fully ASU-credited first year of college via MOOCs under their Global Freshman Academy, at a cost of $45 for identity verification and a $200 'per credit' fee to ASU. Giving away freshman credit is very brave unless it is at scale and many learners continue into the next year paying full cost. At that point, perhaps, the move could be sustainable.

On top of these initiatives, in 2014 Udacity announced that it would team with various companies, including AT&T and Google, to provide 'nanodegrees' in areas such as programming and data analysis. The proposition is that employees would gain certification from completing online modules over a period of six months to one year, at a monthly cost of $200, and that these certificates would be recognised and valued by the relevant partner company. In 2016 Udacity announced a further innovation: for those who pay for and complete an enhanced nanodegree course there will be a guarantee of employment within six months of graduation or the course fee will be refunded. There is some fine print attached to this. For example, graduates must submit at least three job applications each week and must accept any offers that fit with their Udacity Professional Profile, but it could well be an attractive offer and will be followed with considerable interest by observers of the evolution of online courses.

New MOOC providers have also come onto the scene. In 2012 the UK Open University launched its FutureLearn online learning platform, which by 2015 hosted some 54 UK and international courses. In 2013 another company emerged from Stanford,

NovoEd, which promised a platform which could provide richer interaction and collaborative opportunities for students.

In the space of a few years the MOOC phenomenon has undergone rapid change. In addition to expansion of the original concept of openly available online subjects offered by major universities, the above moves show that some MOOC providers have pursued business models by becoming platform providers to more traditional university-owned courses, in some cases dropping the massive and open aspects. Others such as Udacity have sought a future by moving into corporate and short-length vocational education.

These are still early days and many of the new initiatives may well flounder before the future direction of MOOCs and related developments in commercial involvement in online higher education become clear. One difficulty is that while students are willing to sign up in large numbers, completion rates have been very low with only the most highly motivated – and in many cases those who already have university level qualifications – staying the distance. Indeed this led to the unwinding of the Udacity–San José State University partnership after less than a year of operation.

Low completion rates have been generally associated with online education. Partly this is because this form of delivery has often been offered to non-traditional types of students who, for reasons of time pressure, competing priorities or other factors have been less likely to complete whether they study online or on a traditional campus. But the massive impersonal MOOC environments, with limited credit and little financial or other motivation, greatly increase the likelihood of students dropping out. This is more likely a problem of early design than something intrinsic to online delivery: some well-designed and supported online courses have shown comparable retention rates for comparable populations of students. It is also not a concern if students do not incur significant costs. However, incorporating online learning into formal higher education is challenging for newcomers as well as established players and the initial feverish expectations that 'free courses from great universities' would transform higher education were overly optimistic.

It is important to understand that higher education students are hardly a single group, and the impact of MOOCs and lower-cost online options will depend very much on the reaction of different segments of the global and local student population. MOOCs are particularly attractive to highly motivated learners seeking to explore particular topics as well as to students in countries that do not have accessible quality universities. Caution should be exercised in extrapolating from such groups to the wider populations served by mass higher education systems. There has been a great deal of attention given to the purported characteristics of new generations of students, the 'digital natives', who are by some accounts expected to be 'media savvy' and possess not only the latest communication technologies but also new mindsets that enable them to multitask and think in ways unlike those of previous generations. Conversely, less flattering depictions of the 'millennials' highlight their supposed narcissism, weak intrinsic motivation, inability to marshal their thoughts coherently, and short attention spans. The first set of characteristics might make young people ideal candidates for MOOCs and other forms of online education, while the second set would render them far from a good fit. Such caricatures are of course gross simplifications of complex realities, and tend to distract from, rather than add to, the process of mutual adaptation that is underway between universities and students.[13] Technology offers an increasing range of options for this process, but it is all too easy to make technology-based assumptions about the future of higher education that fail to mesh with the reality of student demand and behaviour.

Many younger students seek a social dimension to their university experience and look for a university that can sustain their interest and motivation as well as provide opportunities for interaction with peers and the formation of social contacts. For those in countries with developed higher education systems such as Australia, blended physical and online facilities are likely to be attractive. However, mature-age students with family and work commitments are likely to be seeking different patterns of contact and convenience, and for many of them online courses will be highly attractive, as will be the opportunity to take a more modular approach to higher learning including professional development. Online delivery and modularity are also particularly important to employers who might sponsor staff to undertake professional education, including programs specifically tailored to corporate needs. Not all mature-age students are seeking fully online experiences. For many the physical environment, desire to build networks and social interaction can also be important motivators, but the momentum toward new forms of provision in postgraduate and professional education is growing.

Ultimately it is what students want and need rather than what academics or entrepreneurs want to provide that will determine the future form of university education. It is important not to over-romanticise the university as a provider of richer learning and social experiences, and critics rightly point out that the programs of our campus-based comprehensive universities do not always live up to their ideals. The financial incentives for faculties to keep their courses and programs within their own fiefdoms are strong, many students do not mix as broadly as they could or take advantage of the range of experiences on offer, and some programs are narrower in their scope and focus than others. However, universities are supposed to provide, for all their students, structure, personal challenge and encouragement of active learning, encounters with stimulating and scholarly experts, curriculum that is close to the cutting edge of knowledge, and breadth as well as disciplinary depth. So too is the promise of development of the mind beyond a simple injection of particular knowledge and skills. This does not mean that the traditional university is always best: there is room for this mission to be interpreted and carried out in multiple ways, but we should be wary of predictions that the features many students want and need can be easily or cheaply reworked.

Proponents of disruption continue to point to examples of technology supplanting long-established institutions, recent examples being Kodak, *Encyclopaedia Britannica*, various book, CD and record shops, and a number of newspapers and other print media. They also highlight slow progress in transformation of the academy from within. Even on the campuses of established universities, where experimentation and innovation have taken shape in myriad ways over many years, no 'killer app' has yet emerged. When MIT OpenCourseWare was first mooted in 2001 one of its pioneering professors said 'once students begin acquiring course content on the web, faculty will be able to pay more attention to the actual process of teaching. OpenCourseWare will enable faculty to concentrate on using classroom or lab time to enhance learning.' Eleven years later, with the launch of Coursera, the same hope was being expressed, but dressed in contemporary reformist jargon about 'flipping classrooms'.[14]

Change usually comes slowly in higher education, in part because of academic conservatism but also for economic reasons. Intensifying on-campus interaction and feedback is important, but it is more costly than a large lecture, and cost containment has become ever more necessary.

The process of blending online materials and activities with on-campus education remains a work in progress – no university can ignore what is going on, and major changes are happening to the nature of interactions between students and universities. But for the most part real progress has been through evolution rather than revolution.

With Amara's Law – when people tend to overestimate the impact of new technology at first but underestimate it in the long run – in mind, it would be complacent to imagine that things will continue to stay this way, and there can be little doubt that online learning will grow in importance and be blended in more innovative ways with face-to-face delivery. Students' expectations and behaviour are changing, reflected, for example, in shifts away from lecture attendance. But popular metaphors of a tsunami of online learning are perhaps less apt than the kind of gradual sea-rise associated with global warming – for some it will come more quickly than for others and some may choose to deny it until they go under. For most, the task will be about continual adaptation, and the end point will see universities transformed in ways that are simply impossible to anticipate.

More importantly, the focus on digital disruption still puts too much emphasis on the 'how' of higher education rather than the 'why' and 'what'. As we saw in chapter two the impact of technology will be felt across all areas of the economy, and perhaps the most important task facing universities is to prepare people to adapt to continually changing environments that demand ever higher levels of creativity and other non-routine cognitive skills.

In this light the other major potential disruptor to traditional higher education – competency-based degrees – also falls short of providing clear solutions. As a movement it is still in its infancy, although it is also possible to envisage a future where assessment, awarding of portable credit for skills and learning, and the issuing of credentials becomes viable as an activity that could compete with the traditional university. However, certification of learning must be credible, particularly to employers. Without compelling new evidence of quality it is likely that conservative attitudes will prevail, favouring known prestige and reputation, and certification of learning will remain a function of universities, although there is considerable scope for it to be made more flexible and outward looking. Deakin University has taken an interesting step in this direction with the establishment in 2014 of a wholly owned subsidiary company, Deakin Digital, which allows people with professional or other experience to obtain various credentials after academic assessment of submitted evidence.

Changes such as those we have outlined in this chapter pose fundamental challenges to universities, in particular to their approaches to credit recognition, local academic ownership and control of the process of education, and more broadly to tired models of academic workload and staff development. Government policy will also need to adapt, and be suitably flexible about matters such as student retention and what constitutes institutional performance in education. Universities should not admit people to formal courses lightly, but they do offer opportunities, not inexorable funnels, to certification and employment.

The traditional form of higher education may have remained dominant to date but vast change is in prospect. Entrepreneurs are actively exploring new ways of breaking old moulds in education, many of them backed by significant funding or powerful institutions. Within the university there are both institutional and academic professional futures at stake. However the future develops, the potential offered by new forms of education should encourage more attention to be given to how universities can add value, and may present a much needed opportunity to reduce the cost of higher education without compromising quality.

Chapter Eight

Picking up the tab:
Cost, quality and sustainability

I would argue that a 1 per cent cut in operating grants next year, leaving universities with more than they had this year, is a very small ask from the sector. So it is with 3 per cent the following year and 1 per cent the year after.

Senator Amanda Vanstone, the minister responsible
for higher education, 1996

The case for reform rests on two facts which cannot be denied. The first is that Australian universities need longer term access to more resources.

Dr Brendan Nelson, the minister responsible for higher education, 2003

I want to make sure that we keep America a place of opportunity, where everyone has a fair shot. They get as much education as they can afford and with their time they're able to get and if they have a willingness to work hard and [have] the right values, they ought to be able to provide for their family and have a shot of realizing their dreams.

Republican presidential candidate Mitt Romney, 2012

In 2012 total student higher education debt in the United States grew, according to some estimates, past the US$1 trillion mark. This number was round and eye-wateringly large enough to focus renewed concerns about the escalating costs of universities and colleges, and those concerns have not been allayed as the debt continues to climb, reaching US$1.2 trillion in late 2014. For many years US college prices have far outpaced inflation and growth in median family income, prompting a flood of reports, claims about causes and solutions, political hand-wringing and government inquiries. Around 89 per cent of those surveyed in a 1989 US Gallup Poll thought that most students would be priced out of higher education in the United States by the year 2000 and, despite the millennium proving not quite so apocalyptic, concerns have only mounted as costs have steadily increased.[1]

Of course the US higher education system is very large, and US$1.2 trillion in total debt may not be such a huge amount when spread across 43.3 million borrowers. The median debt level in late 2014 was around US$15,000 and the average around double that number, meaning that while many borrowers had small balances (40 per cent owed less than US$10,000) a significant number of borrowers had much higher debts.[2] New bachelor degree graduates in the US in 2012 had average debts of nearly US$30,000 (and by 2015 this average was estimated to have risen to around US$35,000) with those from public universities accruing around $26,000.[3] In Australia the average debt in 2014 for graduates under the Commonwealth's higher education loan program HELP was around $17,500 and a bachelor degree student graduating in 2015 could expect to have accumulated a debt anywhere between $18,000 and $49,000 depending on their course of study.[4] Moreover, approximately 70 per cent of US university students go into debt[5], while over 92 per cent of Australian university students accrue some debt via HELP. The question arises: why is student debt a crisis in the

United States but, at least until deregulatory fee policy changes were proposed in 2014, rarely remarked on in Australia?

Part of the answer is the distribution. In the United States some 10 per cent of former students have debts above US$50,000 and for graduate degrees such as law and medicine the average is more than US$100,000 (for private law schools average graduate debt in 2011 was US$125,000).[6] By contrast, only 1 per cent of Australian HELP debtors owe more than $50,000, though the media are fond of chasing down the very small number of students who have managed one way or another to accumulate six figure debts.[7]

Moreover, contrary to common perceptions, many of the elite US universities have the highest 'sticker prices' but combinations of student aid and wealthy parents can produce low average levels of graduate debt, particularly for those completing undergraduate programs. At Princeton, for example, tuition fees are very high but average graduate debt is around US$5,000. A significant amount of the burden of student debt in the United States falls on those from less affluent backgrounds, a situation that has been compounded in recent years by the rapid growth of high-cost for-profit education providers, which have, in the main, recruited less well-off students using federal subsidies and low-interest loans.[8] Bachelor degree graduates from for-profit institutions in 2012 had 57 per cent higher average debt levels than their counterparts from public universities.

Furthermore, the rate of default on US student loans is worryingly high, particularly among those from poorer backgrounds, and the flow-on consequences of such default can adversely impact the lives of those who may have only small debt balances. In contrast, the Australian HECS-HELP scheme is 'income contingent': that is, it does not require people to repay debt until a healthy threshold of income is reached ($54,126 in 2015–16) and those who prove unsuccessful in the employment market are not required to repay their debt. The government estimates around 20 per cent of the new student debt in 2014–15 will ultimately remain unpaid.

The idea of income contingent loans (ICL) arose in the United States but did not take root there. From 1974 to the early 1990s Yale experimented with the approach but discontinued it for various reasons, including limitations on the university's ability to collect what was owed. Australian economist Bruce Chapman, who undertook his PhD at Yale, developed what became the first national-level ICL arrangement for higher education at the time of the Dawkins reforms of the late 1980s, and the resultant package included upfront discounts for early payment and interest rates set at the rate of inflation. Repayments are low compared to take-home earnings and public subsidy is lowest for those who gain the highest incomes after graduation. This scheme has greatly softened the impact of student debt and has stood the test of time as a reasonably fair and effective mechanism for handling the contribution of students to the cost of their education.

But such a mechanism comes at a growing cost to the wider public. Higher education is a service that, like many others, involves public subsidies as well as private payment. Its financing is by no means as fiendishly complicated and difficult for consumers to understand as health care, but the interplay of grants, loans and underlying costs does introduce some complications to people's understanding of what is going on. To begin with, 77 per cent of all domestic students in Australia in 2014 were in courses where the Commonwealth government set the overall income the institution received to teach them, and also set the share of that amount that was to be covered by a HECS-HELP loan. For the 37 public universities, which between them accounted for 93 per cent of all domestic students, over 82 per cent of all students were in this category. Therefore, to a very large extent Australian higher education has been price-controlled and university spending has been constrained by the income determined by government.

In 2015 Australian students contributed an average of around 41 per cent of the income a university received from the government, though this varied greatly depending on which course a student undertook, ranging from around 26 per cent for nursing to 83 per cent for business or law.

Since the first introduction of student contributions in 1989 – after a period of around 14 years when the government picked up the entire tab – Australian university students have experienced periodic increases in the level of contribution, particularly in 1997 and in 2005. In 1997 the increase was part of a program of government savings measures that also included a cut to university grants, while in 2005, following a period of review and lobbying borne of concerns about universities' finances, the increase was allowed to be determined and retained up to a maximum of 25 per cent by universities. In 2007 the government increased its own contribution for a three-year period in return for concessions in the areas of governance and industrial relations.

Through price control and by shifting a greater share of cost burden to students, the public as well as the private cost of higher education has been controlled in a way quite unlike the United States. Indeed, total public subsidies for Australian higher education were around 1 per cent of GDP in the late 1990s and had declined to just under 0.9 per cent by 2013–14, despite domestic student numbers increasing by more than 50 per cent.

However, throughout the period from 1996 to 2008, Australian universities complained that the total funding provided from both students and government had failed to keep pace with growth in university costs. In fact this failure to keep pace was official policy, first introduced by the Labor government, designed to 'encourage' universities to operate more efficiently by having their grants indexed below growth in actual costs.

Over the past three decades there has been a near incessant cycle of lobbying and review in Australian higher education, with universities pointing to their tightened circumstances, governments insisting that universities better control their costs, and students wondering why they are paying more for a system that is regularly subject to restructures and lay-offs and has apparently fewer full-time staff available to teach them. Despite the churn of review it has been difficult for clear messages to emerge about the distinction between what student debt pays for and what it actually costs to provide university education.

Australian universities, unlike many of their US counterparts, generally do not provide residential facilities for students, and they do not run expensive athletics programs or pay for staff healthcare, all factors that have been cited as being part of the cause of high US university costs. Where, instead, do the cost pressures come from in Australia?

Drivers of university costs

One explanation for cost growth that has understandable popularity among many academics is that pressure on university budgets comes from misplaced priorities – vice-chancellors with 'edifice complexes', erecting unnecessary buildings; rampant growth in executive numbers and pay; and general 'administrative bloat'.

Without wishing to defend the merits of each and every capital works project in Australia, for the most part the wave of new buildings appearing on university campuses in recent years has been government funded with institutional contributions that have not placed great strain on university recurrent budgets. A few exceptions, however, are acknowledged. Moreover, almost all new buildings have been for education and research rather than administrative in purpose. They have also been sorely needed after decades of limited support for major campus infrastructure.

Information on executive pay can be assessed from university annual reports, which show that this item generally accounts for between 0.5 and 2 per cent of the total institutional salary bill. More to the point, for many universities this has not been increasing.[9]

The charge of administrative bloat might have more substance. It is a shock to many people when they first hear that in Australian universities staff who are not academics outnumber those who are, and the numbers of these 'non-academic staff' (generally referred to as 'professional staff') have grown by 43 per cent over the period from 1996 to 2013.[10] However, academic staff numbers grew by 45 per cent, against an overall growth in student load of 81 per cent. Over the past 15 years professional staff costs have stayed steady at around 47 per cent of the total university salary bill, and the share of staff in central units – as opposed to those in academic departments or schools – has also remained unchanged at around one-third. National data on university staffing also show that the percentage of staff in 'General Institution Services and Institution Overhead Services' has remained more or less at the same level for many years, with a slight increase from 2010.

Furthermore, over the period 1992–2007 two major international surveys of academic staff found that in Australia there had been no increase in overall working hours and the only significant change was a decrease in teaching time,[11] so the burden of bureaucracy has not been unduly shifted to academics. While there is no doubt that this administrative burden has increased, for a range of reasons, and it is possible to choose earlier starting points to demonstrate disproportionate growth in administrative over academic expenditure, the trends since the mid 1990s make it hard to argue that 'administrative bloat' explains much of the increasing cost pressures within universities. The charge of administrative bloat is also an easy one to make for those academics who choose to remain blind to the reality that the size, complexity and sophistication of modern universities means that they have needed to professionalise their systems and modernise their operations. More is said on this in chapter ten.

Another significant source of pressure has been associated with growing research activities. Universities receive operating grants for each government-subsidised student they enrol, and from this they are expected to cover a range of costs. This range obviously includes the direct costs associated with student education, but also covers a rather fuzzily defined component for scholarship or research, which in practice involves a share of academic salaries. Research grants from competitive sources such as the ARC and NHMRC cover only part of the direct cost of a project.

The balance, including infrastructure such as researchers' salary, facilities and IT support, is expected to be provided by the university. Block grants (so named because they are allocated in a single amount to universities each year) are provided under various headings to contribute to such infrastructure, not only for competitive grants but also for the support of students undertaking research degrees. Over time competitive grants have grown far faster than either operating grants or block grants, leading to increasing cost pressures in research support. In recent years additional funding has been provided to ease some of this pressure, although in 2012 pressures on the Commonwealth budget saw full implementation of this plan pushed back by three years to 2016.

While the increasing scale of research is one source of cost pressure, this growth is very unevenly distributed throughout the sector. Yet the signs of financial stress are more uniform. Moreover, it is evident that some of the strongest cost pressures are felt in the least research-intensive universities. Whatever the merits or otherwise of student to staff ratios as indicators of quality, they provide a useful guide to the extent of resource constraints since the employment of academic staff is strategically important to institutions as well as to staff unions. Such ratios are not made worse by choice in the absence of a change in the fundamental modes of university operation. Data on student to staff ratios are far from precise, and there are important variations among the various fields of education, but they show quite clearly that the most research-intensive universities have more nominally teaching-related staff per student, and their ratios of students to staff have not been increasing faster than the rest of the sector. Furthermore, the research-intensive universities tend to have lower percentages of sessional academic staffing. Something other than research or administrative growth must be at work.

More fundamentally there are two overarching economic theories about what drives university costs. One was set out by economists William Baumol and William Bowen in the 1960s, and related in general to labour-intensive services (their book was about the performing arts), but higher education and research could also be included within this framework. Known as 'cost disease', this theory proposed a fundamental difference in rates of labour productivity between locally provided services and other industries such as manufacturing, where labour productivity refers to the ability to produce more outputs per hour worked. Where technology makes an industry more productive, for example where machines replace human labour, then the value of labour rises in that industry. But local services need to compete for labour, and so their costs rise as technological progress impacts other sectors. In short, the price of such services tends to outstrip the price of goods. This does not mean that productivity increases are impossible in services provided by the university, but it does imply that cost pressures are driven in the first instance by staff costs and that productivity increases can be hard to come by in the basic processes of education and research. It also does not imply that academic salaries will always grow beyond inflation. What matters is labour productivity and wage growth elsewhere, particularly for people with high skill levels.

The other main explanation came from Howard Bowen who, in 1980, set out the 'revenue theory of cost' specifically for higher education. In essence this claims that universities will always try to maximise revenue in ways that boost quality and prestige, and without an externally imposed constraint they will adopt approaches that end up being more costly. From this perspective it is pointless to seek out the 'true cost' of higher education or research, since it will be whatever the revenue is.

It is tempting to simply say that both of these theories are at work. But there are policy implications that follow, depending on which one might think predominates. If cost disease is prevalent, then without any paradigm shift in provision there will be underlying cost pressures that need to be acknowledged if quality is not to be put at risk. If, on the other hand, revenue theory is the main cause of pressure, then costs are a matter of institutional strategy and choice, and discipline needs to be imposed by changing existing incentives, for example by greater government intervention, changing governance structures or driving greater exposure to market forces.

Robert Archibald and David Feldman, economists from The College of William and Mary, point out that costs per student in higher education follow a very similar trajectory to counterparts in other service industries, which rely on highly educated labour, and argue that cost disease is likely to be the major driver.[12] In particular, we can see regular real rises in costs in other specialised labour-intensive service areas such as healthcare, childcare and secondary education. It is noteworthy that while universities have had their grants per student indexed at a rate around 2 per cent each year over the period 2000–10, the Australian government Schools Recurrent Cost index averaged 5.6 per cent.

On the other hand, data from the United States also show that educational spending per student is not only higher in the more prestigious private research universities than in public research universities, it is also increasing at a greater rate.[13] This would seem to favour the revenue theory, as would evidence that public subsidies have contributed to rising tuition prices in the United States, particularly at private and for-profit colleges.[14] It is possible that the two theories apply in conjunction, and while the government controls price to counteract institutional tendencies to charge higher fees, Baumol-like rising staffing costs are causing pressure. Without a paradigm change in university operations, such pressure can put quality at risk.

Thus for Australian universities the short answer to the question of what is driving most of the pressure on university budgets is staff costs. Technology has yet to lead to savings beyond the 'back office' administrative functions and, while it has undoubtedly opened up new avenues for exchange of scholarly information and for research productivity in the sense that more can be accessed and built on in a scholar's working day, technology has probably added to the costs of education by being used to complement and enhance rather than replace the work of academics. Undoubtedly there is potential for new approaches to the design of courses to replace some elements of expensive staff time in teaching – MOOCs, competency-based modularisation or other uses of technology might all be part of this response, as indicated in the previous chapter.

A review of Australian university funding in 2011 was undertaken by an expert panel chaired by former South Australian education minister Dr Jane Lomax-Smith. Her panel's final report noted a point we mentioned earlier, namely that funding per student had been more or less maintained in real terms – in other words, after adjusting for normal (CPI) inflation. What the Lomax-Smith Review did not point out was that over the period 1994–2010 CPI increased by 54 per cent, but adult average weekly earnings (AWE) grew by 97 per cent, and university salaries have moved roughly in line with AWE. The report stated that it 'considers that there is a point at which cost savings are achieved at the expense of quality' but unfortunately it was not able to find a way of telling when that tipping point might be reached.

While pressure on funding undoubtedly has encouraged institutions to focus on areas where they are weakest, and on those areas where they might be operating uneconomically, the 'cost disease' affects all parts of the university. The disparity between university income and costs for Commonwealth-subsidised students could be met in the medium term in only four ways: by subsidising from other income sources; by developing alternative, less staff-intensive models of delivery, which are educationally effective; by limiting salary growth; or by changing the deployment of staff time including, at a more fundamental level, the respective roles of academic and professional staff in the teaching and learning process.

The first of these was an option that could be sustained for a while, particularly by international student income, provided universities were able to charge above the marginal costs involved. A number of factors make that less viable now, including the increasing competitiveness of the international student scene.

The second option is much heralded, particularly by advocates of technology disruption, which we considered in the previous chapter. Other approaches are possible. In response to Texas governor Rick Perry's call in 2011 for degrees that cost less than $10,000 a number of models were put forward, for example by the University of Texas of the Permian Basin. However, these involved combinations of pricing strategies rather than fundamental changes in cost, where lower-demand institutions had unused capacity at the margins, and credit arrangements were developed for work done elsewhere, including in high school. The ability to scale and replicate such arrangements is questionable.[15] It is imperative that universities pursue structural change to lower costs in ways that deliver quality, and a range of measures continue to be pursued particularly in exploring greater efficiencies in 'back office' functions in administration and support, aided by extensive benchmarking with other universities. Strategies for more efficient delivery of academic functions, including opportunities arising from the incorporation of technology in teaching, also need to be actively explored. But we should acknowledge that such strategies have yet to bear fruit consistently in Australia or in established universities elsewhere. High-quality university education is likely to remain labour intensive for some time.

The third option, holding salaries down, is difficult to sustain in an environment with high inter-institutional mobility and where competition for skilled people is intrinsic to the enterprise. Every few years university staff enter into enterprise-bargaining negotiations with universities, and academic unions are well aware that pressure on a few of the more prestigious universities with apparently deep pockets can be effective in setting benchmarks that are hard for the rest of the sector to disregard. Competitive salaries are extremely important in an industry that depends so heavily on attracting and retaining highly skilled and mobile people.

The fourth option, changing the way staff time is deployed, has been pursued on university campuses over the past two decades with good and bad outcomes, and doing it well is perhaps the major management challenge for universities. The increasing availability of information on staff performance and time usage will drive new wedges into traditional industrial expectations, in particular about research time. There has been increased use of sessional staffing (which grew sharply in the 1990s, and levelled off for a while before increasing again from 2010), steady rises in student to staff ratios and a greatly increased focus on academic staff performance.

At a more fundamental level the shift from face-to-face to more blended learning environments is challenging dearly-held and stoutly-defended academic traditions about the locus of responsibility for the ownership, creation and delivery of course content. We are transitioning inexorably from learning environments where the academic has had proprietary rights over all these aspects to more creative learning settings where the academic works as the content expert in a team that also includes professionally trained learning designers, pedagogic and technology specialists. Traditional academics may be deeply disturbed by this trend, and invoke forlorn warnings about a loss of academic autonomy. But the shift toward more team-based approaches to learning and teaching offer the prospect of both an enhanced student experience and a more affordable wages bill.

Nor is a greater reliance on the use of sessional academics necessarily a uniformly bad trend. Sessional-type work and short contracts are typical for a range of fields (including the creative and performing arts), and sessional engagement may be convenient for people with family responsibilities, for postgraduate students wishing to top up their scholarship stipends and gain some teaching experience, and for people who might otherwise be locked out of academic careers. Sessional engagement also provides a valuable avenue for the injection of external expertise into university teaching.

Meanwhile, student to staff ratios are not a direct measure of the quality of education, and a focus on academic performance can ensure that people's work time allocation is aligned with their strengths and that opportunities for productive people are not compromised by those who may be mere 'time servers'. All these strategies can be handled badly or done well. Many universities have not paid sufficient attention to the support and development of sessional staff, and academic underperformance has been able to persist in some places without much serious attention from academic managers and because of little encouragement from the staff unions for it to be addressed. Nevertheless, as the Lomax-Smith panel pointed out, there comes a point when something must give. But how do we know when we arrive at such a point? When is quality compromised?

Measuring the unmeasurable: Quality and standards

For the past two decades there has been a great deal of attention given to the assessment of quality in universities, with Australia and the United Kingdom moving as they so often do in tandem, in this case by establishing agencies charged with auditing university processes. The Australian entity was known from 2000 to 2011 as the Australian Universities Quality Agency (AUQA). While these audits had been termed 'quality assurance', it became clearer over time that neither here nor in the United Kingdom were they providing the reassurance that some might like, particularly because the notion of quality as 'fit for purpose' proved insufficiently specific to make the kinds of distinctions that were becoming necessary in an increasingly diverse sector. Criteria in the form of 'National Protocols' had been adopted in Australia in 2000 to manage the establishment of new higher education providers, and these were extended to cover the activities of existing universities. AUQA was charged with the task of assessing compliance; however, its efforts to do so were hampered by lack of clarity in the criteria and their status as guidelines rather than standards meant that established universities were not bound to observe them. By the time of the Bradley Review in 2008 the need for a clearer and more broadly applicable framework was evident.

In the 2009 Budget the Commonwealth government accepted the Bradley Review recommendation that a Tertiary Education Quality and Standards Agency (TEQSA) be established. This agency would not only oversee the approval of new providers, but also would extend its scope to existing universities, which, for the first time, would be required to be recorded on a national register to operate, with review after a designated period. Universities would also have to comply with a range of new standards, including a revamped set of standards for the course structures known as the Australian Qualifications Framework (AQF). Not surprisingly this caused some consternation in many parts of the established university world, in that any imposed restriction on university activities could be construed as a weakening of autonomy. Yet established universities could not reasonably claim complete immunity from standards that had to be applied to others, and assurances were given by the government that the intention was to apply regulation in proportion to the likelihood of risk, a principle now written into the legislation governing TEQSA's operation.

TEQSA came into operation from the beginning of 2012, after an extended period of development and consultation. We will return to the genesis and wider regulatory role of TEQSA in chapter ten, but of particular interest here is a key innovation in the TEQSA approach – referencing its assessments of universities and other education providers against explicit standards.

The Standards Framework is ultimately decided by the national minister after receiving advice from a Higher Education Standards Panel, and also after consulting with TEQSA and relevant state and territory ministers. The panel is made up of a group of experts from the sector and is independent of TEQSA. Among the various standards it develops are recommendations on any change to the categorisation of universities or other self-accrediting or non self-accrediting institutions. This is important policy terrain for two reasons. First, it goes to the perennial debate about whether permission for the badge 'university', which is much sought after by other players, should be allowed for an institution that does not conduct research. And second, it reopens the matter of eligibility for government support of new players, including private colleges, particularly if they aspire to offer undergraduate education.

While established universities might complain about some curtailment of their ability to do as they please, it is also the case that formalisation of previously unregulated matters can work against the wishes of some external proponents of university reform. In particular, the Standards Framework as it applies to new universities effectively rules out the possibility of Australian 'teaching only' universities along the lines of many of the US for-profit or potentially 'disruptive' competitors, although they could operate as 'higher education providers' under some other title.

TEQSA's role in relation to the assessment of quality comes in essentially two forms, first as a set of threshold standards with which any provider must comply to be registered, and second, a less clearly defined mandate to undertake quality assessments 'to identify, validate, and promote the adoption of good practice in meeting the requirements of the TEQSA Act, and in particular the Higher Education Standards Framework'. The threshold standards were promulgated at the start of 2012 and describe the criteria providers must meet to be registered under various categories – including as a university, university college or university of specialisation – as well as standards for their course structures (the AQF). However, publication of standards is only the first step, the other (and harder) part is to apply them in practice.

The standards are laced throughout with words such as 'appropriate' and 'sufficient', which will require interpretation. For example, under financial viability the relevant requirements state that 'the higher education provider applies, and demonstrates the capacity to continue to apply, sufficient financial resources to ensure the achievement of its higher education objectives'. Similarly, under the AQF graduates of a bachelor degree 'will demonstrate the application of knowledge and skills: with initiative and judgement in planning, problem solving and decision making in professional practice and/or scholarship; to adapt knowledge and skills in diverse contexts; with responsibility and accountability for own learning and professional practice and in collaboration with others within broad parameters.'

Establishing whether or not a provider complies with these kinds of standards is clearly not straightforward. But it has proven even more difficult for TEQSA to undertake the wider quality assessment and quality enhancement tasks. Its first effort, to examine third party arrangements, involved a 47 page survey with 136 questions issued to universities and other providers. Ironically, the survey was distributed the day after a government-commissioned review into universities reporting requirements was published. TEQSA later acknowledged that the survey had been the 'biggest trigger for the greatest attacks' on the agency, and the backlash led to quality assurance being put on the backburner, following direction from the government that TEQSA undertake closer consultations with the sector, and absorbing a budget cut applied from 2014 to help TEQSA 'focus on its core quality assurance activities of registration and accreditation'.

Assessing university quality has proven no easier in other countries. In 2009 the UK House of Commons Innovation, Universities, Science and Skills Committee published a report on higher education that devoted considerable attention to issues of quality and standards. In so doing, it provided a useful illustration of how difficult even simple-sounding concepts can be in this area. The report's authors stated that 'given the amount of money that the taxpayer puts into universities it is not acceptable, as we found during our inquiry, that Vice-Chancellors cannot give a straightforward answer to the simple question of whether students obtaining first-class honours degrees at different universities had attained the same intellectual standards.' Later they observed that:

> students, understandably, want to know the worth of their degrees. We were therefore concerned when staff at Imperial College London informed the Chairman of the Committee during his visit as a rapporteur that some academics had noticed that masters students enrolled at Imperial, who had graduated from certain other universities with first class honours degrees, sometimes struggled at Imperial College. We consider that this could be evidence of a devaluation of degrees in those institutions.[16]

This raises several questions about what people might mean by standards and how they might be measured. Should all students be expected to graduate from broadly similar degree levels with 'the same' standards of learning and ability? How would one tell? Anecdotal evidence such as that presented above is clearly inadequate, but what alternatives might be possible? The House of Commons report rejected standardisation of curricula and testing, and suggested a rather circular solution: 'we consider that national standards can be established and enforced by other methods such as peer review against a national standard – a development of the role conventionally played by external examiners.'

Some idea of the magnitude of the task of developing wider academic standards can be gleaned by contemplating the ever-expanding frontiers of knowledge, the widening array of higher education providers, the proliferation of purposes and aims in higher education from professional training to preparation for further study or general 'cultivation of the mind'. On top of that is the multiplication of sites and methods for teaching and learning including online, in the workplace and at home.

Academic standards in diverse and constantly changing fields of knowledge can be assessed only by competent people; that is, by academic peers. Work is underway on methods of enabling this to happen in ways that are scalable, affordable and complement the existing mechanisms we have in areas such as the accreditation of many professional programs. Ideally we ought to be able to assure the public that Australian standards are up there with the world's best and at the same time contribute to the development of good practice by sharing information. But, as with all areas of TEQSA's operations, a watching eye needs to be kept on the tendency for regulation to drift into formulaic bureaucracy.

The threshold standards provide an important but inevitably imperfect framework for weeding out obviously low-quality activity. But the quality of teaching is not some immutable constant experienced by all students in the same way across a university. Quality depends on a myriad of interactions between individuals as well as on the materials and facilities they use and on institutional policies and characteristics. In practice, university quality remains much like pornography, in the famous words of Justice Potter Stewart: 'I shall not today attempt further to define the kinds of material I understand to be embraced within that shorthand description ... and perhaps I could never succeed in intelligibly doing so. But I know it when I see it.'

Unfortunately, this leaves us in the difficult position of being unable to find the Lomax-Smith tipping point for funding. How do we know if quality is being put at risk because of lack of funding?

Alternative sources for university funding

Higher education and research are intrinsically reliant on specialised and highly skilled labour, and the 'cost disease' phenomenon cannot, at least for the time being, simply be wished away by dreams of online automation. There is certainly room for further adjustment of the deployment of both academic and professional staff time, and for further productivity gains in a range of areas within universities. These, however, will not yield perpetual reductions in cost. Behind much of the 'mission differentiation' and 'diversity' discourse considered in chapter four lies the belief that some institutions should lower costs by opting out of research, though, as we suggest in that chapter, this may be neither desirable nor feasible except at the margins of university policy. Redistribution of research or other funding as a way of making up shortages for some institutions would be both regressive, in the sense that the most privileged students and institutions would gain at the expense of the least privileged, and ineffective as new equilibria would soon be reached with ongoing demands for sustenance. The Lomax-Smith tipping point may not be a clear line, but the principle still holds: unless online disruptive models move from promise to reality (and they show no signs of doing so imminently), and while salaries for highly skilled people continue to rise in real terms, universities need to focus more effectively on their use of staff time and, ultimately, some increase in operating income will need to be found.

The big question is: where will the money come from? To date most attention has centred on students and government, but we often hear claims that the private sector, either business or philanthropy, could step in to shoulder some of the burden. We will return to the newest front in the government–student funding wars in the next chapter, and in the rest of this chapter examine the alternatives.

First, to put things in perspective, in Australia in 2013 donations and bequests amounted to just 1 per cent of overall university revenue, while consultancy income made up 4 per cent, and royalties, trademarks and licences contributed 0.4 per cent. On the other hand, overseas students provided 16 per cent and government grants and loans accounted for around 61 per cent.

Philanthropy

Over many decades a powerful and well-documented tradition of philanthropy has developed and matured in the United States. Observers elsewhere have regarded this phenomenon with a mixture of envy and resignation. Its sheer scale is evident in the multibillion-dollar endowments accumulated by a number of the leading universities. Harvard, with almost $US38 billion in total endowments in 2015, leads the field, though more than 70 universities and colleges in the United States administer endowment pools that exceed US$1 billion. Many of these are public universities, including the University of Arkansas, which, although outside the 'Top 70' just referred to, still ranks as the recipient of the single largest donation to any public university in the United States. This was the US$300 million donated in 2002 by the Walton Family Charitable Foundation.

Around the turn of this century the extent of philanthropic support in the US higher education sector was becoming of particular interest in the United Kingdom, where chill budget winds were placing serious pressure on broad operating costs as well as on the particular funding of research and innovation. In that context, philanthropy was viewed, as it has been elsewhere in the Western world, as a 'third' source of income for universities, the first and second being governments and students.

At that time only a very few well-known UK universities were attracting significant support, and even these were drawing from a limited number of benefactors. The single largest gift, certainly in the modern era, was the Bill and Melinda Gates Foundation endowment of the Gates Cambridge Scholarships, at £200 million. Each year this initiative, announced in 2000, supports some 90 incoming postgraduates from outside the United Kingdom, who receive fully funded scholarships to study for awards across the spectrum of disciplines.

The likelihood of continued public funding pressure was recognised by the United Kingdom's 2003 White Paper 'Future of Higher Education', which encouraged universities to take greater control of their financial future. This led to the establishment of a Task Force, chaired by Professor Eric Thomas, which in 2004 proposed to the UK government a range of strategies to increase the level of voluntary giving to the nation's higher education institutions.[17] These strategies included taxation instruments to encourage charitable giving, and a government matching funds program where private donations to colleges and universities would be 'matched' with public funds. The Thomas Review also pointed, importantly, to the tangible steps the universities needed to take in order to professionalise their fundraising, development, and alumni operations.

In 2008 the UK government responded to the Thomas Review by launching a matched funding scheme for voluntary giving, to be administered by the Higher Education Funding Council for England (HEFCE). The purpose of that program, to which £200 million was allocated over the period 2008–11, was to achieve a 'step change' in voluntary giving. The program catered for institutions at different levels of maturity in their philanthropy culture, by providing the funds on a capped basis across three tiers. For those institutions that were least experienced with fundraising the matching would be pound for pound. A ratio of one pound for every two raised privately would apply for the majority of institutions that had existing development and fundraising programs, while a ratio of one to three would be provided for those institutions with highly developed fundraising mechanisms already in place.

Other initiatives followed. These included a 2011 'Giving' White Paper, outlining the UK government's plans to encourage a community-wide renewal of Britain's culture of philanthropy, and a 2012 HEFCE-commissioned review of philanthropy in UK higher education.[18] This latter study noted the successful delivery by Oxford and Cambridge of the first two £1 billion fundraising campaigns for the United Kingdom. But the HEFCE-commissioned review also noted that by this stage more than 20 UK higher education institutions had received gifts in excess of £1 million, including newer players such as London South Bank University, the University of the West of England and Nottingham Trent University.

Philanthropy has been on the rise also in a number of Asian countries where, significantly, public sector investment in education and research is continuing apace. This should not be entirely surprising. Many leading business, political and industrial figures in China, Singapore, Hong Kong, Taiwan and elsewhere have themselves been educated in the United States or other Western countries, or mix with colleagues who have been, and thus have direct knowledge of the impact this experience has had on their lives. It is also the case, as discussed earlier, that Confucian-influenced cultures place a very high premium on the power of education in terms of personal and family transformation.

Certainly the potential scale of philanthropy in Asian higher education, and the implications of this activity for the competitive environment internationally, are already in evidence. An article by Yojana Sharma in *University World News* in April 2011 reported, for example, a US$120 million donation by the Singapore-based Lee Foundation to Nanyang Technological University, as well as a US$128 million (HK$1 billion) donation by one of Asia's richest men, Li Ka Shing, to University of Hong Kong. But that was dwarfed by the HK$5.4 billion support provided by Li Ka Shing's Foundation to Shantou University, located in the Chaoshan district of China's Guangdong Province. Li Ka Shing was born in that province.

More controversially, in 2011 Lei Zhang – a Chinese businessman who had studied at both Yale and the Beijing-based Renmin University – donated the sum of US$8,888,888 – auspicious because of the good fortune associated with '8' in Chinese culture – to Yale. The significance of the gift was not so much the amount, which is less than many gifts by Asian business figures to universities in their own countries, but rather that Lei Zhang chose to recognise the US institution at which he had studied and which had, he added, educated many other Chinese leaders over the decades before him. In a similar spirit, in 2011 India's Tata Group donated US$50 million to the Harvard Business School (HBS). Ratan Tata, the chair of Tata Sons Ltd, had attended HBS's Advanced Management Program in 1975, and had received the school's highest alumni honour in 1995.

A 2016 study released by the Ash Center for Democratic Governance at Harvard University confirms the emergence of large-scale philanthropy in China. Among that country's top 100 philanthropists, the average donation paid out (as opposed to pledged) in the calendar year to September 2015 was US$8 million, with education, government-backed welfare charities and disaster relief among the favoured targets for support and environmental issues least favoured. The lead author of the study, Peiran Wei, confirmed the attractiveness of education to philanthropists: 'In Asian cultures, we put a high emphasis on education ... But you also see short-term benefits: you have a scholarship or a building named after you.'[19]

In Australia there has been a historical tendency to regard major educational philanthropy as a uniquely American phenomenon. Certainly it is true that philanthropy to all causes in the United States represents a significantly greater share of gross domestic product than it does in Australia, and that the education sector is a much less favoured focus for philanthropy in Australia than is the case in the United States.

At a political level the need to develop a culture of philanthropy was recognised by Julie Bishop when, as the federal minister responsible for higher education, she invited the Business, Industry and Higher Education Collaboration Council (BIHECC) to look into the matter. This led to a 2007 report, prepared by Allen Consulting and endorsed by Universities Australia and BIHECC, recommending a matched funding program as one way of stimulating philanthropic endeavour.[20] The Bradley Review, 18 months later, also recommended matched funding in terms and scale very similar to that announced in the United Kingdom a few months beforehand. That recommendation was not taken up by government here, perhaps for the reason that there were a number of signs emerging from the universities themselves that many were now engaging seriously in the fundraising space.

Simon McKeon, Australian of the Year in 2011 and a philanthropist, was reportedly 'gobsmacked' by tax statistics showing that of the about 8,000 Australians earning more than $1 million a year, more than a third made no gift at all to charity, claiming not even one $2 tax donation.[21] The same article also reported Daniel Petre, a former Microsoft executive who had worked alongside Bill Gates and who has focussed on philanthropy since returning to Australia, as making the even more acidic observation that the average Australian worker gives away more cash than the super wealthy and that 'this is just appalling'. He went on to say, 'Generally speaking, they don't see a moral obligation to give generously to the society in which they've built their wealth.' The comment about the attitude of average workers is in line with Australia's good overall showing on the 2015 World Giving Index, reflecting the comparative generosity of Australians to volunteer and to give money at times of natural disasters.

The journalist who wrote the article referred to above, Miriam Steffens, also made the telling point that the greatest philanthropist in Australian history, Chuck Feeney, is not Australian, but an Irish American who does not live here. That should be clarified because Feeney's personal interest in attending to projects in many different parts of the world makes him somewhat nomadic, and he has spent time each year in Brisbane for the last 20 years. We will say a little more about Feeney shortly.

David Kennedy, who worked as Australian representative for Chuck Feeney for the five years to 2012, is hopeful that the philanthropy tide may be turning.[22] He also attributes Australia's ordinary record in the past to the absence of death duties or estate taxes like those in some other countries, and to challenges around the granting of tax-deductible status to non-profit organisations, thus making Australia's environment less attractive for tax-deducted giving. Kennedy also suggests that Australia's comparatively high personal income tax rates, which help to sustain a broad system of government programs to help those less well off, may mean that top tax payers may feel they are already paying their fair share in taxes and are contributing, through that tax system, to those people and organisations in the community that need support. Kennedy's is a benign assessment.

While philanthropic funding had been scarce for universities in Australia for a very long period, it is noteworthy that the original establishment or development of a number of the nation's universities was facilitated by generous individual or family benefactors. Many of these have been written about elsewhere and they include those of

Walter Watson Hughes (University of Adelaide), John Henry Challis (University of Sydney), John Ralston (University of Tasmania), John Winthrop Hackett (University of Western Australia), three generations of the Myer family (University of Melbourne), and the Mayne bequest (University of Queensland). More recently, Australia's first private university – Bond University – was established in 1987 and its initial development funded by a joint venture between Australian businessman Alan Bond of Bond Corporation and Harunori Takahashi of Japanese entity EIE Development Company.

Don Markwell, at different times warden of both Trinity College at the University of Melbourne and Rhodes House at Oxford, has drawn the entirely plausible link between the growth of government funding and control of higher education, and the decline of philanthropic support. He has also added that as the real level of government funding has generally receded, the need for philanthropic support has grown, but the efforts to secure it have been slow to develop.[23] One of the reasons for this slowness is the condescension sometimes encountered in the traditional academy toward the need to professionalise fundraising, alumni and development. Also, there are those who worry about the potentially directive nature of philanthropy and the implications for other academic priorities.

The potentially game-changing contribution to Australian philanthropy in general, and to higher education and research in particular, has been that of Chuck Feeney, founding chair of The Atlantic Philanthropies (TAP). In the period since 1990 Chuck Feeney, through TAP, has donated at least $500 million to Australian, and Australian-related entities, primarily universities and independent research institutes. Much of that benefaction has been for medical and health research, and a large proportion of his support has been directed toward Queensland-based institutions, including the University of Queensland (UQ), Queensland

University of Technology (QUT), the Queensland Institute of Medical Research (QIMR) and Griffith University, as well as research groups at the Mater and Wesley hospitals. Feeney's interest in Queensland had its roots in personal friendships he had developed, including with a tennis great, the late Ken Fletcher. Feeney and his wife Helga came to love Queensland and make many friendships in the northern state. But what also attracted his interest was the way Queensland had committed itself to a broadening of its economic and social base, which historically had been too narrowly based on mining, agriculture and tourism. And while less generous observers were, for a time at least, sceptical of Queensland's repositioning as the 'Smart State', under the successive premierships of Peter Beattie and Anna Bligh, Feeney could see the potential contribution of education and research to the state's future. His interest was sustained by the cooperative relationships between the state government and higher education, as well as the collegial environment within the state's university sector.

Apart from the sheer level of generosity involved, and the powerful example set, there are several other important features about Chuck Feeney's approach to philanthropy in Australia that deserve mention. The first is the leverage he has been able to secure, because his philanthropic gifts were often contingent on matching funds from the state and/or federal government. It is estimated that Feeney's grants in Australia have leveraged the construction of some $2 billion in new university and research facilities. The most obvious example is that of his $102.5 million contribution toward three major capital projects announced in 2009 (involving UQ, QUT and QIMR). That contribution leveraged support from both the Commonwealth and Queensland governments and resulted in the construction of three major facilities with a total capital cost well in excess of $700 million. Two of these were devoted to the medical sciences, and the third to science and engineering. Second, Feeney has supported some of the most established universities, such as Queensland, Melbourne and New South Wales, as well as emerging research players such as QUT and Griffith. This is similar to his practice in Ireland, where he has contributed hugely to the development of the comparatively new University of Limerick (formed in 1972) as well as to that nation's most established players. Feeney's support of RMIT University is interesting, given it was significantly directed toward the establishment of RMIT's Vietnam campus in Ho Chi Minh City. Feeney had a strong interest in Vietnam dating back to his earlier life experiences.

Feeney has long championed the philosophy of 'giving while living', believing that the best philanthropy is done while the donor is still alive and can be actively engaged with the beneficiaries. His personal connection with the grantee institution and each project, his level of comfort with the 'DNA' of the leadership, the cultivation of partnerships among grantee organisations, and the ability to leverage from government or others, are all important to him. This formula has characterised his gifting in Vietnam, Ireland and California, and of course to Cornell University, his own alma mater. Feeney graduated from Cornell's Hotel School in the 1950s. At the time the Hotel School – according to Feeney biographer Conor O'Clery – accepted the lowest SAT (Scholarship Aptitude Test) scores in that university. But the Hotel School consistently produced the most successful entrepreneurs, such as Jones W. McLamore and David R. Egerton, co-founders of Burger King, and Michael King, who built the Alamo car rental business. The *Cornell Chronicle Online* (20 December 2011) reported Chuck Feeney's benefaction to that institution between 1982 and 2011 had totalled approximately US$600 million. Since then, Feeney and TAP have provided a US$350 million anchor donation to support Cornell's successful bid to develop a Tech campus on New

York City's Roosevelt Island. This brings his total benefaction to Cornell very close to US$1 billion.

That same personal interest in individual projects has been a particular feature of Chuck Feeney's interest in Australia. Clearly he has had a deep belief and interest in the potential of medical and scientific research to benefit humanity, as evidenced by his support of major research precincts. These include UQ's Institute for Molecular Bioscience and the Queensland Brain Institute, the Walter and Eliza Hall Institute in Melbourne, and both the Victor Chang Cardiac Research Unit and the Garvan Institute of Medical Research in Sydney. But he has also supported QUT's Kelvin Grove Urban Village – in this case TAP's contribution was directed to the development of health clinics, recreation facilities and the establishment of the Institute of Health and Biomedical Innovation at that institution.

Notwithstanding the overall reluctance of many wealthy Australians to contribute philanthropically, the numbers seem to be moving in the right direction. It should also be acknowledged that there have been, and continue to be, a number of notable exceptions, particularly generous benefactions in the arts and medical research and, more recently, toward major initiatives supporting underprivileged children, rural and regional education, and Indigenous education, health and aspiration building. Chuck Feeney, however, has raised the stakes and significantly elevated the place of education and research within national philanthropy in Australia. This repositioning is confirmed by a number of other landmark donations made by the alumni of various Australian universities over recent years. The largest of these was Graham Tuckwell's $50 million donation to ANU for undergraduate scholarships, made in February 2013. Other very significant donors include John Grill and Barry and Joy Lambert (University of Sydney) and Andrew

Brice and Graeme Wood (University of Queensland). Another major gift, in favour of the University of Technology Sydney (UTS), was by a well-connected Sydney Chinese businessman, Chau Chak Wing, whose son had studied at that institution. Dr Wing went on, in 2015, to make a major donation to the University of Sydney for a museum to be named after him.

Most of the philanthropy in Australian universities to date has been for medical and health research, sponsored professorships, new and refurbished facilities and scientific equipment. In more recent years benefactors have also ramped up the support of scholarships for disadvantaged students, especially from Indigenous, rural and regional backgrounds. But not all philanthropic support to address disadvantage has come from the 'big end' of town. Back in 1998 QUT established its Learning Potential Fund (LPF) as a perpetual mechanism to provide opportunities for disadvantaged students. After an understandably slow start, the LPF had achieved a balance of $41 million by the end of 2015, a solid start toward a $100 million target. A notable feature of the LPF is that, in addition to the support of alumni and friends, there is a strong level of 'buy-in' by QUT staff. Some 700 staff support the LPF via fortnightly payroll deductions, and more than 20,000 scholarships or bursaries have been financed by the fund since its inception.

Business

Today's universities are far from being ivory towers and the web of connections between them and the rest of society is complex and ever changing, and this is certainly the case for links with business and industry. There are many forms of business engagement at various levels, for example in applied research projects, CRC involvements, science parks, work placements, industry involvement in course development (and in some cases delivery), customised education programs, consultancies and partnerships.

Many sectors of the economy have a stake in what universities do, and universities certainly have incentives to cultivate relationships.

For some in the academy the dark side of such developments includes the potential for distortion and corruption of academic work by commercial considerations, as well as threats to academic freedom and risks of engaging with the wrong business partners. These are not empty concerns – former Harvard University President Derek Bok has discussed them in some depth in his 2004 book *Universities of the Marketplace*. Harvard's own governance and entanglements with the former Enron Corporation attracted much attention following Enron's collapse, while a few years later the potential conflicts of interest of a number of leading US academic economists were aired in the wake of the 2008 global financial crisis. We will be considering some specific examples of where university governance has gone astray, in the next chapter.

However, much of this terrain is manageable in practice, and the dominant concern is that existing links between universities and industry are too weak rather than too strong. In recent years, Australia's poor performance in university-business research collaboration has been the subject of intense scrutiny. Particular attention has been given to OECD figures on 'firms collaborating on innovation with higher education or public research institutions' where Australia is ranked at the bottom of the OECD. While it may be argued, with some justification, that Australia's industrial structure is different from that of Germany or California, Arun Sharma – in an article in the *Australian Financial Review* – argued that a significant contributor may be the differing types of research expenditure made by businesses and universities.

In 2010, businesses spent 52 per cent of their R&D outlay on engineering, while universities spent 9 per cent. Businesses spent 28 per cent on ICT and universities spent 4 per cent. On the other hand, while universities spent 38 per cent of their research expenditure on medical and health sciences, the comparable figure for business is 6 per cent.[24]

The more recent 2012 figures are not much different.[25] Sharma argues that a strong bottom-up peer review system – without a counterbalancing research investment in areas of strategic significance to the Australian economy – has led to Australian universities replicating the disciplinary research mix and the proportional scale of activity of most other advanced economies, to the extent that the research capacity in Australian universities has evolved independently of local innovation needs. This is in contrast to, say, the UK, which has similarly significant university research activity in medical and health sciences, but benefits from the capacity of a large pharmaceutical industry that is able to take advantage of this research activity.

It has often been argued that Australian businesses do not invest in research in universities and that somehow this is different to the situation in other knowledge-intensive economies. Again, the reality may be less clear-cut. Industry is seldom generous with its research funds, understandably focussing support on immediately relevant priorities. Even MIT receives only 19 per cent of its research funding from industry, and MIT ranks first in the United States in industry-financed R&D expenditure among universities without a medical school. When it comes to industry income as a proportion of total research income, Australian universities do reasonably well, in fact they are on par with, or better than some of the Scandinavian countries that do much better than Australia on the OECD university–business collaboration league tables. A partial explanation of this anomaly is that much of the university–business collaboration in these better performing countries is funded by the taxpayer because there is acceptance of spillover effects to the economy if universities and business collaborate on the production of knowledge. Serious funding associated with programs like DARPA in the United States was instrumental in driving the technology revolution through targeted investment and by bringing together industry and universities. Initiatives such as the Technology Strategy Board (now called Innovate UK) have similarly provided investment in targeted areas where business and the research sector have been able to collaborate. Mariana Mazzucato has provided a persuasive case for public investment in her 2013 book *The Entrepreneurial State: Debunking public vs. private sector myths.*

The challenge for Australia will be to provide effective incentives to both universities and businesses to collaborate. The recommendations from the recently concluded Watt review will go some way in providing research block grant incentives to universities to work with end users. Measurement of engagement and assessment of research impact, as signalled in the Turnbull government's innovation statement released at the end of 2015, will also help change behaviour in universities. The review of the R&D Tax Concession provides another opportunity to consider incentives for businesses to collaborate with universities. Ultimately, however, the Government may be persuaded to at least consider some large strategic investment in targeted areas of national significance to correct the significant business–university disparity in expenditure patterns around national research priorities. This may amount to picking winners, and successive Australian Governments have shied away from doing so. Industry Growth Centres are an early attempt to move in this direction, but they appear to be more about better aligning existing funding pools to national needs rather than any significant new investment. The only promise of additional large scale funding has been the Medical Research Future Fund that is targeted to grow to $1 billion per annum, effectively doubling the research funding available from the NHMRC. While this is excellent news for medical research, it does not address the university–business disconnect. More generally, it reinforces Australia's vulnerability to the perception that, in university research terms, it is a 'one trick pony'. Of course advances in medical research are a critical priority for our community. However, given the scale and scope of the economic, environmental and social challenges facing the nation and our region, we will need greater depth and breadth in our national research efforts as well as better bridges to link such efforts with the people in the wider community who might put new knowledge to best use.

Concerns about skills shortages and the quality of graduates have also been raised on a regular basis in the various reviews that have taken place over the years. For example, in the West Review 'one executive in a major firm' was cited as concluding that:

> graduates are much too theoretical in their approach and lack basic management and economics knowledge or understandings. They are unprepared for life in remote settings. They don't understand company loyalty and have an elevated sense of their own importance. They tend to be unaware of issues confronting the industry and are unfamiliar with the importance of occupational health and safety.[26]

More systematic and consistent feedback from industry has been difficult to obtain at a national level, although various universities or areas within them have conducted their own surveys from time to time. Evidently there are different cultures and expectations that persist about the role of education and what graduates ought to be learning during their studies. These matters have only been addressed at a broad level through mechanisms such as graduate statements and national architecture such as the AQF.

The Bradley Review did not address external relationships in great detail, although it did examine philanthropy and skills shortages issues. For the latter it noted that the issue was not just about graduate supply: 'Other factors such as time lags, salary levels and employment conditions can cause skills shortages in specific areas.' The review's report looked briefly at incentives for students to enrol in particular courses, though it noted that this had not been particularly successful in the past.

The contemporaneous Cutler Review of the national innovation system emphasised the need for better collaboration among all the parties involved in innovation in Australia, including universities and business. It noted that innovation was not just about commercialising new knowledge, but that in the past the overwhelming focus of national innovation policy had been on increasing the supply and commercialisation of research, scientific discovery and technological advances. This was and remains an important part of the innovation picture, but the Cutler Review was keen to see a broader approach aimed at developing capabilities within firms and growing national and international linkages.

Australia is not alone in having concerns about perceived lethargy in university–business relationships. As part of its 2011 Higher Education White Paper the UK government announced that Professor Sir Tim Wilson would undertake an independent review of business–university collaboration. Professor Wilson presented his review findings in February 2012. Noting the diversity of the relationships involved, a series of recommendations was made to improve links in education and research, many of which were aimed at university and government policies. In response, Universities and Science Minister David Willetts noted that Wilson:

recognised that it was not an area where there were 'large amounts of levers and instructions to come from Whitehall' ... A lot of it is to do with collaboration and cooperation and growing links between universities and businesses. [Many] proposals in this report are for a number of agencies apart from government and I think that's a very realistic and sensible approach.[27]

One of the centrepieces of direct government support was to give the relatively small sum of £50,000 to the Council for Industry and Higher Education for the development of a National Centre for Universities and Business to strengthen links between the two sectors.

In Australia, as in the United Kingdom, there have been several efforts to lift the level of innovation in industry, and programs have been developed to subsidise some forms of applied research as well as supporting commercialisation of products and services. But it has been difficult to persuade the government to take a more active role in underwriting closer engagement, for example a Universities Australia proposal for a National Internship Scheme failed to make much headway. In fact, some government policy has likely had an unintended negative impact on working with business, particularly in research as higher stakes have been attached to excellence as assessed by academic peers and citations. As noted earlier, proposals have been put forward to measure and reward research 'impact', but the track record of incentive-based approaches by governments to allocating university funding has not been encouraging.

Certainly Malcolm Turnbull, as prime minister, conveyed through his government's innovation statement an expectation that all Australian universities will need to work more system-atically and closely with business whether or not there is explicit support from government. Indeed, this is essential if Australia is to move beyond its current circumstances by developing cultures of innovation within Australian firms. Greater penetration of PhD graduates into Australian businesses will be an important part of developing such cultures and, as noted, Australia lags behind countries such as Germany in this respect. Some of this is structural, in the sense that Australia's economy is remote from the major world markets and dominated by natural resources and service industries rather than the more knowledge-intensive small- to medium-sized companies that may be found in Germany (in manufacturing) or in California (IT and entertainment). However, if it is to change we need more productive links between universities and both existing and emerging industries in Australia. Links have to be allowed to develop organically as well as encouraged and managed from above, and this is sometimes a tricky balance to strike. The best relationships require long-term dedication and the building of close personal connections as well as institutional policies and funding commitments. More can and should be done by universities, businesses and governments to promote and foster productive interactions, however, the likelihood is that for some time we will see the broad components of university income continue in their current form.

If the great majority of university funding has to come from a combination of student and government sources, then in a mass higher education system – one where, say, more than a third of young people attend university at some stage – the issues surrounding balancing wide and expanding access with rising costs for students and limits on public finances become ever more difficult. We have seen that in Australia the move to income contingent loans has provided an excellent balance over the last few decades, but that settlement has relied on some relatively arbitrary decisions about the size of the system, the scope and consistency of coverage across public and private institutions, the level of university funding and the share paid by government and students. Over recent years the balance has been harder to sustain and those decisions have increasingly been called into question.

Up to 2008 the stakes were lower because the government kept a cap on overall student numbers. Between 2001 and 2008 the number of government-supported places grew by only 6 per cent. But after 2008 student numbers increased rapidly and the number of places in 2014 was 36 per cent higher than in 2008. The main impetus for this growth was the 'demand-driven system' that phased out caps from 2009 to a complete removal by 2012. The Labor government was aware that removing caps would drive up enrolments, and as a result would drive additional public spending. In her memoir *My Story*, Julia Gillard, recalled that as the minister responsible for higher education, she witnessed this policy, accompanied by additional spending measures including better indexation of university grants and extra funding for research infrastructure, facing stiff opposition from Treasury and Finance. Indeed, it was eventually secured only by a last-minute ministers-only discussion in the prime minister's office. As it turned out, the appetite and capacity of universities to enrol additional students far exceeded the government's estimates, and what was initially expected to be a policy costing $491 million over four years added around $2 billion to the annual cost of government grants by 2013.

Facing such a blowout, and post-GFC pressures to rein in the Commonwealth deficit by reducing expenditure, the Labor government in 2013, by then with Julia Gillard as prime minister, decided to seek savings from higher education in order to support new reforms to secondary education. These included deferring or discontinuing some of the spending announced in 2009 and introducing an efficiency dividend of 2 per cent in 2014 and 1.25 per cent in 2015. Sensitive to criticism at a time of relentless political pressure being applied by Opposition leader Tony Abbott, Gillard later described the 'vocal and violent' opposition from universities and 'hysterical and immature reaction from the National Tertiary Education Union' as 'politically stupid' given what might be on offer should a conservative government take office. The education minister Craig Emerson personally rang vice-chancellors to convey his displeasure with their reaction, but for their part vice-chancellors feared that the large and arms-length higher education budget was a tempting target for raids from either side of politics.

Some idea of the bipartisan nature of trends in higher education funding comes from the United Kingdom. University tuition fees there were first introduced by the Blair Labour government in 1998, initially at £1,000 and then tripled in 2004. In 2009, while a Labor government in Australia was announcing what in retrospect might have been 'peak public funding' for universities, the UK Labour government sought to meet additional funding demands by commissioning a review headed by Lord Browne of Madingley, a former chairman of BP. The Browne review paved the way for wider application of income contingent loans and recommended removing caps on university fees. The Conservative government which came into power in 2010 used the review to launch a new policy that retained a fee cap but tripled it again in 2012 to £9,000 and used the additional student funding to substitute for direct government grants for teaching in all areas other than high-cost subjects including science, technology and engineering.

The 2012 UK university funding reforms represent the extreme of a shift from government grants to student loans to finance university education. The shift has also been applied to other grants, including support for students' living costs where such 'maintenance' support was moved to a fully loans-based system in 2015. The first step toward a similar transition was made in Australia as part of the 2013 Labor government savings measures, part of which involved converting an additional scholarship that had been made available to financially disadvantaged students to a loan, with an estimated saving of $1.2 billion over three years.

Loans have evident advantages over grants in that they reduce direct spending, and so help improve budget deficits, and the anticipated repayments are counted as an asset. However, income contingent loans still involve public subsidies, first because the public carries the cost of some students not repaying loans because they do not earn enough over their working life (in the UK loans are written off after a 30 year period) and second because of the costs associated with providing the loans, principally arising from the difference between the cost to government in raising the funds for the loan and the interest rate charged to the student (in Australia HECS-HELP loans do not involve a real interest rate, with debts indexed only to inflation).

The reforms introduced by the Conservative party-led government in the UK certainly posed problems for students, who faced debts of £27,000 from tuition for a three-year degree (which would be more than twice the average Australian graduate debt), but they did not cut university income, they did not reduce student demand (at least from the traditional full-time school leaver base) and they did not even dent student satisfaction outcomes. Originally the UK government had expected only a few universities to move to the top price allowed, but when almost all proposed to do so it put in place complicated mechanisms designed to enforce lower fee levels (the preferred being around £7,500), though by 2012 the average net annual fee charged was some £8,330. There was some volatility in student demand, with notable falls for part-time and older students, but by 2015 almost all English universities enjoyed solid financial surpluses.

In 2013 the prospects facing Australian universities and their students involved a pursuit by both sides of politics of savings from the sector in order to reduce calls on direct government outlays, and an increasing trend toward loans. When in government the ALP had undoubtedly invested extra funding to expand the number of student places and provide for new buildings. However, the refusal to countenance real increases to funding per student and delays and cuts to the funding promised to relieve pressures on underlying operations seemed to follow the White Queen's promise to Alice in *Through the Looking-Glass*: 'the rule is jam tomorrow and jam yesterday – but never jam today.' Among the Opposition, few doubted that the UK reforms would pass unnoticed, or expected that rivers of gold would flow to public providers of higher education. But it was also abundantly clear to those in the sector that a change of government was likely and that higher education was not a core election issue. In an address to the peak body Universities Australia in February 2013 the leader of the Opposition, Tony Abbott, described liberal conservative governments as 'patrons of higher learning' but pointed to budget pressures and suggested that a period of policy stability, even 'masterly inactivity', from government was probably what universities most needed.

Chapter Nine

The big deregulation gamble

Only the Coalition can provide the policy certainty that
our higher education sector so badly needs.
Senator Brett Mason, shadow minister for universities
and research, 15 April 2013

The Abbott government came to office in September 2013 and
immediately set about laying the groundwork for widespread reform
to government funding. In October a National Commission of
Audit was appointed, a strategy that had been employed by incoming
Australian conservative governments in the past to formalise a sense
of urgency around the need to reduce public expenditure and to
float sometimes politically risky options. The Commission's report
was not released until May the following year, just before the federal
budget, and for higher education it recommended shifting the share
of government grant funding for tuition from 59 per cent of the
total cost to 45 per cent, and reducing the HECS-HELP repayment threshold by 37 per cent while charging interest at the 10 year
bond rate to match the cost of government borrowing.

Meanwhile, in November of 2013 the government commissioned a review of the demand-driven system, which had resulted

in massive growth in enrolments in public universities and driven up related government grant funding from around $4 billion per year in 2009, to $6 billion by 2013 and a projected $7 billion by 2016. The reviewers chosen for this task were the authors of a proposal to move to deregulated university fees in the late 1990s, former Howard government education minister David Kemp and his policy adviser Andrew Norton. The earlier plan had been vetoed by Prime Minister John Howard in 1999 to neutralise negative reactions following the leaking of a draft cabinet submission. Since that time, Andrew Norton in particular had been a consistent advocate of reducing government involvement in and controls over higher education funding, and was a strong supporter of removing both government caps on enrolment and special access to subsidies by public universities. Moreover, the original Bradley review, which instigated the demand-driven system, always envisaged it would be a staged process that would begin with public universities and eventually be extended to other providers, subject to approval by TEQSA. So it was no great surprise when the Kemp-Norton report was released in April 2014 that it recommended dropping the previous government's targets for growth and access, removing special arrangements for public universities and extending subsidies to private providers, and extending the removal of caps to sub-degree programs and, to a limited extent, to postgraduate programs. While noting that specific recommendations on financing were beyond the review's terms of reference, particular mention was made of the potential benefits of removing controls on institutional fees and student contributions.

Also in November 2013, the Abbott government – despite having criticised the previous government's cuts only a few months earlier – introduced legislation to enact two key university savings measures put forward by its predecessors. These were an efficiency dividend and the conversion of assistance for financially

disadvantaged students from a grant basis to a loan. But with the tables now turned, the ALP announced it would oppose the cuts it had put forward while in government, ostensibly on the grounds that the school reforms (for which the putative savings were to be directed) had not been fully implemented by the new government.

To add to the mix in the lead-up to the Abbott government's first budget in May 2014 some vice-chancellors, particularly those from the Group of Eight, took the opportunity of the unsettled policy and budget environment to further their longstanding advocacy for deregulation of undergraduate fees. The vice-chancellor of ANU, Ian Young, along with chancellor Gareth Evans, wrote in April of that year that lack of ability to set their own fees meant that universities like ANU could not offer unique, elite programs or offer extension programs to students living on campus. Invoking again the magical word 'diversity' they suggested that more flexibility would allow emulation of Harvard or Stanford, with offsetting equity scholarships 'to enhance, not in any way diminish, access to students from disadvantaged back-grounds'. Meanwhile, an 'incoming government brief' emanating from Parkville (the suburban base of the University of Melbourne) had been circulating for some months within ministerial and departmental offices. That 64-page document advocated similar measures, in the name of 'microeconomic reform'.

With these ideas in play, expectations of the first Abbott budget ranged from maintenance of the status quo through to anticipation of some cuts and extension of subsidies to private providers. In spite of reports of Minister Pyne referring to price competition in a speech to a private audience shortly before the budget was brought down, few expected the scope of reform that was actually put forward.[1]

The 2014 budget went for wholesale deregulation of higher education, removing caps on sub-degree places, removing all limitations on fees and extending subsidies and loan arrangements on an equal footing to all providers, whether public or private, on the condition they were registered with TEQSA. To help pay for this expanded system, government contributions would be reworked into a simplified set of course groups and cut by an average of 20 per cent, student loans would attract interest at the long-term bond rate to reflect the cost of government financing up to a limit of 6 per cent, and the repayment threshold would be reduced by 10 per cent. Universities that charged more than the existing student contributions would be required to spend $1 of every $5 of additional revenue on scholarships for disadvantaged students. Despite these scholarships not involving any government funding, but rather requiring students at a given university to carry the cost for additional support for disadvantaged students at that university, they were to be designated as 'Commonwealth Scholarships'.

The complexity of the package meant that it took some time for its detail to be absorbed within the sector, and more widely by the public and the media. Moreover, the changes to university funding were only one part of an ambitious set of changes proposed by the Abbott government which sought to use the Commission of Audit and advice from various quarters to launch a comprehensive program to reduce public spending, including in the various social service areas of healthcare, welfare and education. Initial reactions from the media and Opposition focussed far more on items such as a $7 patient co-payment for GP visits than on the many interconnected and moving parts of the higher education reforms.

Over the next few months lines of lobbying and reaction were becoming staked out more clearly. Most vice-chancellors were, with varying degrees of enthusiasm, willing to advocate for the reforms, albeit with some concessions from the government. The minister responsible, Christopher Pyne, had signalled early on that he was willing to discard the most unpopular element of the reforms – the high interest rate on student loans. The prospect of additional concessions enabled Universities Australia to secure almost universal agreement in support of the legislation, subject to changes that ranged from the hopeful, such as removal of the cuts to government contributions, to the usual rent-seeking moves such as a weakly argued 'structural adjustment' package for those universities that feared they might not be able to charge fees as high as some others. One particularly egregious example of such behaviour was a proposal from the regional universities group and the Group of Eight to have funding for equity outreach and support preferentially directed toward the regionals. On the other hand, another bid from regional universities to have the Commonwealth Scholarships pooled centrally, rather than earmarked for the university from which the money came was described by the Group of Eight chairman as 'immoral'.

The government itself was not beyond criticism in its selling of the package. From the start some of the framing was highly implausible, with the budget papers referring to Australian universities occupying only five of the top 100 positions in the 2014 *Times* rankings compared to 6 in 2013 – as if the slip by the University of New South Wales from 85 to 114 was a national problem (all six improved their position the following year) and as if deregulation of student fees had any relevance for such rankings. The treasurer, Joe Hockey, also sought to claim that public funding of university education was regressive since only 40 per cent of taxpayers had degrees. This position was echoed by Group of Eight spokesman Michael Gallagher, but it was ably debunked by Geoff Sharrock from the LH Martin Institute, who pointed out that the government was also highlighting that most tax was paid by a relatively small proportion of taxpayers and that university graduates had relatively high incomes, and so were disproportionately likely to be in this group.[2] The prospect of lower fees arising from competition was also touted by the minister, just as it had been in the United Kingdom and in the changes to student contributions allowed by Brendan Nelson in 2005. However, as we will see, this was by no means a straight-forward proposition.

Fears of rampant fee increases were certainly not damped by the announcement from the University of Western Australia (UWA) that it would, if allowed, charge each student an annual fee of $16,000, an increase of between 55 and 125 per cent. This amount was, perhaps coincidentally, the equivalent at the time of the UK £9,000 fee. But whereas that was the total income per student for an English university, UWA would in addition expect to receive around the same amount again on average by way of government contribution given its own adoption of a variant of the Melbourne model. Echoing the stance that saw the 1999 deregulation changes shot down, the ALP announced that they would not support '$100,000 degrees'. This was politically effective, but misleading, and in an effort to provide some balance to the debate QUT later published estimates of the fee increases it envisaged. These esti-mates were considerably more modest than those of UWA and far from the $100,000 mark, even for five-year double degrees.[3]

In the lead-up to the introduction of the relevant legislation to the Senate in September 2014 the lobbying efforts had intensified, with stakeholders and their representatives beating well-worn paths to the doors of the eight independent senators, the support of six of whom would be needed to secure passage of any legisla-tion that was opposed by the ALP and the Greens, as was the case with the higher education reforms. Three of the eight initially were part of the Palmer United Party, headed by Clive Palmer, an eccentric self-proclaimed mining magnate who held the House of Representatives seat of Fairfax. The name of this party became increasingly ironic as two of the Palmer senators left it to become independents, but on the issue of the university reforms they were indeed united in opposition. Despite persistent, perhaps overly persistent, lobbying by the minister and various groups within the sector, and despite the removal of the loan interest rate and provision for extra rural scholarships, the legislation was rejected by the Senate in December 2014.

Undaunted, Christopher Pyne immediately reintroduced a similar bill for reconsideration by Parliament, and it was again voted down by the Senate in March 2015. Declaring, 'You couldn't kill me with an axe, I'm going to keep coming back,' Pyne again asserted that the plans would still go ahead, and they were duly factored in unchanged to the 2015 federal budget, though the stated intent to reintroduce them for a third time to Parliament seemed little more than obduracy given that there was little sign evident that any opponent's position was likely to change.

Careful assessment of the merits and drawbacks of deregulation was almost impossible in the frenetic climate of lobbying, competition for media attention and pursuit of last-minute compromises that characterised 2014–2015. One of the criticisms of the reforms was that they were unveiled as a surprise and a fait accompli, rather than emerging from the traditional process of discussion and consultation about options. On the other hand, the government could reasonably have argued that such a process was unlikely to generate anything fundamentally new, particularly given the raft of policy and funding reviews to which the university sector had been subject over the preceding decade or so. The government's thinking may have been that it was better to start from a position of perceived market purity and negotiate from there. Unfortunately the decision to unveil a complex surprise, and to defend it without a solid and broadly accepted foundation of evidence of the need for change, meant that too much reliance was placed on selective quotes from vice-chancellors and general assertions about unsustainability. These evidently were insufficient to sway broad public opinion and the crucial independent votes in the Senate. Christopher Pyne repeatedly referred to a 'slide into mediocrity' without the reforms, echoing the phrase with which we chose to close the first edition of our book, a claim that was 'fact checked' by the national broadcaster the ABC with a conclusion that it was 'far-fetched'. But we used that phrase to warn of what might happen if the chipping away at university budgets continued indefinitely, not as an inevitable consequence of the continuation of current policy. However, we do believe that a case can and should be made for change.

Defenders of the status quo could start with the proposition that Australia has a high-quality university system, rated among the world's best, with a presence of universities in the world rankings above that expected for a nation of our size, short history and our distance from the intellectual and industrial powerhouses of the northern hemisphere. Student places in our universities are highly sought after by overseas students. Though we could do better, we have been able to provide this high quality in a relatively uniform way across the nation, without stark disparities in access to good universities arising from wealth or geography, and without opportunistic low quality providers being allowed to emerge to exploit students. We have done this while keeping a lid on both public and private costs, indeed we have among the developed world's lowest public investment in this area of education.

However, this comfortable outlook has some challenges. There are pressures for further increases in the higher education system in Australia, both within the boundaries of current policy and beyond those boundaries. Within current policy, ongoing enrolments in bachelor degree programs at public universities, although unlikely to grow as rapidly as the initial burst between

2009 and 2013, could still be significant, particularly with growth in online enrolments and in states such as Queensland with under-lying demographic growth. Another source of potential growth comes from the push to extend subsidies to sub-degree level and also to private and non-university providers such as TAFE. The latter types of provider experienced buoyant growth prior to the demand-driven system as they catered for demand that, at the time, was unmet by public universities. But since the demand-driven system was introduced they have been a less attractive option. While they can set their own fees they have operated at a relative disadvantage without subsidies other than a loan system that had an associated surcharge designed to cover potentially higher public costs. Yet maintaining such different treatment is politically contentious: in almost all other areas of service activity, from secondary schooling to health care, a mixture of public and private provision is the norm, and if providers can meet certain standards of quality then why would we not want to see greater competition, variety and choice?

In addition to growth in the overall number of students, we have argued that the cost of educating students to the standards we expect as a community will continue to rise, even as we pursue efficiencies and new ways of organising and providing higher education.

If we are to maintain the vigour of our universities and, more importantly, if we do not reimpose limits on growth and, even more importantly again, if we extend the current boundaries on access to subsidies and loans, then we need to consider from where the additional funding will come.

We see no sign of an appetite for increasing the national taxation base to cover increased social expenditure, and even if this were to change there is no sign that higher education would be a particularly high priority for public spending given the rising health and welfare costs associated with an ageing population and rising levels of obesity. Even if an enlightened government did give priority to public expenditure on higher education, experience has shown that the expansion of student numbers always takes precedence over efforts to meet rising institutional costs.

We have also argued that efforts to centrally manage higher education through compacts or crude incentives factored into funding formulas are misguided and likely to be counterproductive. We do not favour attempts to engineer institutions into less costly academic activities by squeezing them out of research activities, or to suggest that regional and rural Australians should make do with access to institutions that are not fully engaged in all forms of scholarship. We have also argued that government should not seek to keep a cycle of strangulation and occasional relaxation on the income universities receive to teach their students, even if such an approach is the norm for government departments and various other public agencies via regular efficiency dividends and other enforced productivity measures.

Deregulation therefore offers an attractive alternative. But its detractors have some potent objections, principally based on the prospect of steep rises in student fees, with a consequent potential to disrupt the equity and accessibility of higher education across the nation.

Yet there are general theoretical and practical reasons for believing that market-based competition can constrain prices – largely based on the premise that consumers can 'shop around' if they feel they have not received value for money. In a speech to the National Press Club in August 2014, Christopher Pyne cited Jim Barber, former vice-chancellor of the University of New England, who said, '... we are likely to see prices move in both directions following deregulation and the prestigious university brands will find themselves going head-to-head with a raft of cheaper but equally high-quality competitors.'

Others, such as University of Melbourne vice-chancellor Glyn Davis pointed to the fact that other parts of the higher education sector were deregulated, namely undergraduate and postgraduate education for overseas students as well as parts of the domestic postgraduate system, without rampant fee inflation. Part of the second iteration of the deregulation package involved setting the international student fee, presumably reflecting a global fair price, as a cap for the total of whatever domestic students might be charged plus the government contribution. This was an effort to preserve the effectiveness of the government subsidy as a means of reducing the price to domestic students.

Unfortunately the interplay of government subsidies, income contingent loans and years of government control over university prices means that matters are unlikely to be so simple. The downward pressure on university income exerted by government meant that when Brendan Nelson allowed Australian universities to charge an additional 25 per cent in 2005, and when the UK government allowed universities to charge up to £9,000, almost all universities quickly moved to levy the maximum amount despite earlier predictions by government of lower prices as a result of competition. In New Zealand tuition fees were deregulated in 1992 and they then increased at an average of 13 per cent each year for the rest of the decade, in part due to reduction in government subsidies. Nor did widening competition exert any downward pressure: the New Zealand reforms also allowed new non-university providers to offer degrees but the cost of provision to the state grew dramatically as entrepreneurial responses manifested themselves. For example, one institution (Te Wananga o Aotearoa) went from receiving less than $5 million in government funding in 1999 to over $230 million in 2004.[4] By 2008 government controls over higher education funding in that country were reinstated. Similar rapid growth occurred when fees were deregulated in British Columbia in 2002.

The proposed withdrawal of 20 per cent of government subsidies as part of the Australian deregulation would be expected to drive around a 25 per cent increase in student fees just to maintain the pre-existing level of university income. Even without that cut driving up prices there are grounds for being sceptical about the scope for competition to drive prices down. Higher education is not a typical service: as we have argued it is very difficult to judge quality when outcomes emerge from years of immersion in study where students are driven by their own motivation and circumstances as well as interacting with other students and with the environment that a university provides. 'Shopping around' is effectively impossible in such conditions. Instead, higher education is often driven by prestige and relative position, in turn influenced by past selectivity and intellectual standing derived from previous research performance, the net effect of which is to disrupt normal understandings of the relationship of price to demand. At one end of the higher education spectrum, just as for other goods and services that convey status, higher education may even become more desirable if it is highly priced and more exclusive. On the other hand, lower pricing can be a signal that reduces demand. If we add to such a situation the availability of loans that defer the cost on attractive terms, as well as direct public subsidies on price, it is not hard to see the potential for prices to rise.

Despite this, there are also grounds for expecting that competition could exert some restraint on university fees under deregulation in Australia. The very lack of apparent diversity among its public universities that some have been decrying in Australian higher education means that there are good universities offering a broad range of subjects in most of the major population centres across the country. The great majority of the established order in Australian higher education is public rather than private, and able to be held accountable for public expectations about transparency in pricing and accessibility. Australia has not built over time institutions that cater for elites in the way that some institutions do, for example, in the United States, and so the self-reinforcing cycle of demand and exclusivity has not emerged as starkly in this country. Presumably this might limit the ability of institutions at the top of the pecking order to 'test the market' or to attempt to recoup shortfalls in research funding from their students.

However, it might reasonably be argued that a full-scale deregulation could over time shift us to a sector that is more hierarchical, allowing more unbalanced competition to emerge over time. The risk of significantly increased fees is not just a concern for students, it could also have major implications for government finances. A shift from grants to loans might solve some immediate issues about budget deficits, but the public cost arising from subsidised loans that might not be repaid is certain to mount in the years ahead. This has been a particularly pressing issue in the United Kingdom, even when the government has retained the ability to cap university prices, and according to some estimates the new loans-based policy may in fact end up costing the public more than the previous system. As a report from the UK Higher Education Policy Institute pointed out in 2015 the accounting technicalities surrounding student loans are far from straightforward and there is a real risk of 'prioritising private-sector accounting methods over good public policy', particularly if harsher conditions are imposed on student repayments to recoup growing public debt and loan costs. Changing student loan repayment terms could, as the report's author Andrew McGettigan warns, 'undermine public goodwill toward higher education and bring more fundamental questions about sustainability to the fore'.[5]

In Australia's subsidised higher education system, and even more so in an unrestrained subsidised market, we can be assured that the issue of unpaid HECS-HELP debt will be more prominent in future policy debates around higher education. This is by no means an argument for discontinuing public subsidies for higher education, or for removing the beneficial elements of income contingent loans; rather, it is a simple acknowledgment that there are no simple solutions.

With comprehensive deregulation of higher education in Australia seemingly defeated, at least for the moment, we will return in the final chapter of this book to what we see as the most feasible possibilities for the future.

Chapter Ten

The scholarship of fools?
Governance and management

The title of this chapter about university governance and management is a mischievous adaptation of the fifteenth-century allegory, the 'Ship of Fools'. This depicts a vessel inhabited by deranged, frivolous or oblivious passengers travelling without a pilot, and seemingly ignorant of their own destination. Such an assessment may be ungenerous and dated. Nevertheless, universities continue to attract a mainly bad rap when it comes to how well they are run and how relevant they and their programs are to the modern world.

It is said that universities cost too much, there are too many or too few of them, and they are about to be swept away by new breeds of nimble, high-quality providers operating effortlessly in a technologically ubiquitous environment.[1] And despite at least two decades of reforms ostensibly directed at making them better, more efficient and more accountable, universities are still chided for being closeted from reality, impenetrable in their manner of operation and seemingly challenged by the notion of presenting a united or coherent front on matters of funding or broader policy. The latter characteristic means that, more often than not, universities are seen by politicians as able to be picked off easily.

The critics are lined up not only on the outside. Many academics see themselves as demoralised because of overall workload and the increasingly difficult task of juggling teaching and research, or because of the perception that their institutions are being ground down to soulless teaching sweatshops run by managerialist ideologues. Of course, there are kernels of truth in all these assessments. It should also be said that the negative mood is pronounced in the United States, the United Kingdom and some countries of the European Union. This is hardly surprising, given the impact of cutbacks associated with the global financial crisis on higher education budgets. In the United States such measures, described earlier, have contributed to a thriving industry in books decrying the state of universities. Some commentators have pointed the finger at capitalism and the commodification of learning and research, or suggested a trend of declining standards. Still others have targeted the recalcitrance of reform-averse ageing academics threatened by generational change within the ranks.

Australian commentary largely follows suit. Older academics in particular may be unhappy about the pace of change, while younger folk seeking to build their careers struggle with the demands of balancing their teaching and research while dealing with complex administrative systems and new technologies, not to mention the demands of students who increasingly see themselves as customers. The latter phenomenon is hardly surprising, given the increased fees they are paying in many places.

A 2011 report to the Commonwealth government in Australia confirmed this commentary, reporting that few academic staff believed either that the higher education sector was heading in the right direction or that there was strong government support for the university sector.[2] The latter underlines the problem politicians and governments have with universities, given the significant investment made in Australian higher education over recent years, especially so in the wake of the Bradley Review. An illuminating 2009 report by the LH Martin Institute was equally instructive. It noted that while Australian academics were among the world's better paid, they were second only to UK academics in discontent about workload and over-management.[3]

Central to the apparent surliness of the older generation of academics is the perception that traditional notions of collegiality, academic freedom and autonomy have been abandoned. These concepts derive from the operation of a university as a medieval guild.[4] Although Australian universities were not established along the lines of Oxbridge-style federal structures based on self-governing colleges, traditions of academic practice and governance draw largely from these models coupled with nineteenth-century German influences. This somewhat idealised 'golden era' of democratic collegiality lasted in Australia until the 1980s, when universities began to feel the chill budget winds blowing across the broader public sector both in Australia and elsewhere. Accompanying these budget pressures were demands for enhanced accountability and financial management reform. Meanwhile a 1986 national review of efficiency and effectiveness in higher education, conducted by the Commonwealth Tertiary Education Commission, focussed a spotlight on a wide range of matters spanning institutional strategic planning, use of assets, performance assessment and academic staffing. The replacement of the so-called binary system of universities, colleges and institutions with a unified national system of 35 universities stepped up the pace of management reform, with government funding contingent on negotiation of institutional course, student and research profile, mission statement, capital management and an agreed response to national policy imperatives.

In the early 1990s the Commonwealth government turned its attention to quality assurance, in line with developments occurring in other Western countries – three rounds of investigation into procedures and outcomes relating to quality occurred. Then in June 1995, the minister for Employment, Education and Training, Simon Crean, announced the establishment of the Higher Education Management Review (chaired by prominent banker David Hoare).[5] This group focussed not only on the broader management issues that had interested politicians for some years, but also, for the first time in Australia, addressed directly questions of university governance as well as that of workplace reform, where the university sector lagged behind the changes occurring in other taxpayer-funded sectors of the economy.

It would be fair to say that the report of the Hoare Committee, presented in December 1995, was not enthusiastically embraced by many vice-chancellors, who probably hoped that its proposed measures to reform governing bodies would be quietly shelved. And while the specifics of some of the Hoare recommendations (such as a limit of 15 members for the governing body) were softened, many of its recommendations in at least a modified form were embraced in the subsequent period.

The Hoare Committee's interest aligned with demands by governments everywhere for improved quality and better accountability and efficiency in the use of public funding. An Australian Qualifications Framework (AQF) was implemented in 1995 to provide national articulation of university and vocational education awards. All universities were then required to provide quality improvement plans as part of their annual planning and reporting to the Commonwealth and, in March 2000, the Commonwealth State Ministerial Council on Education, Employment, Training and Youth Affairs (MCEETYA) approved the establishment of an Australian Universities Quality Agency (AUQA).

Separate legislation, the *Education Services for Overseas Students Act 2000* (ESOS), was passed to ensure the quality of education and services for overseas students in Australia.

Over the subsequent decade AUQA was to conduct two separate rounds of institution-specific audits. In effect, the process was one of moderated self-assessment for the universities. The first cycle focussed on 'whole of institution' considerations while the second cycle, from 2007, not only followed up on the previous audits, but also looked at internationalisation and other issues mutually agreed with each individual institution. The focus on internationalisation reflected the importance of the international market to Australia, increasing sensitivities about international dimensions in their curricula and supporting the needs of international students.

Toward a national regulator for higher education

In the previous chapter we noted the announcement, in the 2009 Commonwealth Budget, of the Tertiary Education Quality and Standards Agency (TEQSA). Our interest there was in the complexities involved in TEQSA's mandate to base its activities on specific standards for universities. Here we focus on the role of TEQSA as an all-encompassing national regulator of higher education and research, not just for universities. Indeed, the Commonwealth's original preference was that such a body embrace the vocational education and training (VET) sector as well. This probably would have been a logical step for a nation of 23 million seeking to position itself as a quality player in the vast and complex international education environment. But it was a step too far for the states, who were being heavily lobbied by the VET sector. VET feared its voice would be drowned out by the universities. For their part, some folk in the university sector also disliked the all-encompassing regulator model, worrying that the association with VET would lower their status. In the end the Commonwealth, concerned about its ability to enforce such a takeover, relented by opting – at least for the foreseeable future – to establish separate regulatory bodies for the two sectors.

The move toward a national regulatory framework should also be considered in the context of the diversity of Australia's higher education system. This diversity is not widely appreciated, even among those in universities. At the time that Bradley's reform agenda was being rolled out by government, the sector was comprised of more than 170 registered providers. In addition to the 39 Australian universities at that time, there were varying numbers of public and private, for-profit and not-for-profit, single discipline and multidisciplinary institutions offering the full spectrum of Australian higher education qualifications from diploma to doctoral studies. Many operated across more than one state jurisdiction and therefore were required to deal with multiple regulators. About half of them were operating in both higher education and vocational education and training, including many universities and more than a dozen public TAFE institutes. Two major higher education proprietors (Navitas and Seek) were publicly listed on the Australian Stock Exchange. The predominant field of study among these providers is business, but there is a significant presence of providers teaching theology, ministry and divinity programs and smaller operators working in 'niche' areas such as graphics and animation, education, allied and alternative health, engineering, law and accounting. While higher education enrolments were overwhelmingly university based (94 per cent), the growth of private, sometimes for-profit interests in the sector was considerable.

The main arguments for a national regulator were set out in the Bradley Review, which drew on a study commissioned by MCEETYA. Bradley highlighted the significant existing pressure on state and territory-based arrangements in achieving consistent regulatory outcomes, commenting that 'the risk of ignoring these deficiencies and concerns is considerable' and that 'there is no defensible argument for the fragmentation and variation in requirements which is apparent across jurisdictions and sectors'. There was understandable and predictable resistance to the idea of a national regulator from some of the existing state-based higher education agencies.

Victoria was the most resistant, followed by Western Australia. This attitude mirrored their similar opposition to the notion of a single VET regulator. They were particularly resentful at losing any influence over the development of higher education stand-ards on which they had some influence through the ministerial council's ownership of the old protocols. This prompted the Commonwealth not to pursue constitutional referral (as they had to with VET), but to use corporations law powers instead, in order to guarantee universal coverage. South Australia's attitude was also interesting. While broadly supportive and constructive in the multi-state policy dialogue, South Australia was an activist in executing its legislative responsibility right up to the eleventh hour. This was reflected in its decision to approve the establish-ment of Torrens University. Victoria had also approved the MCD University of Divinity (Australia's first university of specialisation) in this twilight period of state regulation.

The Indian student crisis in Australia during 2009 provided significant propulsion to the case for a national regulator. This was because that crisis highlighted not only shortfalls in visa policy, but also duplication and inconsistencies in state-based regula-tion of education providers and an unwillingness or inability at state level to control suspect private operators. It will be recalled that at this time Australia was suffering serious collateral damage abroad as a result of a number of highly publicised physical attacks on Indian students and the forced closure of a number of private colleges. Some of these institutions were private VET colleges and others were English-language colleges. A significant number were new outfits operated by marginal players that applied for status as registered training organisations to enrol large numbers of mostly Indian students in apprentice hairdressing or hospitality courses. Many of the students who travelled to Australia to undertake these certificate-level training courses were also hoping (and being led to believe) that qualifying as pastry chefs or hairdressers would lead to both good employment and permanent residency in Australia.

At the time there was little the Commonwealth government could do to align the state-based regulatory arrangements, though a review of the ESOS Act allowed the opportunity to amend the visa settings that quickly sank a number of the private colleges. And, of course, many students were left high and dry. Australia's universities were caught in the crossfire. For the most part this may have been unfair, though there was chatter about the practices of a few universities putting the good overall name of the system at risk. Moreover, while AUQA had pursued its quality audits conscientiously, its approach was seen to have become formulaic. Nor did AUQA, as a quality audit agency, have the regulatory authority to deal with some of the troublesome issues that had emerged over a decade during which the higher education sector had become much more complex.

All these factors assisted Minister Chris Evans to press the case for a single national regulator to oversee tertiary education. The university sector too was alive to all these realities and was, through its peak body Universities Australia (UA), cautiously supporting the establishment of the national regulator. In particular, there was support for a regulatory risk framework, which was couched in terms of the risks to students, sector reputation and protection against provider collapse. In turn, the TEQSA legislation emphasised the need for a proportionate approach to risk being adopted, while explicitly recognising the self-accrediting status of universities. UA had set this requirement as a condition of support of the legislation. Moreover, TEQSA would assume the accreditation responsibilities of the states, regulate international tertiary education under the ESOS Act, and assume AUQA's audit role (that body having been abolished). A new set of Provider Standards would replace the national protocols, the upside of the standards model depicted as providing a focus on the assumption that graduates and qualifications were what universities claimed them to be.

No other country has a body quite like TEQSA, but a number of places have several of the components. Several countries have federal systems where regulation is at state or provincial level, so the extent and nature of regulation can vary. However, qualification frameworks and statements of standards are not uncommon. They may be found, for example, in England and New Zealand and are also reflected in the development of the Bologna process.[6] Meanwhile, quality assurance mechanisms are nowadays near universal. Also, wider regulation is often in place but equally often is poorly coordinated and piecemeal. For example, in the United States – a much larger and more diverse system than Australia – federal regulations apply to the allocation of student loans and grants. However, state-level regulations vary and there are well-recognised, albeit sometimes confusing, accreditation programs at the major regional level.

It is certainly the case that Australia's decision to establish a national higher education regulator attracted a polarised reaction. In September 2012 TEQSA's first chief commissioner, Dr Carol Nicoll, made a presentation to the OECD's IMHE biennial conference of higher education officials, university administrators and scholars. At one end of the spectrum, the reaction to her remarks by some of those present was pure horror at the thought of the impact a national regulator might have on academic work and freedom. At the other, Nicoll was bombarded with interest from officials of other OECD countries about how such a mechanism could be introduced in their national systems.

TEQSA has two particularly noteworthy features. One is the comprehensiveness of its coverage; that is, of all universities plus other higher education providers. The other is the legislative 'teeth' it has been given – an ability to intervene with defined powers under defined circumstances. With regard to its comprehensiveness, this also extends to its regulatory powers under the Commonwealth ESOS Act, the legislation that had been in place for more than a decade to provide targeted protection of the interests of international students studying in Australia. The consequence of the TEQSA legislation is to remove the relevant Commonwealth department from having any regulatory responsibility in Australia – just as the states and territories lost their higher education regulatory role, so too did the Commonwealth in this area.

The agency has faced a number of tests in its early years. None has been more important or difficult than the settling and implementation of the Standards Framework. The second test has been of TEQSA's own approach, and the perceptions thereof. Universities were prepared to support the establishment of a national regulator because the TEQSA legislation guaranteed their self-governing autonomy and specified that TEQSA's actions would be proportionate to the inherent risks. Also, there was a reasonable expectation that the new arrangements would provide a simpler, more manageable framework, though in this respect the universities certainly want to have their cake and eat it too. On the one hand the universities wanted simplicity of arrangements but, on the other, they had no appetite for an all-powerful regulator and preferred a separate standards body. Indeed, that is why a separate standards panel was established.

Further complexity is provided by the reality that TEQSA's accreditation occurs against the AQF, a creature of MCTEE. The AQF Council spent two years reworking the AQF to develop greater clarity and consistency, proposing a structure of ten levels of qualifications with defined learning outcomes and expected time of study and volume of learning attached to each. Particular friction was generated between the council, which saw itself as protecting the integrity of qualifications levels, and the Go8 institutions over the issue of courses to which the title 'Doctor' could be attached. The disagreement was ironic. The AQF Council preferred that the Doctor title belong solely to traditional research-based PhD-style programs, whereas the Go8 proposed that some liberalisation be introduced to allow the graduates of certain professional degrees at Masters level, typically in the medical and health spheres, as well as the Juris Doctor (JD), to use the title Doctor.

The challenge for bodies like TEQSA and the AQF Council is not merely to protect the integrity of the system and stay relevant, but to keep pace with a rapidly changing educational and technological environment. The ubiquity of mobile devices, the emergence of online open courseware, e-portfolios for student assessment, rich technology learning support and the incorporation of these and other elements in hybrid physical–virtual learning environments are destabilising and sometimes confounding traditional assumptions about what constitutes outstanding learning and teaching, the campus experience, and the student–teacher paradigm. TEQSA will need to ensure that its regulatory framework is meeting expectations and in this regard may look to the strong student and learning outputs focus increasingly required at the international level by discipline-based accreditation bodies such as the American Association of Colleges and Schools of Business (AACSB). Much the same applies to the AQF Council, if the Australian qualifications framework is to be internationally relevant.

All this underlines the point that the role of a body such as TEQSA is to streamline and coordinate regulation in an increasingly diverse and rapid-paced environment. In December 2015 the Federal parliament progressed this agenda, passing legislation to harmonise the requirements of ESOS and TEQSA.

In summary, TEQSA has an important role to play in assuring the quality of our system and in protecting students. The temptation it has to guard against is being unnecessarily interventionist, to overly standardise requirements or otherwise constrain institutions as they seek to respond to that dynamic environment.

The broader compliance burden

For its critics TEQSA is the epitome of all that universities dislike about the burdens of accountability. Certainly TEQSA has imposed new requirements, as we have seen from the previous discussion, and there is always a latent concern that such a body can exceed its brief. Obviously too there is a complexity in TEQSA having to work alongside a standards panel as well as the AQF. But there are other realities of the Australian operating environment that provide challenges for universities. The most important of these is the congestion imposed by our federal structure.

The regulatory burden imposed on our universities by the federal system has, in fact, been ameliorated by the establishment of TEQSA and the abolition of quasi-quality higher education bodies at the state level. It remains the case, though, that all but one of Australia's universities are established or authorised by state or territory legislation, yet the overwhelming public funding portion of their income derives from, or is controlled by, Commonwealth laws. Indeed, in only two states – Queensland and Victoria – has funding of universities by state governments over the last decade approached the level of state taxation contributed by the universities in those jurisdictions.

While constitutionally some areas of Commonwealth and State power are clear, in others the apportionment is ambiguous or shared. And beyond those, universities – like other organisations in the community – will be required to observe international treaties and laws to which the nation is signatory. None of this is exceptional, though it is worthwhile to reflect on the sheer weight and impact of the regulatory burden that falls on universities.

Let us take a typical university, Queensland University of Technology (QUT) in a typical state (Queensland). As with other Australian universities QUT is the subject of its own Act, as well as more than 120 acts of either a Commonwealth or state nature, many of them having associated Regulatory Instruments. In addition, there are local government ordinances and by-laws to meet. A good number of these acts are specific to universities or the education arena more broadly, while many others set standards of behaviour and conduct about health and safety, workplace requirements, crime and misconduct, energy and environment, financial reporting, immigration and visas, competition policy and procurement practices, professional conduct, and corporate law as well as public sector standards of various types.

Quite beyond these Commonwealth, state and local laws, most universities have over the years developed their own associated regulations, university policy and procedures, statutes and rules, governing council procedure, authorities and delegations, and enterprise agreements or other employment contractual frameworks for academic, professional and senior staff. In the case of QUT, the manual of policies and procedures contains nine chapters and some 260 policies, and runs to many hundreds of pages. Moreover, individual faculties and divisions often seek to develop their own mini-manuals, allowing them to contextualise or interpret for their own convenience university-level rules that are deemed too generic.

Sometimes this proceduralisation can assume farcical proportions, a good case in point being policies for the allocation of workload for academic staff. There is a good reason for an industrial interest in workload, in particular to protect sessional and more junior staff and other newer academics from being professionally exploited. However, the codification of workload policies and practices that takes place within many universities at discipline or faculty level is absurd in its detail, and may sometimes be used more as a manual, setting out the ways in which academic staff, especially at the more senior end of the spectrum, can evade their core responsibilities in teaching and research by engaging in other second-order activities. Some law faculties have shown a particular penchant for such antics.

And more serious problems can arise, as happened between 2007 and 2011 when the University of South Australia (UniSA) received qualified audits of its financial statements from the auditor-general of South Australia. This was because the university was judged as not complying with an Australian accounting standard. UniSA's position resulted from a conservative approach to recognising grants from government by deferring the recognition of this revenue. In so doing, it was seeking to achieve a better match against expenditure that was consistent with not-for-profit entities complying with International Public Sector Accounting Standards (specifically, IPSAS 23). However, this international standard conflicted with the requirements of Australian Accounting Standard AASB1004, which required immediate recognition of the revenue.

The point being made here is that simultaneous compliance with the requirements of both jurisdictions was not achievable. The matter was also a challenge for comparability of performance with other universities in Australia. We see echoes of this issue every year, with reports to auditors-general complying with state government requirements but masking the true underlying position of particular universities. It is for this reason that an increasing number of institutions have adopted the additional internal practice of calculating what they believe to be both 'unadjusted' and 'adjusted' financial outcomes by excluding one-off capital and other grants. Nor are they dealing with small numbers, because for a large sandstone university there can be a difference of $100 million or more (for an organisation with a $1 billion turnover) between the 'unadjusted' and 'adjusted' (or underlying) financial outcomes in a given year.

The challenge for universities in dealing with compliance, and particularly with risk, is to retain the same sense of proportion that we expect of the national regulator. This is oftentimes not achieved. Over the last two decades universities (and many others) have developed whole new industries around quality (TQM, QA, Six sigma, triple bottom line, and so on) and risk. Obviously some of this activity is important for quality assurance, safety and reputation. But at other times it signifies faddishness and overreach, as arguably was the case with the response to Y2K and as seems to be the case with workplace health and safety more recently. It also invites distraction of managers' attention from assessing the risks that matter most in particular circumstances. This is a challenge for universities not only because of the resources available, but also because of their wish to be seen to be responsible organisations in the community.

Unfortunately, it seems to be an ironclad rule of bureaucracy that any attempt to systematically tackle red tape ends up creating more.

This has certainly been the case with Australian university reform, each wave of which comes with the delusional promise that it will be accompanied by more simplified and streamlined regulation. This is, of course, not a peculiarly Australian phenomenon. President Ronald Reagan was elected to the White House in 1980 on a platform of dismantling red tape – at the time the Code of US Federal Regulations, when consolidated, amounted to more than 85,000 pages. Eight years later, when Reagan departed from office, the Code had doubled in length. It beggars belief as to what might have happened if he had not pursued his deregulatory policy with such zeal.

Ministers and buffer bodies: Be careful what you wish for

Governments are greatly interested in universities being efficient and responsive, and universities are equally interested to protect their independence from outside influences that might compromise their autonomous operations. There will always be, therefore, very close interest in how the formal relationship of government and universities is transacted.

As in so many other areas of university activity, Australia has been influenced strongly by British practice in the way our universities report and formally deal with the government of the day. Indeed, the landmark 1957 report by the Committee of Inquiry into the Future of Australian Universities was chaired by Sir Keith Murray, who was at the time the chair of the United Kingdom University Grants Committee. Murray recommended an essentially identical body for Australia, though Prime Minister Sir Robert Menzies – keen for any such body to have a broader remit than the allocation of grants – established in 1959 the Australian Universities Commission (AUC) as a statutory body. Its brief was to be a buffer oversighting the relationship between the government of the day and universities, with responsibility for allocating funding.[7]

Such a buffer body still exists in England, although in a significantly modified form, and is these days known as the Higher Education Funding Council for England (HEFCE). In Australia, the AUC was subsumed in 1977 into the Commonwealth Tertiary Education Commission (CTEC), which advised the Commonwealth on universities as well as the colleges of advanced education (CAEs) and technical and further education (TAFE) colleges. Then, in 1988 the Commonwealth Department of Employment, Education and Training took over responsibilities from CTEC for student profile and other negotiations with institutions. A National Board of Employment, Education and Training (NBEET) was formed to advise the Commonwealth, with subsidiary councils including a Higher Education Council (HEC) and an Australian Research Council (ARC). John Dawkins was the Commonwealth minister responsible for universities at the time of the abolition of CTEC and the creation of the new unified national system of universities. He made very clear his reasons for taking this action:

> the trouble was that the CTEC was organised in such a way that it actually was a barrier to significant change. CTEC had a considerable amount of power and whoever was the chairman of CTEC was essentially the Minister for higher education ... I thought that if the Government had views about what it wanted to do and wanted to commit huge additional resources to the system, then I thought it needed to have its hands more closely on the action.[8]

Over the last 25 years ministers from both sides of the political divide have been happy to retain this direct model of interaction with the university sector. More recently, there have been murmurs from some folk within universities that, perhaps, it would be better for Australia to return to a buffer body.

The arguments for such a return are several: it would reduce the possibility of government interference, which may compromise institutional autonomy or academic freedom; it would allow for long-term decisions to be made about the university system outside the hurly-burly of the political cycle, thus preventing short-term political cycle factors interfering with good policy; and it would allow important decisions to be taken by experts. A further recent argument advanced in favour of a buffer body is that it could replace the recently established national regulator for Australian higher education, TEQSA.

The arguments against such a development, however, invite caution. First, if the objective of creating a buffer body (such as an Australian Universities Commission) is to remove politics from higher education funding and regulation, it will almost assuredly fail. Governments bear responsibility for the allocation of monies and direction of policy traffic. More to the point, ministers and governments enjoy these activities, and they are keen to make – and be seen to make – decisions that they think will matter and result in improvements. Although an opposition without power might flirt with the idea of a buffer body and a correspondingly weaker department, a minister once installed and keen on exercising the levers of power will quickly find such a body irritating and see it as rivalrous. Dawkins made precisely this point.

Second, and potentially more lethally for the universities, such a buffer body would be a convenient vehicle for an incoming government to create an arms-length mechanism to implement a substantial Commonwealth funding cut and, through the apparent independence of the commission, provide a degree of political cover for the government doing the cutting.

Third, a universities commission-style body adds a potential layer of bureaucracy and complexity to a system already heavily burdened with reporting and compliance, and certainly invites the institutionalisation of conflict not only with the minister and department, as already mentioned, but also with advisory bodies such as the Office of the Chief Scientist or the Australian Research Council.

There would certainly be very little support for a buffer body if, in practice, it was to be a supreme authority or even an authoritative advisory mechanism. The very essence of good policy-making involves a healthy contest of ideas sifted through the political process. Furthermore, the idea of conflating or aligning the roles of TEQSA and an AUC is flawed: one is a buffer body, the other a regulator. There is plenty of evidence in Australian higher education about the governance dangers of creating a single entity with divergent functions. A good example in the recent past was Australian Education International (AEI), when it was responsible for both the promotion of Australian international education and its quality regulation through the ESOS Act. AEI was not able to credibly balance the two, and the quality function was shifted to the national regulator.

There are other challenges. Recent history in Australia reminds us of the vulnerability of separate bodies that hang off ministerial portfolios. The establishment of such new and separate bodies also has been frowned on by the Commonwealth, certainly since the Department of Finance 2005 directive, extending the principles outlined in the Uhrig review two years earlier that 'there is a policy preference to curb unnecessary proliferation of Government bodies. Consequently, a function, activity or power should, if possible, be conferred on an existing department, or another existing Australian Government body, rather than on a new body.'[9]

This goes to the sphere of responsibility of a buffer body and that, in turn, to the composition of such a supposedly independent commission. Universities almost take for granted the case, based on traditions of self-governing autonomy and academic freedom, that they should be treated differently to the VET sector, but politicians are likely to see the two as part of the one education continuum. As for the composition of a buffer body's board of governors, the university sector itself is likely to be more comfortable with a minister making decisions about sector shape and priorities, rather than a handpicked commission of experts and worthies – at least a minister is a clear target and focus for lobbying.

None of the above is to suggest that the idea of a buffer body is without merit. It has some attractions in a reasonably perfect world, but we should not be blindsided about the ease or relevance of transplanting models, even in a modified form, from elsewhere. It is true that there is still a buffer body in England, but it is not the case that these days HEFCE operates as its predecessors did. The golden age of the buffer body was certainly evident in 1981 when – as recounted by Peter Scott[10] – the chair of the University Grants Committee, Sir Edward Parkes briefed journalists about institution-by-institution decisions in relation to funding cuts. Significantly, he did this before Secretary of State for Education and Science Mark Carlisle was informed. That would not happen now.

These days there is both a HEFCE and a director-general of education, institutionalising the potential rivalry between minister and buffer referred to earlier. HEFCE also has become more a regulator than a buffer, constantly wedged between the decisions of government and the determination of universities to retain their autonomy. Bahram Bekhradnia, director of the Higher Education Policy Institute at Oxford, captured the situation at the Wellington Group meeting in 2006:

There was a time when Governments thought universities too unimportant or too arcane to want to be bothered with. That was, in England anyway, the golden era of the buffer body. The government's job was to set the total public investment in higher education and to hand it over to the buffer to allocate as it saw fit. Those days have passed. Governments now think universities are more and more important, and so they want to be more and more involved in what they do and how they are run. We have seen that very strongly in England where the Government has intervened increasingly in functions that would previously have been reserved to the buffer – in matters which, frankly, would previously have been of little interest to the Government. And that is a trend I have observed around the world. That is, in fact, a measure of the importance of universities. But it does undermine the concept and the purposes of a buffer body.[11]

New Zealand and Hong Kong are two countries that retain a buffer body. In New Zealand the Tertiary Education Commission (TEC) is required by its legislation to provide 'system steward-ship', but the ministry of education assumes the role of principal policy director on tertiary education matters. The TEC's remit includes ensuring coherence of the system as a whole, comprising universities, institutes of technology and polytechnics, industry training organisations, private training establishments and schools. The legislation governing TEC mentions the need to safeguard academic freedom and institutional autonomy, while the govern-ment monitors both TEC's own management and budget and influences the TEC through board appointments. In summary, the minister directs most of the action and TEC ticks the boxes.

Those familiar with the Hong Kong University Grants Committee point to a level of consistency and stability of policy-making, the avoidance of splinter groups among universities, and universities being provided a direct say on policy settings as argu-ments in favour of such a body. But Hong Kong is a small and designed system, and has its own tests to face. There is a level of concern that the cherished independence of its universities may be compromised by political influences from the mainland. In early 2016 protest followed the appointment by the Chief Executive of the Hong Kong SAR of a former Education minister as chairman of the governing board of the University of Hong Kong. This incident followed another at the same university in October 2015, when the governing council was reported to have rejected the promotion of a pro-democracy law professor to pro-vice-chancellor.

In any case, Australia's arrangements resemble those of England much more than those of Hong Kong. In England the operation of HEFCE has not prevented the flourishing of splinter groups – those lobby groups do so, in fact, because the government largely dictates what HEFCE can do, rendering it a fairly weak buffer.

Those who are attracted to a buffer agency tend to believe that such a body will protect them from unwelcome government decision, interference and regulation. But a buffer body also might operate unpredictably, as shown in the United Kingdom by HEFCE's response in late 2012 to a combined push by both the government and the Russell Group (of older research-intensive universities) for the scaling back of quality audits. The Russell Group had argued that its members, in particular, should not be subject to the regular review that might apply to other universities. But HEFCE rejected this push, explaining that it was not appropriate to have one rule for the research-intensive institutions and another for everyone else. In this case the buffer body functioned, on this core issue of quality audit, as a buffer body for the rest of the university sector against exception status for the oldest and most established players. Nor should it be assumed that the elite institutions are immune from the pitfalls that await all unwary players in the higher education sector. The most obvious of these are financial risks, including budget exposure.

The struggle to lobby effectively

Universities struggle to register on the political radar. This is despite the number of students enrolled and graduating from them, the high proportion of the national research effort derived from them, and the dominant role played by our universities in education as one of our foremost export industries. So, why do universities have this problem in engaging political interest? The most ready explanation is that over the years universities, and vice-chancellors in particular, have been poor advocates. We will examine this truism momentarily and there are other contributing factors.

In the first place, what universities do – educate people at a higher level and conduct research – are activities that have more long-term than immediate impact. True, the fruits of an undergraduate education may be obvious in the case of a graduating engineer proceeding directly into a well-paid job. But other qualifications may provide more of a personal or professional foundation and perhaps lead graduates in different directions. Moreover, as an activity, research by its nature involves complexity, and the development of knowledge requires the sifting of evidence and the weighing of uncertainty. The public's attention may be momentarily captured by a ten-second media clip of a medical discovery promising a cure for a major disease but, on the other hand, that same attention span will struggle with research that identifies potential long-term threats or the disruption of popular sentiment, especially if that research invites costly public policy responses. We have witnessed this over a long period with the tobacco-smoking issue. And over the last decade we have seen it with the rising debate over climate change. In the case of the latter, the task of shifting public opinion is also made more difficult when scientific methods attract adverse attention. This occurred with the work of the University of East Anglia Climate Research Unit when emails were hacked and wide publicity given to the implications of improper data manipulation. Multiple inquiries have since exonerated the researchers but the perception remains widespread among many people that a tainted air hangs over some climate change research.

In Australia, the vice-chancellors' lobby group (AVCC) was first formed in 1920, representing a very small number of institutions with similar missions.[12] It remained 'the voice of the universities' as the system grew in size and complexity in the post-war period, although, as Peter Quiddington has pointed out, fractures became more evident from the 1980s. These derived from the natural challenge for a single lobby group seeking to represent the interests of a university sector now embracing institutions with different history, levels of wealth, prestige and mission. Meanwhile, there had also emerged, alongside the AVCC, a number of other advocacy and professional groups as well as the discipline-based academies. The most prominent of these were the Council for the Humanities, Arts and Social Sciences (CHASS), the Federation of Australian Scientific and Technological Sciences (FASTS), the Australian Academy of Science, as well as the National Union of Students (NUS) and the National Tertiary Education Union (NTEU).

The growing complexity of the university sector, and increasing competition for resources and jockeying for strategic positioning, led to the formation of lobby subgroups such as the Group of Eight (Go8), the Australian Technology Network (ATN) and the Innovative Research Universities (IRU). Universities based in major regional centres also sensed the opportunity to flex their own political muscle, forming the Regional Universities Network (RUN), while other universities preferred to remain unaligned or independent of the formal lobby subgroups. Many other collaborations exist beyond these formal mechanisms. Some are strategic, others project based. In Brisbane the three large universities have worked together in the delivery of languages teaching, while in a number of regional areas recent changes in the policy and funding of vocational education are encouraging universities and TAFE colleges to work together more closely. Victoria hosts several 'dual-sector' universities, and some other universities, such as CQUniversity, have strategic collaborations with TAFE institutions.

The emergence of university subgroups was probably an inevitable part of the journey for a sector experiencing simultaneously the pains of growth and competition, the latter with an increasingly international dimension. This pattern was also occurring in the United Kingdom – in both places previously separate institutes of technical and advanced education had been merged with older universities. In the United Kingdom the Russell Group of research-intensive universities had emerged, as had the so-called Redbrick universities.

While the AVCC had retained its position as the overall lobby group of universities in Australia, as did the equivalent body in the United Kingdom, there was increasing acceptance that no peak body could speak for all universities on all issues. And, not surprisingly, the most obvious fault line was around research policy and funding. However, there was also tension emerging among some of the vice-chancellors, including senior players feeling or choosing to be dislocated from the plenary. This was very evident during the AVCC presidency of Di Yerbury, with dark intimations from some vocal Go8 members that withdrawal from the AVCC might be contemplated.

The AVCC responded to this situation in 2006 by commissioning an external review of its own operations and approach.[13] Again, developments were occurring elsewhere where similar groups were positioning themselves as major industry peak bodies, rather than as clubs of vice-chancellors as CEOs. This was both a symbolic and substantive shift, because vice-chancellors were being publicly portrayed – and even mocked by some government ministers – as self-absorbed members of a privileged club, focussed narrowly on extracting maximum funding for their own institutions rather than on ensuring that benefits were delivered to students and the wider community.

In the United Kingdom the longstanding Committee of Vice-Chancellors and Principals (CVCP) had reinvented itself as Universities UK, with a mandate to develop strategic alliances with other groups. In Canada, on the other hand, the peak body – the Association of Universities and Colleges of Canada – was based on institutional memberships, with links to universities extending beyond CEOs in the form of collaborative networks of academic and administrative organisations that have associated membership. In both cases the peak body is headed by a serving vice-chancellor but the CEO is not a former vice-chancellor.

The Go8 had originally proposed that the AVCC should be replaced by a federation of university subgroups chaired by a former vice-chancellor who would serve as both president and CEO. Such an outcome would have ensured the new body would be weak, reinforcing the fragmentation of the voice of universities along the lines of age, income and historical reputation. Any rolling together of the CEO and presidential roles into one position for a former vice-chancellor would have been a curious proposition for vice-chancellors to entertain, given their usually firm views about the separation of governance and management in their own universities.

For a time there was some uncertainty that all universities would join the new body, Universities Australia (UA), although they ultimately did so when UA commenced operation in July 2007. This was despite the disinclination of one or two vice-chancellors to attend plenary meetings. And although matters of research funding are always the most likely to cause fracture within the UA, over recent years the plenary has come together not only on the relatively straightforward matter of grant indexation, but also on cautious support for the establishment of TEQSA and on the need for a broader national higher education strategy.

Nevertheless, vice-chancellors can sometimes remain their own worst enemies. A good example was the response to the Labor government's decision in 2010 to legislate for the indexation of university grants. The new arrangements provided for significant improvements to the policy that had been in place since 1995 and, significantly, the new legislation secured bipartisan support. The old arrangements had indexed operating grants in line with the consumer price index (25 per cent of the weighting) and provided only a limited safety net weighting. This resulted in annual indexation of around 2 per cent, a figure well below actual cost increases.

On the other hand, the new grant index, enshrined in legislation, was based on a discounted (90 per cent) measure of professional salary movements. However, the first cycle of the new salary index was affected by the global financial crisis, thus there was a drop in the financial quarter that was to be used to determine the indexation for 2011. In other words, even though the result was a disappointing one for universities in the first year of its operation, the new formula provided a much better level of sustenance for universities in the longer term, as was demonstrated in the following two years. This did not stop a few vice-chancellors from suggesting that UA should go back to Minister Evans and ask for the whole matter to be reconsidered and perhaps even re-legislated. This would have been, at best, ill-advised – the legislation had been endorsed by both sides and was seen as a solid outcome. This assessment has been reaffirmed by the attitude of the Department of Finance, which in subsequent pre-budget manoeuvrings, agitated for the new indexation formula to be overturned to achieve budget savings.

The most obvious challenge for UA in the years ahead will be its ability to balance the vocal self-interest of individual members with the imperative to develop policy positions in the broader public interest. This is no easy task, especially as the rationing of dollars – and research dollars, in particular – tightens. The other matter for attention is for UA, as the higher education peak body, to develop much deeper ties with other professional bodies, especially those in the business sphere, around improving national productivity. A feature over recent years has been the increasing engagement of lobby groups, professional groups and think tanks in debates about the future of education policy and funding.

University governance, and inevitable hiccups

Much has been written about the governance of universities and it is not our intention to review that material here. Suffice it to say that the responsibility of the governing body of a university – whether it be a university council or senate, or boards of regents or trustees – is comprised of three key tasks:

- to appoint, work with, keep to account and, if necessary, to sack the vice-chancellor or president;
- to approve and monitor the university's budget and strategic plan, keeping them aligned; and
- to monitor the performance of the university, especially via key performance indicators (KPIs) and external benchmarks, all the while attentive to both internal and external environmental factors and risks.

The relationship works best, of course, when there is a trusting and substantial working relationship between the governing board and the senior management team and, more particularly, between the vice-chancellor (or president) and chancellor (or the chair of board of regents or trustees). The relationship quickly breaks down if either the chancellor seeks to run the university or the vice-chancellor seeks to prevent the governing board from probing issues and performance. The relationship is also likely to be guided these days by the relevant national voluntary code of best practice for the governance of universities such as that endorsed by the Australian Universities Chancellors Committee and UA, the peak body of universities.

The sheer size and complexity of universities has also helped to reframe the priorities and modus operandi of the governing board. The era has passed when governing bodies could afford to be distracted by parliamentary-style theatrics, the personal crusades of elected staff, the pet hobby horses of external members or, for that matter, by vice-chancellors more skilled at talking than listening. Nowadays, governing bodies are focussed on corporate governance challenges in much the same way as are public company boards, though, in the case of universities, some legitimately different and arguably broader notions of 'shareholder' and 'bottom line' apply.

Inevitably, there will be periodic and well-publicised examples of untidy or even failed university governance. These will be painful, and occasionally tragic, for those involved, though at a broader level should be seen as the natural accompaniment of contemporary organisational life. Usually they will involve the breakdown of the relationship between the governance and management arms in general, or the personal relationship of the chancellor and vice-chancellor in particular. Usually, but not always, the vice-chancellor is the casualty because he or she is the officer accountable to the governing body. Vice-chancellors and presidents know that this is the reality, but perhaps no one has responded to the application of it to their own situation better than

American Clark Kerr on the occasion of his removal by the Board of Trustees of the University of California. He commented somewhat wryly that he left the role as he had commenced it – 'fired with enthusiasm'.

Legislation passed in New South Wales in 2011 suggests, though, that in the future it is more likely that chancellors of universities in that state will also be held to account for their performance. The legislation referred to provides a mechanism to remove chancellors from their posts, under certain circumstances. This legislation was passed in New South Wales in response to difficulties that had occurred at the University of New England between the chancellor and the vice-chancellor, and the university council's loss of confidence in the chancellor. In that instance, the chancellor's term was not renewed.

Three recent cases of governance frailty – one each in the United States, Canada and the United Kingdom – are interesting insofar as they do not conform to the usual script of governance breakdowns. In June 2012 the Board of Visitors of the University of Virginia sacked the president, Teresa Sullivan, who had been in her post for slightly less than two years. Just two weeks later, Sullivan was reinstated. Clearly the Board of Visitors had misjudged the situation, and the reporting of the crisis suggested not only the predictable breakdown of trust, but also serious dysfunctional activity within the Board of Visitors.

Reverberations from the Virginia case were felt internationally as demonstrated by strongly worded correspondence from Richard Legon, president of the Washington DC-based Association of Governing Boards of Universities and Colleges, which was circulated internationally. Legon acknowledged the dual responsibilities of such boards to be accountable for the mission and heritage of their institutions, and accountable to the public and their institution's legitimate constituents. He went on to highlight the lessons from the Virginia situation for getting the balance right between 'board oversight and today's increased public expectation for transparency and candour, including between the Board and the President'.

Pleasingly for the University of Virginia, the leadership tensions did ease. The chair of the Board completed her term the following year and remained on the Board thereafter, while the president also survived.

After only a year or so in his post in Canada as the president and vice-chancellor of the University of British Columbia (UBC), Arvind Gupta resigned in the summer of 2015. He did so as a result of friction with UBC's board of governors and with some internal elements over matters of institutional strategy and management style. There was also dysfunction evident in the board of governors itself. Nor was Gupta, who later publicly regretted his decision to leave (after having the opportunity to peruse 860 pages of accidentally released unredacted documents), the only casualty. The chair of UBC's board of governors, John Montalbano also resigned following an internal investigation that concluded that the university had failed in its obligations to protect the academic freedom of a UBC professor who had written a blog supporting Gupta. The allegation was that the chair of the board had attempted to gag the professor by complaining about the post.

The example from the UK is that of London Metropolitan University (LMU). In August 2012 the UK government, through the Home Office and the UK Border Agency, made a decision that in effect revoked LMU's ability to host foreign students from outside the European Union. The decision, if confirmed, would be to ban LMU from teaching and recruiting overseas students and thus effectively threaten the university with closure. Understandably, the matter prompted huge concern for more than 2,000 international students who could have been forced to leave the United Kingdom if they were unable to transfer to another university. The matter was resolved in April 2013 when LMU was provisionally returned the authority to recruit internationally. And although controversial, the public authorities obviously had harboured significant concerns about the legitimacy and quality of students enrolled at LMU. This raised questions about the quality of governance at LMU as well as about whether HEFCE was aware of the issues. The unfortunate person caught in the middle of the crisis was the newly installed vice-chancellor, Malcolm Gillies. His task in taking his institution forward, given the reputational damage inevitably sustained, was large.

One of the most difficult episodes in university governance in Australia over the recent period involved Central Queensland University (CQU), more recently rebadged CQUniversity. Originally a regional university based in Rockhampton, CQU hosted five campuses in its local catchment, two major offshore partnerships, four other Australian campuses in Sydney, Melbourne, Brisbane and the Gold Coast that targeted the international market, and a campus in Fiji. The four Australian international campuses (AICs) were conducted in partnership with C_Management Services (C_MS) Pty Ltd, which CQU half-owned.

At the core of the issue was a governance structure that gave rise to the practical reality that the governing Council of CQU was not in control of the span of the university's intricately configured academic and commercial interests. Essentially, CQU – with partner Kallawar Holdings Pty Ltd – established a private for-profit arm, C_MS, to operate both the four AICs and the Fijian campus. In turn, Campus Group Holdings, a company wholly owned by Kallawar, was contracted to actually run the AICs.

C_MS was listed as a controlled entity of the university, though CQU and Kallawar were each 50 per cent stakeholders. In turn the C_MS board comprised four members (two each from

CQUniversity and Kallawar), while CQU's chancellor chaired the board and held the casting vote. However, the agreement between the parties required any casting vote to be cast in favour of C_MS. This implied, as the February 2006 AUQA report on CQU[14] found, that CQU might be unable to direct the activities of C_MS, purportedly a controlled entity. The same AUQA report went on to point out that the board membership gave rise to a possible conflict of interest, given that CQU's two representatives on the board were the chancellor and the deputy chancellor. This certainly would be the case in the event that CQU found itself in significant dispute with C_MS. And, indeed, this was to occur.

More than 50 per cent of CQU's students were studying in the AICs, thus being sourced from and serviced by C_MS. And while the move to establish these AICs was initially seen as a bold response to the challenges of demography and financial sustainability facing a regional university, the AICs were extremely vulnerable to fluctuations in the international student market. Meanwhile, CQU was attracting criticism from the local community for having forsaken its central Queensland base in favour of building its international student profile at the modest end of the market, although it was able to mount a partial defence of its strategy around the nest egg (at one stage reportedly exceeding $70 million) it had accumulated. But while it was making money from its international students, its Queensland-based regional campuses were failing to meet Commonwealth-funded student load targets.

The other area of contention was operational. The model had some advantages for CQU in that C_MS was able to deal more flexibly with industrial relations and property, which went to the cost base of the enterprise (C_MS had a separate and cheaper industrial agreement for the AIC campuses). In the case of property, the ability of C_MS to lease typically CBD property in metropolitan centres rather than to own it meant a better ability to match space with teaching requirements. Also, other services provided to the Brisbane campus were furnished by various Kallawar-owned companies (cleaning, maintenance, and so on), and the usual requirements for contestable procurement applying to a public sector entity were bypassed, and Kallawar and its subsidiaries were able to take value out of the relationship at other points. A harsh analysis of the situation would be that CQU was effectively conferring on a commercial partner the capacity to make a commercial venture out of its legislatively based power to confer degrees. CQU's defence was that C_MS was partly its own.

The point about the approach to property is ironic, given that political notice of CQU's governance arrangements had begun with a relatively benign property matter. Specifically, CQU had sought a Queensland Treasury guarantee on a long lease for new premises it was seeking because it had outgrown the facilities it occupied at that time in Sydney. The problem for the Queensland government was that CQU had not tested the market, as required under the relevant state legislation. And the reason it had not tested the market was that Campus Group Holdings (the wholly owned subsidiary of Kallawar) had developed the idea and had not seen the public accountability dimension that was involved. In other words, it had not done its due diligence on the relative merits of leasing or purchasing or on whether the property for which they sought the guarantee was best value.

The various issues stemming from what was a flawed governance model congealed and the partnership became gridlocked: if Kallawar did not approve a matter being submitted to the C_MS Board, there was no quorum and, thus, no outcome. The endeavour finally ended in tears, with the rebranded CQUniversity effectively buying out C_MS for a reported $12 million. It was only once this point had been reached that CQUniversity was able, in effect, to reconnect with its geographical base and begin the process of rebuilding its position. New Vice-Chancellor Scott Bowman was given this large task.

Over the years a number of vice-chancellors have been moved or fired, but very few treated quite as brutally as was Rory Hume. An Australian by academic training with a distinguished international career both in dental research and as the executive vice-chancellor of the University of California Los Angeles (UCLA), Hume had a tumultuous two-year term as vice-chancellor of the University of New South Wales (UNSW) between 2004 and 2006. His period in office was marked by public disagreements within UNSW's governing council, in particular regarding his handling of investigations relating to the conduct of a senior medical researcher. Hume cited the reason for his departure as vice-chancellor to a breakdown in his relationship with the governing body. There were suggestions that the UNSW Council may have struggled with Hume's US-influenced management style, but there is little doubt that the UNSW Council was at odds with itself.

Macquarie University experienced difficulties at the point of changeover of vice-chancellors. Di Yerbury had been vice-chancellor for the remarkable period of 19 years at the time of the appointment of her successor, Steve Schwartz. Schwartz had come to the role having been a successful and prominent VC at both Brunel in the United Kingdom, and Murdoch University in Perth. The public dimension of the dispute was very much centred around the contested ownership of several hundred artworks. Yerbury remained on staff following the arrival of her successor and had been retained, it was reported at the time, in order to perform ambassadorial roles for the university. Behind the immediate issues were the serious matters of governance and the responsibility of the chancellor of the day to ensure a smooth and clear transition between vice-chancellors.

In late 2011 the University of Queensland was caught up in a controversy surrounding alleged admission irregularities, which resulted in the resignation of the vice-chancellor, Paul Greenfield. The issues at hand attracted much public attention, and probably led to some short-term reputational harm, especially among UQ's alumni. Those matters also reflected as much on governance and culture as on the incident that had sparked the controversy in the first place. Yet very little attention was given in the public domain to the role of, and the handling of the issues by the UQ senate.

Occasionally, governance frailties can have their amusing side, even if this is only recognised in hindsight. In mid 2004 the vice-chancellor of the University of Southern Queensland (USQ), Bill Lovegrove, was slightly perplexed to receive an email that was purportedly a job application for the position of academic director of the USQ campus in Dubai. This was interesting because, as far as Lovegrove knew at the time, and as far as his governing body knew, USQ did not have a campus either in Dubai or, for that matter, anywhere else in the Middle East. Lovegrove then did the sensible thing and logged on to USQ's website, only to see a photo of the official opening event for that campus, featuring government officials from both Australia and the locate emirate. The campus was, indeed, already fully operational.

At QUT an innocent lapse in communication between Vice-Chancellor Peter Coaldrake (one of the co-authors of this book) and the senior deputy vice-chancellor, David Gardiner, resulted in the 2008 purchase of an aircraft by the university. The intention was that the plane would be used as part of QUT's unmanned vehicle research program. The plane in question was a second-hand Cessna 172 and the purchase took place without the knowledge of the vice-chancellor, the university's Audit and Risk Committee, or the governing council. In this case the issue was not about the cost of the purchase – it was well within delegations – but the level of risk involved. This risk included making the vehicle airworthy – it was not – flying it 1,500 kilometres to Brisbane – it was in Victoria – and the licensing and insurance arrangements to cover the university staff piloting the vehicle. As it transpired, Gardiner – an outstanding administrator – had attended to all these points of substance in his approval of the transaction while the vice-chancellor was away from the university. But the matter had slipped through the formal reporting cracks.

Management realities

Clark Kerr, the great American educationist referred to earlier in this book, once quipped: 'I find the three major administrative problems on a campus are sex for the students, athletics for the alumni, and parking for the faculty.' A similar observation would be unlikely from any vice-chancellor or university president today. The macro challenges nowadays are much more likely to be presented as universities being required to do more with less, driving for performance in an increasingly competitive environment, or responding to the variegated needs of a student body contributing more to the costs of its education.

Among the most difficult internal issues for contemporary universities, especially those in the western world, is the ageing of the academic population and managing the transition and replacement of this group. In Australia, for example, academics are the second-oldest occupational group after farmers and, thus, older than two other groups publicly identified as facing a demographic crisis – nurses and school teachers. Many universities have begun to grapple with this challenge, recognising that the tasks of rejuvenation and improving quality sit alongside each other. In practice this means that universities are simultaneously hiring early career academics, seeking to retain their best mid-career talent, and searching for the professorial stars of the future.

Some universities, and some countries, are in a better position to respond than others. Budget limits are obviously one potential impediment; another is academic culture and the related preparedness of academic managers to deal with performance issues. Sometimes the laws under which universities operate may discourage action. In Australia, for example, academic managers may be cautious about addressing performance issues if doing so is likely to invite charges of bullying, harassment, age discrimination or unfair treatment. In other words, industrial laws and enterprise bargaining frameworks – which are there to protect staff and defend against management overreach – are seen by many people (not just managers) as impediments to effective management of staff. And while universities are generally doing better in the ways they recognise good performance, they have learned to devise other ways to deal with the other end of the spectrum. These include the offering of departure packages, pre-retirement contracts and redundancy payments (even for people well above the traditional retirement age). Rarely, however, are departures forced for those with ongoing appointments because of the performance management process – it is simply too long, too expensive, and too uncertain in its prospects.

While much of the discussion about the challenges of university leadership and management tends to focus at the most senior level, arguably the very hardest positions are several rungs lower. These are the heads of school or department, or similar posts, and they are the first level of academic management. Thirty years ago such positions would be occupied more often than not by a senior professor, sometimes serving in rotation. They were, essentially, collegial roles that exercised a very 'light touch' responsibility for the activities of colleagues or the organisation of classes and timetables.

Such characterisation is no longer relevant. A person holding such a position nowadays is just as likely to be a mid-career colleague plucked out on account of their teaching or research leadership and, usually, without any serious prior management experience.

The typical spread of responsibilities of such positions entails academic and resource oversight as well as collegial support and the management of performance. It also requires the building of bridges laterally in the organisation as well as accountability and responsiveness to university directives from above. But despite the complexity of the role, and the usual lack of preparedness of incumbents for it, the development needs of this most critical level of the organisation are often overlooked by the leadership strata above.

It is also at the head of school or department level where the stresses on the traditional model of academic work are engaged with at a very practical level, via the allocation of teaching, research and other responsibilities. These stresses derive from the pressures of a mass and diverse system, the increasingly harsh rationing of the competitive research dollar, local budget conditions and the operational reality that while good research should inform good teaching, there are no guarantees of this. It is also the case that more than half of Australia's undergraduate teaching is undertaken by staff engaged on a sessional basis; that is, for particular course units and specified times. These sessional workers include PhD students supplementing their income and wanting to develop their teaching. They also include industry professionals and others who do university teaching for the usual combination of reasons of economic necessity and personal reward. Many are women seeking to balance family life with a career.

Although national-level surveys referred to earlier indicate that it is the established academics who are vocally critical about their lot, it is both sessional staff and those at the 'early career' phase of full-time academic life who are under the most pressure. Early career academics often teach and supervise large teaching teams in heavily enrolled units, particularly at the first-year level; and at the same time, they are under pressure to succeed in the competitive research arena. And the option to break away from the usual all-rounder profile and try for a research-only pathway is even more fraught with career risk.

The other group frequently overlooked is the professional staff, still dubbed somewhat patronisingly in some universities as 'general' or, worse, 'non-academic' staff. These people make up more than half the total staff complement in our universities. Some of those who pine for the return of a golden era point to the growth of the professional staff as clear evidence of the rise and overreach of managerialism. It may be true that 30 years ago universities with small numbers of students and staff and little external accountability had no great call on professional assistance beyond administrative and clerical support, but those days are long gone. The student and staff populations of universities are now often as large as regional cities. Universities have had to learn to professionally manage multimillion-dollar budgets, complex technology-based systems and the array of accountabilities and efficiencies faced by any modern organisation. In addition, universities have particular obligations to internationalise their reach, cultivate their alumni, manage their laboratories and workshops, and commercialise their research. The professional staff in our universities, who are responsible for running many of these activities, need to be equipped to do so and, indeed, many hold higher level academic qualifications and occupy roles that require them to explore the frontiers of innovation.

An obvious example is the learning and teaching sphere, where academics now work alongside professional staff with positions such as pedagogical advisers, online content producers, learning and teaching designers, curriculum developers, knowledge managers and technical writers. And for any traditionalists who doubt the necessity of such roles, the development of MOOCs in particular, and the evolution of the hybrid environment of blended learning in general, provide the answer.

What all this says is that in the same way that universities are coming to grasp the complementary roles of governance, leadership and management, they are also now required to accept the inevitable blurring of the lines between academic and professional staff roles. With the stakes involved in higher education and research being raised ever higher, and resources likely to be more tightly constrained in the years ahead, the capacity of universities to productively manage themselves and their relationships with the wider world will become increasingly important. Some universities will find this more of a challenge than others.

Chapter Eleven

Facing the realities

Universities are, rightly, seen as essential parts of an adaptable and resilient society. All countries face the challenges of competing and flourishing in a globalised economy dominated by knowledge-based services that are being continually reshaped by large-scale technological and other disruption. While most attention is focussed on the potential of world-class research breakthroughs, universities have an even more fundamental role in preparing people for the future. If innovation is to be embedded in Australian workplace cultures then we need more than a few more entrepreneurs, scientists and venture capitalists, we need high quality and widely accessible universities to help people understand the complexities of the world and to rethink assumptions. The idea of a community of scholars may be over-romanticised, but a significant part of the value universities can bring to the economy is to educate the students who will constitute our future workforce in rich learning environments that can pass on disciplines of thinking as well as the best knowledge available to us in various areas.

This is of course a rather narrow economic conception of what universities can offer, but it is the one that is most important to those capable of supporting universities: governments and students. While there are many who will defend the broader ideas of universities as engines for social good and for fostering curiosity and broader intellectual development, the great majority also expect some enhancement of their job prospects and the skills to thrive in a profoundly changing and increasingly disrupted environment. With sluggish post-GFC economic growth and the prospect of ongoing job disruption coming from advances in computer science and robotics, the stakes involved are higher than ever. Almost every government knows this, and almost every country has moved from elite to mass higher education. Universities are important, and they need to deliver.

The good news is that they have. For what is a comparatively modest public investment Australia's university system is in good overall shape. Universities are under financial pressure, but they have coped without major problems. Australia features prominently in world rankings for research. Students record high levels of satisfaction with their university experiences, they are not financially exploited, and their debts are manageable and equitably handled by income contingent loans. Students anywhere in the country and from all socioeconomic backgrounds have reasonable prospects of enrolling in a university that offers education developed and delivered, albeit not entirely, by scholarly communities linked to the forefront of their areas of expertise and also to relevant professions.

However, there is a downside. There is a large price tag attached to the traditional model of university education that promises to bring students directly or even indirectly into contact with the world of scholarship as constituted by a group of people who enjoy significant academic freedom and who are active in their areas of specialty. Almost all of the chronic policy problems of contemporary higher education trace back to two questions: 'where does the money come from?' and 'can we be sure that academics and institutions will act in the best interests of those who support them?' These questions are of course common to almost any service, such as health, childcare or school education, but universities and higher education have features that make them especially difficult.

Our knowledge about the world is constantly changing and branching in different directions. The point of higher education is to introduce people to this changing frontier, and for them to learn from their own efforts, and from the work of teachers, the experiences and facilities provided by universities, the interface with the outside world, and many other factors. There is no fixed curriculum and we simply do not have reliable standardised ways to measure many of the fundamental aspects of what universities are expected to provide: from the quality of teaching to employment advantage and more generally the public and private benefits of what might be learned. We have many partial measures, and within universities academics certify the achievement of students in particular courses. However, we just do not have available the kind of information that those paying the bills might like, that might for example clearly distinguish one university from another on education quality as opposed to the ability to select high performing or otherwise advantaged students. There have been efforts to grapple with this problem, but solutions have been elusive.

This poses a real dilemma for both those who favour government control of the sector and those who favour market competition. There is no objective evidence to say how much higher education should cost, or how much of that cost should come from the public and how much from the student. In education more so than research, there is little robust evidence to either condemn or commend current practice beyond eliminating obvious fraudulent behaviour. The standard arsenal of government management tools – targets, compacts, financial incentives, efficiency cuts, targeted funding, performance funding – delivers diminishing returns. Like the buttons for pedestrians on many traffic lights in New York some policy levers give the appearance of effective action without being properly connected to where the change occurs. All too often the envisaged changes to behaviour do not emerge and in fact existing patterns of behaviour are reinforced. Market forces will not come to the rescue because markets cannot operate as intended if student consumers do not have proper information. Publishing a patchwork of broad averages is useful accountability, but not so useful to students who want to know about specific subjects. Market signals are further diluted by covering the cost of student loans that are repaid when above average earnings are achieved.

In the absence of solid evidence about quality and standards, widespread concern has emerged that our university system is unsustainable. Those providing the money worry that it is unsustainably expensive, while many of those inside the sector catastrophise that it is under-resourced to the point of becoming unsustainable. These concerns persist despite decades of almost continual review and re-review, much of which have produced little tangible evidence about perceived problems. To date Australia has managed to strike a balance which has seen public expenditure for higher education and research stay at around 1 per cent of GDP over the past quarter of a century, compared to around 1.4 per cent across the OECD, despite massive increases in research funding and a doubling in the number of Australian students enrolled in universities. This has been achieved by controlling access to public subsidies, capping numbers of students, controlling fees and increasing the share of fees to be repaid by students.

Now things have changed. The aim of extending higher education to all those who might benefit from it was always somewhat at odds with the maintenance of caps on student enrolments.

And the removal of the lid in 2012 led to enrolments shooting up, further cementing the idea of university as a mainstream aspiration. There was little political support for reapplying caps on student numbers; however, rapid growth in enrolment meant that government spending also rose rapidly. Whether the spending growth driven by unchecked university expansion can be sustained within current settings is debatable, and growth has slowed in more recent years. The sector cannot hope to be protected indefinitely from cuts when the government is under pressure to support costs associated with ageing, defence and healthcare, and broader national infrastructure. Nor is the university sector by any means the government's major priority in education: funding for schools and vocational training are both acute challenges and universities are just part of the continuum needed to educate and develop the workforce of the future. Governments might acknowledge the importance of higher education and research but they have been exasperated on a regular basis with the sector's tendency to be self-absorbed about its importance, to complexify and exaggerate its problems, and to be habitual mendicants. One of the results of this has been to seek reductions in government spending on universities.

Throughout 2015 and into 2016 the savings associated with the 2014 deregulation package continued to be factored into government budgets despite ongoing rejection of the reforms by the Senate. This amounted to a shortfall of some four billion dollars, and while the 2016–2017 budget reduced the expected savings to around two billion dollars the sector remains highly vulnerable when reality finally hits. Savings will either be forgone, testing further the willingness of government to increase direct outlays to universities, or they will not, and other offsets will need to be found. Put even more bluntly this means either that students will pay more or universities will take a cut, or a combination of the two will emerge.

What is even more clearly unsustainable is the situation in research. Over the ten years to 2013 governments doubled medical research grant funding in real terms and increased general university research grants from the ARC by 70 per cent. In contrast, infrastructure grants only grew by 25 per cent. Over this time the number of academics notionally involved in research grew by 37 per cent, slightly less than growth in student load. Yet despite increases in grant funds far outstripping growth in the academic population, demand for research grants has far exceeded supply, with success rates for grant applications falling to record lows. This has come about partly because more funds have been concentrated on the most successful applicants, and proposals to extend the duration of project funding would exacerbate this. Perhaps more significantly it has also come from the heightened stakes attached to external research funding for individual academics and for institutions. Global and national rankings, national audits of quality and funding formulas with further rewards for the successful all serve to reinforce the primacy of academic research as a marker of excellence directly impacting on reputation. Australia must strengthen its research base, but governments will not pour more money into the black hole of research indefinitely, even for medical research which usually and understandably attracts political favour. The solution is not to spiral inwards with an ever greater concentration on past glories or to pick winners or favoured universities. However, Australia's future challenges are diverse and demand a research base that is also diverse and vibrant. The reality is that most research funding will find its way into the most research-intensive universities. Yet we need to be able to develop new fields, including interdisciplinary work that tackles our greatest national and global challenges. We must find ways of sustaining excellence on many fronts and in many places, which in turn will need sustained commitment of public funding together with healthy competition and fundamental changes in research expectations, academic roles, and institutional ability in order to match rhetoric about strategy and selective strength with effective action.

The challenge of supporting students and funding tuition in an environment of growing concern about public spending and deficits has led to a new appreciation of the potential for income contingent loans to take the place of direct grants. While Australia pioneered the mass provision of HECS/HELP loans to cover university costs, in post-GFC England the prospect of turning current spending into a loan asset that might even be sold to generate more revenue for current spending has gained traction, and the 2012 reforms in that country have moved much further along that path than we have seen in Australia. In England the bulk of public grant money has been replaced by student fees covered by loans, helping to relieve government deficits but creating substantial debt-related burdens for students. English students now pay the highest fees for public higher education in the world, and the government there faces an uncertain future burden of debt that might not be repaid, dependent as it is on the strength and rewards of future labour markets. The deregulation reforms proposed in 2014 in Australia did not involve such a large government-mandated increase to student debt, beginning with an average increase of around 20 per cent, but the extent of the market impact on student fees was unknown. It seems likely that the future will involve a greater emphasis on student loans as a way of handling rising costs. Thus one major focus of future government policy, given the weak track record of past efforts to use financial incentives to change the status quo in universities, will be on loans policy and the maximisation of repayment and minimisation of loan subsidies.

There are some limits that should apply to this trend. In England grants that formerly were provided to financially disadvantaged students for living costs are to be converted to loans. This will be combined with a reduction in real terms of the threshold for debt repayment, and so students who by accident of birth do not have family money to draw upon will face greater financial penalties should they go on to earn a decent income than their peers from more affluent backgrounds. This is effectively a tax on social mobility as noted by higher education analyst Andrew McGettigan. Australia has begun to take steps in this direction with the recasting of top-up scholarships for poorer students as loans, a policy that began under Labor and was confirmed under the Coalition government. Such shifting of support for the disadvantaged, from a grant when needed to a loan to be repaid if the recipient's circumstances improve, deserves wider debate than was possible amid the flurry of measures that were put forward over the 2013–2015 period.

Another potentially bad idea in loans policy is that universities should contribute to the unrepaid debt of their graduates, as for example has been proposed in the United States from time to time. While universities should do all they can to improve the job and career prospects of their students, there will be problems if they are expected to help repay to the government the debt of students who do not earn enough after they have left the university. It could deter universities from enrolling students at greater risk, which largely includes students from disadvantaged backgrounds. The government might offer compensatory rewards but this would only amplify bureaucracy and create problems around timing and definitions of risk.

In general, the move from grants to loans and increasing the student share of university costs is about transferring the risks in undertaking higher education from the public to the individual. This is of course part of a wider shift in the relationship between governments and citizens that has taken place over many years in countries similar to Australia. But at a time when graduate employment prospects are more uncertain than ever, and the national need to make the best use of its intellectual firepower is greater than ever, we should be particularly cautious about the impact on current disadvantaged students and on future generations of graduates.

Having institutions share in this risk might seem sensible, but as we have argued in this book this is not best done by penalties or rewards attached to simplified measures of complex outcomes. Institutions do have responsibilities to their students, and interest in their future success, and their best contribution to lowering the risks of an uncertain future is to provide the best education possible and to support students in their studies. There is a great deal that can and should be done within universities to adapt to uncertain and challenging times. We do not expect that students or governments will be willing to underwrite whatever universities and academics might want, and so rationing of research funding and pressure for cost reduction in all areas will inevitably continue. Even if universities can and wish to operate in the future more or less as they do today, the pressure on traditional modes of academic work will become overwhelming, and the stresses are already showing. The spectral threat of technology-driven disruption is taking increasingly clear shape: universities might be able to survive by absorbing and adapting technology – we know that in a general sense they are resilient institutions – but they will not be able to do so while staying the way they are now. Changes are coming whether egged on by government incentives or not, and they will demand far-reaching changes in the way we organise and conduct academic and university work. They will require patience and competence, with governors, university managements and professional staff working with highly mobile academic communities whose allegiances are as much or more to their disciplines and careers as they are to a given institution. Our best hope for quality improvement, indeed conceivably for survival in the face of fundamental dislocation, will not come from bureaucratic oversight, but from having institutional directions aligned to academic cultures that are ambitious and as externally attuned as internally reflective, and that have strong peer respect for the quality of teaching as well as research. In practical terms, institutions need to know what underlies their costs and be able to take hard but broadly accepted decisions if they are to sustain a viable and vibrant university.

The main task confronting Australian universities over the past few decades has been the development of institutional strategies and cultures that enable them to adapt to fluid and demanding educational missions within limited resourcing and many demands for accountability, and to find their place in the hyper-competition for research resources. It is a task that is far from complete and if anything, universities are distracted rather than aided by the constant churn of policy ideas that seek to shift the locus of attention to issues of access to government money. The future will require much more unpredictable adaptation by institutions, particularly if the efforts of any of the many start-ups and new higher education models that are being actively developed in the United States and elsewhere prove successful.

Government funding is of course important, and is especially necessary in areas of particular imbalance such as support for research infrastructure and in general to enable universities to prosper and students to attend university. Public funding is also necessary to lubricate the wheels of collaboration, whether between universities and industry or among universities on various matters. However, the question of how much public funding is needed for the general operations of universities has had no clear answer. Universities can cover their costs by charging students for expenses not covered by government grants, as with overseas students, and in areas of burgeoning potential such as corporate education and fee-based postgraduate programs. But when it comes to the large majority of Australian students who are in receipt of a public subsidy, there are a number of options for sustaining or improving the resource base. With all of them, however, we can expect that students would incur greater debt.

At the most basic level there are really just two choices. First, the government might continue to control the fees that can be charged for students who are in receipt of public subsidies. If the government sought savings, or if universities needed extra income, then the government could set corresponding increases in student fees. This has the virtue of simplicity but the vice of putting the onus on a remote and sometimes unwilling government to set the appropriate fee levels. The other option is to have some greater scope for institutions to set their own fees for publicly subsidised students. In this scenario, government and students will share a common concern about possible runaway increases in fees and student debt, and will want assurances about the rationale for fees and the uses to which fee income might be put. There have been various proposals put forward to counterbalance possible fee increases. The ANU's Professor Bruce Chapman outlined an option for reducing government subsidies as institutions charge higher fees,[1] while the Vice-Chancellor of Victoria University Professor Peter Dawkins set out a variant on this idea together with an enhanced program of support for disadvantaged students.[2] Meanwhile Professor Peter Noonan, from the Mitchell Institute, has revived the idea of an independent 'buffer' body of experts to oversee a new financing system.[3] Unfortunately the more flexibility institutions have to set their own fees the more these issues grow in complexity and the more potential there is for adverse consequences, particularly if the architects of policy seek to build in new incentives and accountabilities for additional funding.

Our present university system and its funding arrangements have resulted from years of compromise, lobbying and review, along with implementing and often later dismantling specially targeted funding. The idea that there are major changes for the better to be made without additional funding is not futile and should not be dismissed, but we do not need yet more reviews to revisit the same old issues. If we accept that the budget position of government is difficult, and that higher education is not a sufficiently high priority to warrant sustaining – let alone increasing – public funding at suitable levels, and that higher education and research are strategically important to Australia given developments in Asia and elsewhere across the globe, then the possible options for a realistic response to university funding policy are relatively few.

Funding from philanthropic and business sources should be encouraged, but we need to be realistic about the scale and scope of such endeavours: they will remain relatively small components of university budgets. The main game will involve new mixes of public funding and student contributions. The priority for public funding should continue to be undergraduate education and mechanisms to allow institutions some discretion to set their own fees should be put in place. Such mechanisms should be designed to provide a robust level of consumer protection and also to ensure that a more deregulated system does not entrench or exacerbate existing inequalities of access and opportunity. This will need both continuation of programs of direct public support for disadvantaged students and accountability from universities for their own efforts to improve social mobility and opportunity. It could take the form of an interplay between rising tuition fees, reductions in government grants, and increases in institutional commitments to equity programs. However, we need to be careful to avoid our national predisposition to develop an overly cumbersome architecture of countermeasures to fee increases.

Universities should be accountable for their level of fees and their use of fee income. But equally we should be realistic that institutions will have legitimately different strategic imperatives. There has been much hand-wringing about the apparent evils of universities cross-subsidising research from fee income, but an interesting silence on the necessary cross-subsidy of niche courses or regional campuses. And, of course, there is little airing of the biggest cross-subsidy of them all, that of international student fees supporting university operations in a range of ways across the sector. These are all matters for institutions to weigh, rather than for government to seek to micro-control. In the event of egregious abuses this approach might need to be revisited, but for research, as well as for teaching, there needs to be some scope for institutional choice in light of the evident inability or unwillingness of governments to provide what universities regard as sufficient base support.

We have acknowledged the limitations of market forces in higher education, but competitive constraints on institutional behaviour do exist. A period of testing the nature of institutional fee strategies within a relatively simple system of government controls should be allowed, with regular review undertaken to assess the direction of the new funding environment and its effect on participation, equity and other considerations relating to the public good, along with consequent revision of policy settings.

We also need to be very careful of arguments for special treatment and where they are raised to encourage informed public debate about such proposals, rather than seeing last-minute deals struck behind closed doors. Greater flexibility for institutions should encourage our political masters to be more sceptical of the outrageously self-interested lobbying we have seen in the past. Sometimes this lobbying is dressed in the apparently respectable clothing of encouraging excellence or diversity. At other times, it presents in the more tawdry garb of marginal seat politics and is manifested in bids for new campuses, or even medical schools.

Relinquishing government control over undergraduate student fees may be a practical response to the need to sustain our universities in the light of the realities of public finances, but it is no panacea. The real action is not about how higher education is funded, which is the primary focus of policy interest, but about what universities do in defining their own futures. Their individual paths will differ, but for all the task will involve reconciling their culture with financial realities, a rapidly changing professional landscape, technology-driven change, legitimate demands for accountability and, crudely, the obligation to deliver quality and value for money.

We should not expect that governments will relinquish the desire to exert some discipline on university funding, or exercise some level of influence over what is done with it. Where grants are made there will be demands for accountability and measurement, and broad priorities in areas such as research are a legitimate aim of public policy. But the limitations in both practice and principle, of government as a driver of change in academic activity and culture should be acknowledged. Governments cannot shepherd universities through potential technological disruption, nor can they orchestrate the diversity of approaches that are needed to adapt higher education to new models of work and to the bewildering pace of changes to knowledge and technology that we see across society.

Rather than categorising institutions into neat boxes or rewarding or penalising institutions with simplistic measures, we need to allow the emergence of different ways of adapting the university ideal to meet society's changing needs within the resources society provides, whether these be public or private, campus-based or online, research intensive or otherwise. The goal should be to ensure that the various forms of a quality university education are widely available and seen as financially attainable by those with potential and regardless of background. Within a given envelope of funding from government and students, government policy should be less preoccupied with efforts to cajole, second guess or nudge institutions and more focussed on how governments can best provide support. For students that means through consumer protection and support for the disadvantaged, and for research it means policy settings that enable universities to move beyond their traditional paradigms, and in the Australian context, this certainly means engaging better with business. The focus on addressing disadvantage cannot rely on government alone: inequalities of opportunity are complex and there are limits on public financial commitment and on the scope of government agencies to respond flexibly to the diversity of need. Too often poverty is connected with rural or regional location, and policy becomes distorted by politics. Stronger cultures of philanthropy need to be developed throughout the community and importantly in higher education institutions. And for research it means making strategic choices and investments of scale to better align university research capacity in order to support sectors of the economy that are Australia's strengths and providing settings and incentives that enable universities to better engage with businesses. In the absence of such an alignment, there is a distinct possibility that Australian university research will become a one-trick pony focussed on huge investments in medical and life sciences research, but without the thriving local life sciences industry that can take advantage of these investments. Put a different way, when discussions of university policy centre as much on students in need and on the innovation needs of the economy and society as they do on institutional horse races we will have made progress.

Much of this book has been about money, accountability and economics, because those have been the principal interests of government policy and most students. Policy makers will acknowledge wider benefits of universities, for example in helping us to understand and address future challenges such as climate change or improving health or building a sustainable role for Australia as Asia develops in influence. There are even more intangible benefits of having Australians educated in institutions that promote reason-based understanding and exploration of the world and our place in it, and that can help realise the potential of human intelligence and creativity. We cannot clearly quantify these benefits, or parse them neatly into public and private components. We can neither accurately measure the risks or opportunities of expanding university education at a time of increasing disruption of the workforce or, conversely, the risks we take as a society by restricting the scope and reach of university education and research. However, in an uncertain world the value to the nation of having strong universities available to a wide cross-section of society is such that we should be prepared to absorb a substantial part of the financial and employment risks involved through public financial support, rather than have them sheeted home to individual students. And we should do so in a way that enables universities to adapt and thrive and students to have the best chance of securing a better future regardless of their background.

We can afford to sustain and even improve a university system in Australia that is already one of the world's best. This is not just about peaks of research performance but also about ensuring that this research is aligned to the innovation needs of the Australian economy. But, above all this is about a broadly accessible higher education system where the full promise of the university – that of linking what is taught with the changing frontiers of knowledge – is available not only to an economic or social elite. There is much yet to be done but there are no simple solutions to the challenges we all face: what is certain is that the fate of our universities is the fate of our society.

Acknowledgements

We gratefully acknowledge the support and guidance of a number of colleagues and friends who have reviewed draft material or made significant textual suggestions to either or both editions: Sam Nielsen, Anne Statham, Peter Corke, Jane den Hollander, Peter Noonan, Carol Nicoll, David Fagan, Mandy Thomas, Peter Little, Andrew Dempster, Andrew Norton, Don Markwell, Glyn Davis, Arun Sharma, Ian Hawke, Leigh Tabrett, Scott Sheppard, Myles McGregor-Lowndes, Carol Dickenson, Shard Lorenzo, Suzi Vaughan, Tom Cochrane, Sheel Nuna, Dave Kennedy and Carl Cartwright.

Special thanks to Kathleen O'Hare and Lee Coaldrake for proofing the entire manuscript, and to Jennifer Petley for her deft juggling of script changes and ensuring version control. Several other staff members of the QUT Chancellery team – Romaine Carpenter, Kathie Thomson, Angela Young, Georgina Maguire, Teresa Short, Gabrielle Kavanagh and Amara Nazim – also provided valuable support to the project.

Of course we are indebted to Sean Leahy and Brett Lethbridge, the *Courier-Mail*'s resident cartoonists, for their drawings, which do so much to sharpen some of the themes and messages of the book.

Madonna Duffy at UQP believed in this book from the moment we outlined some initial ideas, and we warmly thank her for her advice and encouragement throughout the process for both editions. We also thank Beth Barber for her work on this edition.

Finally, and most importantly, we thank our respective partners, Lee and Robyn, for their love and patience during the many months of distraction associated with the preparation of both editions of the book and the actual writing of the manuscript.

Peter Coaldrake and Lawrence Stedman

Notes

Chapter Two: The role of universities in the twenty-first century

1   The four-volume *A History of the University in Europe* (Cambridge University Press) gives a comprehensive overview from medieval to modern times.

2   Two such polemics appeared in 2012: *Whackademia: An insider's account of the troubled university* by Richard Hil (New South) and *Australian Universities: A portrait of decline* by Donald Meyers (self-published e-book).

3   We have drawn much of our short account of the economic shifts in Australia and elsewhere, and the role of technology in driving different returns to different education and skill levels, from Frijters and Gregory (2006) and Acemoglu and Autor (2010).

4   See Frey and Osborne (2013), *The Future of Employment: How susceptible are jobs to computerization?*, University of Oxford.

5   Frey and Osborne (2013) and Durrant-Whyte et al. (2015).

6   Beaudry et al. (2013)

7   Coelli (2015).

8   This was the conclusion of an update of calculations on the private rate of return to higher education undertaken by Daly et al. (2011) and used as part of the review of higher education funding (Lomax-Smith Review, HEBFR [2011]).

9   See Diane Coyle (2008) for an accessible overview of the development of these theories and their influence on policy in the United Kingdom.

10 It ought to be a salutary lesson in the folly of grand government target setting: ten years later the measure used to gauge progress against Blair's target had barely moved. While perhaps not in the class of Bob Hawke's 1987 pledge that in three years no child would (have to) live in poverty, this failure in no way diminished attachment to the idea that large social aggregates can be the subject of such targets as if they were the result of industrial production methods.

11 Cambridge University's Alan Hughes (2006) has described much of this pursuit of science and innovation policy as a 'cargo cult', whereby it is hoped that replication of some of the institutions of Silicon Valley will lead to the emergence of innovation.

12 See Dodgson et al. (2011).

13 Nowotny et al. (2001).

14 See Wheelahan (2010) for an account of how proponents of practical outcome-focussed training were able to appropriate constructivist ideas and terms to isolate academic knowledge from the curriculum, particularly in vocational education and training (VET), to the disadvantage of students.

15 Frank and Meyer (2007).

16 Marginson (2011a) and Liu (2012).

17 Program for International Student Assessment

18 Yu He and Yinhua Mai (2015)

19 Altbach (2009).

20 See for example Marginson (2011b).

21 World Economic Forum (2012).

Chapter Three: Models of the Australian university

1 Cited in Douglass (2000), p. 191.

2 Marginson (1997), p. 44.

3 For an excellent account of the influence of particular political actors in the development of the Australian higher education sector from the 1950s to the turn of the century, see Madeleine Laming's 2001 paper. Accounts of the influence of individuals and political inclinations in the beginning (Ansell 2008) and the end (Kogan and Hanney 2000) of the binary system in the United Kingdom may also be found. However, despite political differences between Australia and the United Kingdom

their paths of higher education policy have followed very similar trajectories, suggesting demographic and global factors may well trump local politics.

4 The 15 to 25 per cent differential is from CTEC (1986), p. 193. The issue has become more topical with the rise of non-university providers of higher education that do not undertake research. The 2011 Lomax-Smith Review (see chapter 2, note 4) recommended that a discount of 10 per cent be applied to funding of non-university providers, a rate that was disputed by Universities Australia (UA) in its response to the review. UA drew on biennial university research expenditure survey data from the Australian Bureau of Statistics (ABS) to arrive at an estimate of 30 per cent.

5 Wark 1969, cited in Mahony (1992).

6 Douglass (2010).

7 Kerr (2001), pp. 186–89.

8 Kevin Kiley (2011). 'UC a Better Idea?' in *Inside Higher Ed.*, cited at http://goo.gl/IlBAL in October 2012.

9 Gabriel et al. (2007).

10 Vogel (2009).

11 Schleicher (2006).

12 Ahola et al. (2014).

13 Svein Kyvik, *Experience with Mergers in the Norwegian University College Sector*, presentation to the Hedda 10th Anniversary Conference, November 2011.

14 Stabile (2007).

15 Margaret Simons documents a number of these perceptions in her article in The Monthly (Simons 2010).

16 The Group of Eight or Go8, sometimes called the 'sandstone universities', refers to the eight most research-intensive capital-city based universities on the Australian mainland. All were established more than half a century ago, all are comprehensive in scope and they are united through their domination of Australian university research funding, particularly in the medical and physical sciences.

17 Conversely, 32 out of Australia's 40 universities maintain a metropolitan campus, that is, within 10 kilometres of a capital city, and this includes several 'regional universities'.

18 Coates et al. (2009) reported that around half of the academics they

surveyed had 'taken concrete action' to change jobs to another Australian university.

Chapter Four: Driving mass diversity

1 Cited at http://economics.com.au/?p=8306 on 6 February 2012.

2 The number of 128 registered institutions in 2016 is not directly comparable with the 89 reported private providers in 2010 as there has been a level of turnover in ownership and structure among these organisations.

3 Most public universities also offer a third 'summer' semester, in some cases formalised as a trimester system, for example at Deakin University. These enable some compression of degree length for those willing to undertake additional study, but generally they are not marketed as 'a degree in two years'.

4 Trounson and Puddy (2011). The university formally commenced operations in November 2012 and in December of that year Professor Fred McDougall was appointed as vice-chancellor. In 2014 Torrens enrolled 325 students, nine of whom were from overseas.

Chapter Five: Funding for performance: The case of teaching

1 Critics have accused universities of heightening 'publish or perish' environments by pressuring academics to produce more publications, particularly in 'top journals', as part of institutional strategies of responding to funding driven by measures of publications. Some universities have also pushed the definitions of particular categories of funding, for example counting research outputs from allied medical research institutes even when they did not pay the salaries of the researchers involved. Performance-based funding for research training also generated close interest in encouraging shorter completion times for PhD and other research students, but this is a complex matter to measure and, while the focus is desirable, it is not clear whether in fact such interest actually generated real improvements.

2 In 2015 Umbricht et al. found that performance-based higher education funding in Indiana did not increase graduation numbers but instead led to institutions becoming more selective and taking in fewer students. They noted that their study 'provides evidence that well-intentioned

state policies may actually exacerbate some of the challenges facing public higher education'.

3 Peter Ewell, 'Some Thoughts on Pay-For-Performance in Higher Education', L.H. Martin Institute Newsletter, June 2010.

4 Sanford and Hunter (2011).

5 Cited in *Times Higher Education*, 7 May 2015.

Chapter Six: Being world class

1 Christopher Ball, Chairman of the National Advisory Body, cited in Kogan and Hanney (2000), p. 98.

2 Watson (2011).

3 Cited at http://goo.gl/kQnt0 on 2 June 2011.

4 Cited at www.nature.com/news/a-question-of-science-1.10461 on 18 April 2012.

5 Salmi (2015).

6 *The Star* online, 'Push for Rankings Stirs Trouble', cited at http://goo.gl/ SNYv2 on 28 August 2011; *The New Straits Times*, cited at http://goo.gl/ vcz6p on 4 May 2012.

7 In October 2012 the Australian government released a White Paper on Australia's place in the 'Asian Century', which set a target that by 2025 ten of Australia's universities would be in the top 100 of the ARWU ranks.

8 Adams (2013).

9 A proposal to merge Erasmus University in the Netherlands with the University of Leiden and the Delft University of Technology was motivated by a desire to move up the world rankings, but was dropped 'because of a mix of political unease, fierce alumni loyalty to the existing "brands", and an "angry" response from research staff' (Baty 2012).

10 Cited at https://www.polytechnique.edu/en/paris-saclay, February 2016

11 *Times Higher Education*, Overseas briefing, 4 March 2010.

12 Bhattacharjee (2011).

13 'Nayang Technological University benefits from tough leadership', *The Australian*, 2 December 2015.

14 Salmi (2009), p. 44.

15 University of Manchester 2020 Strategic Plan.

16 Marginson et al. (2008), p. 22.

17 Before 2002 the ANU was ineligible to compete for Commonwealth research grants and to access some associated block grant support. It was granted access in return for making 20 per cent of its special block grant contestable.

18 See Pettigrew (2012) for a summary of OECD data. The citations comparisons are based on scientific publications normalised to the world average.

19 Hazelkorn (2011).

Chapter Seven: Weapons of mass instruction

1 Cunningham et al. (1998, 2000); Ryan and Stedman (2001).

2 A thorough post-mortem on the UKeU may be found at http://goo.gl/OFGYT.

3 Data from Eduventures, reported in the *Chronicle of Higher Education*, retrieved June 2012.

4 Strauss (2015).

5 Data from the National Student Clearinghouse Research Center, retrieved May 2015.

6 Allen and Seaman (2015).

7 Economists David Deming et al. (2015) found some evidence of an average link between online course provision and lower prices, but noted a number of studies which had found problems in the quality of learning online and also their own research showing that employers were less likely to follow up applications from graduates of online for-profit universities. Researchers from Stanford University (Bettinger et al. 2015) studied data from the large for-profit DeVry University and found that on average online classes were associated with reduced student learning and higher rates of dropout. Deming and his colleagues noted that we are still only in the early days of online university education, and relationships between cost and quality are likely to change.

8 Cited at www.universitybusiness.com/article/what-went-wrong-alllearn on 6 January 2006.

9 Christensen and Eyring (2011).

10 Special arrangements were put in place in the United States to recognise WGU programs, including a provision that could qualify students for federal aid based on competency rather than credit hours.

As it turned out, WGU chose not to use this provision, instead translating competencies into units that paralleled credit hours, because these were better recognised by employers providing tuition assistance and students transferring to other institutions. Thus the competency model has in practice morphed into a hybrid competency/credit-hour model, which no doubt will lessen its impact as a mould-breaking template for others to follow. See Lederman (2012).

11 In June 2012 academic publisher McGraw-Hill announced that it had entered into a performance-based deal with WGU, whereby the university pays a significantly discounted flat fee for McGraw-Hill's course material plus a premium for each student who uses the materials and passes the course.

12 Cited at www.wgu.edu/tuition_financial_aid/overview in June 2012.

13 Jason Sternberg provides a critique of generational stereotypes in Sternberg (2012).

14 Cited at http://goo.gl/OGWsi on 18 April 2012.

Chapter Eight: Picking up the tab: Cost, quality and sustainability

1　National Association of College and University Business Officers (2002), *Explaining College Costs*, Final Report.

2　Federal Reserve Bank of New York, *Student Loan Borrowing and Repayment Trends, 2015*.

3　The Institute for College Access and Success, *Quick Facts About Student Debt*, March 2014.

4　Education and Training Portfolio Budget Statements 2015–16.

5　A 2011–12 survey of US higher education, which included 1084 families with students attending public or private four-year universities, found that 53 per cent took out loans – 63 per cent of those attending private universities and 48 per cent of those attending public institutions (Ipsos 2012).

6　See *High Debt, Low Information: A Survey of Student Loan Borrowers* cited at www.nera.com/nera-files/PUB_Student_Loans_0312.pdf on 21 March 2012.

7　*The Sunday Telegraph* reported in 2012 that the highest HECS-HELP debt owed by an individual student was $400,000, with the number two spot held by a graduate who owed the government $272,000 (Maiden 2012).

In the United States something like 0.2 per cent of undergraduate student debtors owe more than US$100,000, though there too they receive much public coverage.

8　Relative to other institutions, for-profits educate a larger fraction of minority, disadvantaged and older students, and they have greater success at retaining students in their first year and getting them to complete short programs. But for-profit students have much worse degree completion times, end up with higher unemployment and 'idleness' rates, have lower earnings six years after entering programs than do comparable students from other schools, and have far greater student debt burdens and default rates on their student loans (Deming, Goldin and Katz 2012). Although for-profits enrol only around 10 per cent of undergraduate students, their students make up almost half of all student loan defaults, and many of these are students who have dropped out without gaining a degree and who have no better job prospects than those without any college education (Lewin 2011). In 2012 the US Senate Committee on Health, Education, Labor and Pensions published a report that documented operations at more than 30 of the largest for-profit providers and found numerous instances of problems with aggressive recruitment and poor student outcomes (see www.gpo.gov/fdsys/).

9　For example, at Griffith University it has declined slightly over the decade to 2010, while at the University of Queensland and Queensland University of Technology it has remained the same. The University of Melbourne and the University of Sydney both had slight increases.

10　These numbers include casual staff and are expressed in full-time equivalent terms. Staff termed 'non-academic' in official government data can include some people who also have a teaching or research function, and institutions do not have uniformly consistent methods of classification, so changes in such numbers should be treated with caution.

11　Coates et al. (2009), p. 25.

12　Archibald and Feldman (2008).

13　Delta Cost Project (2008), *The Growing Imbalance: Recent trends in U.S. postsecondary education finance*.

14　Much attention has been given in the United States to the so-called Bennett hypothesis, named after a former secretary of education who claimed that tuition fees had risen as a result of increases in financial aid. Studies found that at public universities and colleges there was little evidence for this, but some found evidence of increases in for-profit colleges. Andrew Gillen from the Center for College Affordability and Productivity has pointed out that the type of aid matters, and that untargeted assistance coupled with uncapped ability of providers to raise tuition is likely to drive an upward spiral with aid chasing increasing unaffordability.

In October 2012 two US economists, Robert Martin and R. Carter Hill, published an econometric analysis of university costs that suggested that the ratio of tenured academic staff to non-academic staff was a key driver of costs, with more administrators associated with higher costs (Martin and Hill 2012). What was needed, they claimed, was greater academic constraints on administrators' powers and control over budgets. They extrapolated their models well beyond existing data points to conclude that the optimal ratio of tenured academics to professional staff would be around 3 to 1 (the actual average is around 0.5 to 1) and claimed that Bowen effects were twice the size of Baumol effects in driving university costs. No doubt further research will explore the method, but the prospects of moving to their optimal staffing ratios are remote.

15 See Kevin Kiley's article 'What Will $10,000 Get Me?' in *Inside Higher Ed*, 9 May 2012 (www.insidehighered.com).

16 House of Commons Innovation, Universities, Science and Skills Committee (2009), *Students and Universities: Eleventh Report of Session 2008–09*, Volume I, p. 114.

17 *Increasing Voluntary Giving to Higher Education*, Task Force Report to the UK Government (chaired by Professor Eric Thomas), May 2004.

18 *Review of Philanthropy in UK Higher Education, 2012 Status Report and Challenges for the Next Decade*, Report to HEFCE by Marc Partnership, September 2012.

19 Katia Savchuk, 'Doing Business with China: The face of China's new philanthropy', *Forbes*, 27 January 2016.

20 *Philanthropy in Australia's Higher Education System, Final Report to Universities Australia on behalf of the Business, Industry and Higher Education Collaboration Council*, prepared by Allen Consulting Group, May 2007.

21 Miriam Steffens, 'Frankly, They Don't Give a Damn' in *The Age* Business Day, 4 June 2011.

22 David Kennedy, *Philanthropy in Australia: Can we create a 'new normal'?*,

address to The Wesley Research Institute, Brisbane, 2 November 2012.

23 Don Markwell, *Broadening the Culture of Educational Philanthropy in Australia*, speech to BHERT/Campus Review Summit, Sydney, 17 May 2006.

24 Arun Sharma, 'Disconnect between research and national needs', *Australian Financial Review*, 16 September 2013.

25 In 2012, businesses spent 47 per cent of their R&D outlay on engineering while universities spent 10 per cent. Business spent 30 per cent on ICT and universities spent 3 per cent. On the other hand, while universities spent 38 per cent of their research expenditure on medical and health sciences and biological sciences, the comparable figure for business is 6 per cent.

26 Department of Employment, Education, Training and Youth Affairs (1998), p. 56.

27 Gibney (2012).

Chapter Nine: The big deregulation gamble

1 Glenday (2014).

2 Sharrock (2014).

3 Julie Hare, 'New fees still cut it, says Queensland University of Technology', *The Australian*, 5 December 2014.

4 Strathdee (2011).

5 Andrew McGettigan, *The Accounting and Budgeting of Student Loans*, Higher Education Policy Institute Report 75, 2015.

Chapter Ten: The scholarship of fools? Governance and management

1 This paragraph paraphrases an opinion article by co-author Coaldrake, 'Too Much Self-interest From Too Many Doomsayers' in *The Australian Financial Review*, 14 May 2012.

2 Bexley, James and Arkoudis (2011).

3 Coates et al. (2009).

4 Coaldrake and Stedman (1998), p. 46.

5 Co-author Coaldrake was one of four members of the Hoare Committee; see *Higher Education Management Review*, Report of the Committee of Inquiry, December 1995.

6 The Bologna Process began in 1999 as a set of agreements between European countries to work toward more consistent structures and processes in higher education. The aim is to build a European Higher Education Area that makes student and staff mobility easier and that enables degrees to be better recognised.

7 Quiddington (2010).

8 *The Weekend Australian*, 12 September 1992, as cited in DEET's *National Report on Australia's Higher Education Sector*, p. 109, 1993.

9 Department of Finance and Administration, *Governance Arrangements for Australian Government Bodies*, August 2005.

10 Scott (2007).

11 Bahram Bekhradnia (2006), *Buffer Bodies*, paper presented to Wellington Group, 15–17 March, New Zealand.

12 Quiddington (2010).

13 This discussion of the 2006 AVCC Review is based on a commentary piece by co-author Coaldrake.

14 AUQA, Central Queensland University Report, 2006.

Chapter Eleven: Facing the realities

1 Chapman (2015).

2 Dawkins and Dixon (2015).

3 Noonan (2015).

References

Acemoglu, D. and Autor, D. (2010), 'Skills, Tasks and Technologies: Implications for Employment and Earnings', *NBER Working Paper No. 16082* (National Bureau of Economic Research).

Adams, J. (2013) 'Collaborations: The fourth age of research'. *Nature*, 497, pp. 557–560.

Ahola, S., Hedmo T., Thomson, J-P. and Vabø, A. (2014), 'Organisational features of higher education: Denmark, Finland, Norway & Sweden'. *Working Paper 14/2014*, Nordic Institute for Studies in Innovation, Research and Education (NIFU).

Allen, I.E. and Seaman, J. (2015), 'Grade Level: Tracking online education in the United States'. Babson Survey Research Group.

Altbach, P. (2009), 'One-third of the Globe: The future of higher education in China and India' in *Prospect*, 39, pp. 11–31.

Ansell, B. (2008), 'University Challenges: Explaining Institutional Change in Higher Education' in *World Politics*, 60 (20), pp. 189–230.

Archibald, R.B. and Fedman, D. H. (2008), 'Explaining Increases in Higher Education Costs', *The Journal of Higher Education*, 79, 3, pp. 268–95.

Barlow, T. (2006), *The Australian Miracle: An innovation nation revisited*, Pan Macmillan

Baty, P. (2012), 'Rankings Without Reason', *Inside Higher Ed*ucation (see http:// goo.gl/Aruj6).

Beaudry, P., Green, D.A. and Sand, B.M. (2013), *The Great Reversal in the Demand for Skill and Cognitive Tasks*, NBER Working Paper No. 18901.

Benneworth, P. et al. (2011), *Quality-related Funding, Performance Agreements and Profiling in Higher Education: An international comparative study*, Centre for Higher Education Policy Studies (CHEPS), University of Twente.

Bettinger, E., Fox, L., Loeb, S., & Taylor, E. (2015), *Changing Distributions: How Online College Classes Alter Student and Professor Performance*, CEPA Working Paper No. 15-10, Stanford University.

Bexley, E., James, R. and Arkoudis, S. (2011), *The Australian Academic Profession in Transition: Addressing the challenge of reconceptualising academic work and regenerating the academic workforce*, Centre for the Study of Higher Education, University of Melbourne.

Bhattacharjee, Y. (2011), 'Citation Impact: Saudi Universities Offer Cash in Exchange for Academic Prestige', *Science*, 334 (6061), pp. 1344–45.

Bok, D. (2004), *Universities of the Marketplace: The commercialization of higher education*, Princeton University Press.

Bowman, N.A. and Bastedo, M.N. (2011), 'Anchoring Effects in World University Rankings: Exploring biases in reputation scores', *Higher Education*, 61 (4), pp. 431–44.

Brown, R. (2010), *Comparability of Degree Standards?*, Higher Education Policy Institute (see http://goo.gl/9F0KY).

Chapman, B. (2002), *A Submission on Financing Issues to the Department of Education, Science and Training Inquiry into Higher Education*, Centre for Economic Policy Research discussion paper no. 456, Australian National University, Canberra.

Chapman, B. (2015), A Submission to Senate Enquiry on Higher Education Reform, February.

Chowdry, H., Dearden, L., Goodman, A. and Wenchao, J. (2012), 'The Distributional Impact of the 2012–13 Higher Education Funding Reforms in England', *Fiscal Studies*, 33 (2), pp. 211–36.

Christensen, C. and Eyring, H. (2011), 'Why You Should Root for College to Go Online', *The Atlantic*, 6 September.

Coaldrake, P. and Stedman, L. (1998), *On the Brink: Australia's universities confronting their future*, University of Queensland Press.

Coaldrake, P. and Stedman, L. (1999), *Academic Work in the Twenty-First Century, Changing Roles and Policies*, AGPS, Canberra.

Coates, H., Dobson, I., Edwards, D., Friedman, T., Goedegebuure, L. and Meek, L. (2009), *The Attractiveness of the Australian Academic Profession: A comparative analysis*, see http://research.acer.edu.au/higher_education/11.

Coelli, M. (2015), 'Stability of education earnings gaps in Australia', *Australia's Future Workforce*, Committee for Economic Development of Australia, June.

Commonwealth Tertiary Education Commission (CTEC) (1986), *Review of Efficiency and Effectiveness on Higher Education*, AGPS, Canberra.

Coyle, D. (2008), *The Soulful Science, What Economists Do and Why It Matters*, Princeton University Press.

Cunningham, S., Tapsall, S., Ryan, Y., Stedman, L. and Flew, T. (1998), *New Media and Borderless Education*, AGPS, Canberra.

Cunningham, S., Ryan, Y., Stedman, L., Tapsall, S., Bagdon, K., Flew, T. and Coaldrake, P. (2000), *The Business of Borderless Education*, Department of Education, Training and Youth Affairs, Canberra.

Daly, A., Lewis, P., Corliss, M. and Heaslip, T. (2011), 'The Private Rate of Return to a University Degree in Australia', *The Centre for Labour Market Research*.

Dawkins, P. J. and Dixon J.M. (2015), 'Alternative Approaches to Fee Flexibility: Toward a Third Way in Higher Education Reform in Australia', Centre of Policy Studies Working Paper No. G-252.

Deming, D.J., Goldin, C. and Katz, L.F. (2012), 'The For-profit Postsecondary School Sector: Nimble critters or agile predators?', *Journal of Economic Perspectives*, 26 (1), pp. 139–64.

Deming, David J., Claudia Goldin, Lawrence F. Katz, and Noam Yuchtman (2015), 'Can Online Learning Bend the Higher Education Cost Curve?', *American Economic Review*, 105(5), pp. 496-501.

Department of Education, Employment and Workplace Relations (2008), *Review of Australian Higher Education*, Final Report (Bradley Review).

Department of Education, Employment, Training and Youth Affairs (1998), *Learning For Life: Final report of the review of higher education financing and policy* (Roderick West, Chair), AGPS, Canberra.

Dodgson, M., Hughes, A., Foster, J. and Metcalfe, S. (2011), 'Systems Thinking, Market Failure, and the Development of Innovation Policy: The case of Australia', *Research Policy*, 40(9), pp. 1145–56.

Douglass, J.A. (2000), *The California Idea and American Higher Education: 1850 to the 1960 Master Plan*, Stanford University Press.

Douglass, J.A. (2010), *Re-Imagining California Higher Education*, Research & Occasional Paper Series, CSHE.14.10 (see http://goo.gl/kS53d).

Downer, A. (2005), *Federal Parliament Gives Green Light to Carnegie Mellon*, Media Release, 9 December (see http://goo.gl/Xkko5).

Durrant-Whyte, H., McCalman, L., O'Callaghan, S., Reid, A. and Steinberg, D. (2015), 'The impact of computerization and automation on future employment', *Australia's Future Workforce*, Committee for Economic Development of Australia, June.

Eley, M. (2001), 'The Course Experience Questionnaire: Altering question format and phrasing could improve the CEQ's effectiveness', *Higher Education Research & Development*, 20 (3), pp. 293–312 .

Frank, D. and Meyer, J. (2007), 'University Expansion and the Knowledge Society', *Theory and Society*, 36(4), pp. 287–311.

Frey, C.B. and Osborne, M.A. (2013), *The future of employment: how susceptible are jobs to computerization?*, University of Oxford.

Frijters, P. and Gregory, R. (2006), 'From Golden Age to Golden Age: Australia's "Great Leap Forward"?', *Economic Record*, 82 (257), pp. 207–24.

Gabriel, G., von Stuckrad, T. and Witte, J. (2007), *Up and Down We Wander: German higher education facing the demographic challenge*, Centre for Higher Education Development (CHEConsult), Germany (see http://goo.gl/jOIP3).

Gibbons, M., Limoges, C., Nowotny, H., Schwarzman, S., Scott, P. and Trow, M. (1994), *The New Production of Knowledge: The dynamics of science and research in contemporary societies*, London, Sage.

Gibney, E. (2012), 'Keep Up the Good Work: Willetts', *Times Higher Education*, 28 June.

Gillen, A. (2012*)*, *Introducing Bennett Hypothesis 2.0*, Center for College Affordability and Productivity.

Glenday, J. (2014), 'Education Minister Christopher Pyne announces support for fee competition among universities', *ABC Online*, 8 May.

Harvard Graduate School of Education (2011), *Pathways to Prosperity: Meeting the challenge of preparing young Americans for the 21st century*.

Hazelkorn, E. (2011), *Rankings and the Reshaping of Higher Education: The battle for world-class excellence*, Palgrave Macmillan, Houndsmills.

He, Y. and Mai, Y. (2015), 'Expansion in China and the 'Ant Tribe' problem', *Higher Education Policy*, 28(3), pp. 333–352.

Higher Education Base Funding Review (HEBFR) (2011), Final Report (Lomax-Smith Review) (see http://goo.gl/DLrUk).

Hughes, A. (2006), 'Optimal Innovation Systems: Lessons from the UK and the USA', *Proceedings of the Innovation Leadership Forum*, December.

Ipsos Public Affairs (2012), *How America Pays for College: Summary Report*, SallieMae/Ipsos (see http://goo.gl/KRGBD).

Johnson, H. (2012), *Defunding Higher Education: What Are the Effects on College Enrollment?*, Public Policy Institute of California (see http://goo.gl/w28DF).

Kahneman, D. (2011), *Thinking Fast and Slow*, Farrar, Straus and Giroux.

Kerr, C. (2001), *The Gold and the Blue, Volume One: Academic triumphs*, UC Press.

Kogan, M. and Hanney, S. (2000), *Reforming Higher Education*, Jessica Kingsley.

Korn, M. (2011), 'Party Ends at For-Profit Schools', *The Wall Street Journal*, 22 August.

Laming, M. (2001), 'Seven Key Turning Points in Australian Higher Education Policy 1943–1999', *Post-Script*, 2 (2), pp. 239–73 (see http://goo.gl/DDNlY).

Lederman, D. (2012), 'Credit Hour (Still) Rules', *Inside Higher Ed.*, 30 April.

Lewin, T. (2011), 'Student Loan Default Rates Rise Sharply in Past Year', *The New York Times*, 12 September.

Liu, J. (2012), 'Examining Massification Policies and their Consequences for Equality in Chinese Higher Education: A cultural perspective', *Higher Education*, 64 (5), pp. 647–660.

Mahony, D. (1992), 'Establishing the University as the Sole Provider of Higher Education: The Australian experience', *Studies in Higher Education*, 17 (2), pp. 219–37.

Maiden, S. (2012), 'Uni students leave with a degree in debt, collectively owing billions', *The Sunday Telegraph*, 5 February.

Marginson, S. (1997), *Educating Australia, Government, Economy and the Citizen since 1960*, Cambridge University Press.

Marginson, S., Weko, T., Channon, N., Luukkonen, T. and Oberg, J. (2008), *OECD Reviews of Tertiary Education: Netherlands*.

Marginson, S. (2011a), 'Higher Education in East Asia and Singapore: Rise of the Confucian Model', *Higher Education*, 61, pp. 587–611.

Marginson, S. (2011b), 'Higher Education and Public Good', *Higher Education Quarterly*, 65 (4), pp. 411–33.

Martin, R.E. and Hill, R. Carter (2012), *Measuring Baumol and Bowen Effects in Public Research Universities* (see http://ssrn.com/abstract=2153122).

Noonan, P. (2015), 'Building a sustainable funding model for higher education in Australia – a way forward', Mitchell Institute discussion paper, January.

Norton, A. (2012), *Graduate Winners: Assessing the public and private benefits of higher education*, Grattan Institute, August 2012.

Norton, A. (2014), *Mapping Australian Higher Education 2014–15*, Grattan Institute.

Nowotny, H., Scott, P. and Gibbons, M. (2001), *Rethinking Science*, Polity Press.

O'Cleary, C. (2007), *The Billionaire Who Wasn't. How Chuck Feeney Secretly Made and Gave Away a Fortune*, BBS Public Affairs, New York.

Pettigrew, A. (2012), *Australia's Position In The World Of Science, Technology & Innovation*, Australia's Chief Scientist Occasional Paper Series, Issue 2, May (see http://goo.gl/x7POL).

Powell, W. and Snellman, K. (2004), 'The Knowledge Economy', *Ann. Rev. Sociol*, 30, pp. 199–220 (see doi: 10.1146/annurev.soc.29.010202.100037).

Quiddington, P. (2010), 'The New Politics of Australian Higher Education: Why universities get rumbled in the budget', *Higher Education Research & Development*, 29 (4), pp. 475–87.

Ryan, Y. and Stedman, L. (2001), *The Business of Borderless Education 2001 Update*, Department of Education, Science and Training, Canberra.

Salmi, J. (2009), *The Challenge of Establishing World-Class Universities*, The World Bank, Washington DC.

Salmi, J. (2015), 'Excellence strategies and the creation of world-class universities', *WCU-6 Proceedings of the 6th International Conference on World-class Universities*, 1–4 November, Shanghai, China.

Sanford, T. and Hunter, J. (2011), 'Impact of Performance-Funding on Retention and Graduation Rates', *Education Policy Analysis Archives*, 19 (33), (see http://goo.gl/UzHkO).

Schleicher, A. (2006), *The Lisbon Council Policy Brief: The economics of knowledge: Why education is key for Europe's success* (see http://goo.gl/OxhMb).

Scott, P. (2007), *A Personal View of the Funding Council: Perspectives on success ... and failure*, Occasional Paper 31, Oxford Centre for Higher Education Policy Studies, University of Oxford (see http://goo.gl/3DRDv).

Sharma, Y. (2011), 'Asia: The Rise of Higher Education Philanthropy', *University World News*, 24 April.

Sharrock, G. (2014), 'Students versus taxpayers: decoding the Pyne-Hockey script', *The Conversation*, 27 June

Simons, M. (2010), 'Dangerous Precedent: The Melbourne model', *The Monthly*, March.

Stabile, D. (2007), *Economics, Competition and Academia*, Edward Elgar.

Sternberg, J. (2012), '"It's the End of the University As We Know It (and I feel fine)": The Generation Y student in higher education discourse', *Higher Education Research & Development*, 31 (4), pp. 571–83.

Strathdee, R. (2011), 'Educational reform, inequality and the structure of higher education in New Zealand', *Journal of Education and Work*, 24:1-2, pp. 27–48.

Strauss, V. (2015), 'Largest for-profit university in U.S. loses hundreds of thousands of students', *The Washington Post*, 26 March.

Trounson, A. and Puddy, R. (2011), 'First Private Uni in 24 Years Led By Clinton', *The Australian*, 18 October.

Umbricht, M., Fernandez, F. and Ortagus, J. (2015), 'An Examination of the (Un)Intended Consequences of Performance Funding in Higher Education', *Educational Policy*, Online First, 9 December.

Vogel, M. (2009), 'The Professionalism of Professors at German *Fachhochschulen*', *Studies in Higher Education*, 34 (8), pp. 873–88.

Watson, D. (2011), *Misunderstanding Modern Higher Education: Eight 'category mistakes'*, Higher Education Policy Institute.

Watts, D. (2011), *Everything is Obvious, Once You Know The Answer*, Crown Business, New York.

Weinberger, D. (2011), *Too Big To Know*, Basic Books.

Wheelahan, L. (2007), 'How Not to Fund Teaching and Learning', *Australian Universities Review*, 49 (1 and 2), pp. 31–38.

Wheelahan, L. (2010), *Why Knowledge Matters in Curriculum, A Social Realist Argument*, Routledge.

Wolf, A. (2002), *Does Education Matter?: Myths About Education and Economic Growth*, Penguin Books.

World Economic Forum (2012), *Global Risks 2012*, Seventh Edition (see http://goo.gl/g81WQ).

Index